For Love of a
WILD THING

For Love of a WILD THING

Ernest Dudley

Further Chapters From
The True Story of
RUFUS The Loving Fox
And His Friends

FREDERICK MULLER LTD

First published in Great Britain 1973 by
Frederick Muller Ltd, London NW2 6LG

Filmset and Printed Offset Litho in Great Britain by
Cox & Wyman Ltd, London, Fakenham and Reading

ISBN 0 584 10095 7

THE HUMANS

Don MacCaskill
Pakistani Girl
McNab
Mrs Turk
The Turk Family
Iris

THE ANIMALS

Shuna the Labrador
Frieda, Rufus's Mate
Robbie, their Cub; and
The Other Cubs
Cronk the Raven

Contents

Introduction

The creative writer, in depicting an animal's behaviour, is under no greater obligation to keep within the bounds of exact truth than is the painter or the sculptor in shaping an animal's likeness. But all three artists must regard it as their most sacred duty to be properly instructed regarding those particulars in which they deviate from the actual facts. They must indeed be even better informed on these details than on others which they render in a manner true to nature. There is no greater sin against the spirit of true art, no more contemptible dilettantism than to use artistic licence as a specious cover for ignorance of fact.

KONRAD Z. LORENZ

1 The Secret of the Glen

The storm was receding. The rain slashed at my shoulders as I huddled the raincoat-collar round my ears. Lightning ripped the sky and thunder rumbled and reverberated round the forest, and down by the loch the waters zig-zagged in a white, foaming edge along the sandy stretch of shore. It was a passing storm, now it crashed against the hills in the distant darkness; its echoes and re-echoes were what I was hearing.

The force of wind had lifted off half the roof of Stalker's Cottage, and I wasn't looking forward to sleeping there tonight. I muttered my dismay and half-turned back to my car, my mind already made up to return to the Fasganeoin Hotel for the night.

I had left the hotel only half an hour before, where after dinner I'd sat over coffee and a brandy with Mrs Turk and Norbert and Sabrina, her son and daughter, listening to "Boris Karloff", as I'd privately nicknamed their uncle, playing Rachmaninoff's Second Symphony at the piano. He was an ex-German Army officer, now helping to run the hotel. The first time I'd stayed there, I'd arrived late at night after driving through the dark, spectral glens, and their eeriness had still darkened my imagination as he greeted me in the dim hall, and a whine of wind sounded underneath the eaves. (I knew Boris Karloff, as a matter of fact. Off-screen he was really a distinguished-looking English ex-public schoolboy; nothing like his horror-film characters.) They were full up with tourists, but I knew Mrs Turk would find a bed for me.

I paused as I made for the car. I had forgotten to call Rufus's name. I had done this every night since the night two weeks ago

when he and Frieda and the five cubs had vanished from their
home, the glen by Ennochdhu Wood. I turned and opened the front
door of the cottage and switched on the light. The living-room was
a mess of rain-soaked furniture and broken tiles which had fallen
in. I turned back to the darkness and called.

"Rufus . . . Rufus . . ."

No answer. No movement from the direction of the forest.
No cry of recognition from Rufus, or Frieda, his mate; no squeak
from any of the fox-cubs. An echo of thunder drowned my
voice.

I went into the sitting-room, the door slamming behind me,
reminding me of the strange, ominous way the mantelpiece had
cracked that night. I meant to give the place a closer once-over
before I went back to Mrs Turk's. I had no intention of attempting
to clear up the broken tiles, the rain-sodden furniture tonight. It
looked to me that the storm had done its worst, it had passed, and in
tomorrow's daylight it wouldn't look so bad as it did now. I would
be back in the morning and with help would clear things up;
there'd be a bit of a problem over getting the roof repaired, but a
temporary tarpaulin covering would take care of that. It was early
summer: bad storms like the one we were experiencing – this was
the second in the past couple of weeks – weren't the rule, even in
the Scottish Highlands, not noted for the driest, sunny days at the
height of summer.

I caught the movement underneath the armchair out of the tail
of my eye. I was just about to switch off the light and go out. With
the movement in the shadow of the chair came a faint whimper.
I was down on my knees and pushing the chair aside, grabbed the
dark, furry body, wet, with blood-streaks on its tiny face, and held
it up. It was one of the cubs. As I stared at it I could feel its little heart
racing, its eyes, which seemed swollen, glimmered feebly back at
me.

I held the cub close, and it gave off a faint, musky scent which
reminded me so much of Rufus. It attempted to push itself inside
my jacket in the old familiar way. But it pushed very feebly; I took
it out and, sitting in the chair, held it on my lap and examined it
coolly and carefully – I was shivering with the excitement of having
found the cub – and right away I saw that both its fore-paws were
damaged. They looked as if they had been crushed. There were no

signs of blood, the skin hadn't been broken. The blood I'd noticed had come from the side of its mouth, as if the cub had received a blow in the jaw.

I handled its fore-paws as gently as I could. The cub didn't react as if it felt any pain, but that could have been due to its not having recovered from the shock of the injuries it had suffered. By now as I stared at it I was pretty sure it was one of the dog-foxes – there had been two dogs and three vixens – in fact, I felt certain it was the eldest of the litter. The one Don MacCaskill and I had said should be called Robbie, after Robbie Burns, or King Robert Bruce, because we were sure that he would prove to be such a handsome, distinguished-looking fox.

Still clutching it with one hand to my coat, with the other I poured some milk into a saucepan and put it on the cooker. I wasn't really thinking what I was doing, it was more of a reflex action, an effort to do something to help the cub, to do something in an effort to save it from dying. It seemed to me even as I poured out the warm milk into a saucer that it was a forlorn hope. The cub half-knelt, half lurched forward on the table where I placed him in front of the milk. Response, nil. I tried to get it to lap up some of the stuff, put some on my finger and tried to get the cub to lick it off. It suddenly occurred to me that perhaps I wouldn't have wanted warm milk, myself – I wasn't too keen on it, I much preferred it cold. Some people, I believe, can't touch the stuff warm. Not if you paid them.

I got a fresh saucer and poured some cold milk into it. Unhopefully I pushed the saucer under Robbie's nose. He slowly rested his little jaw on the saucer's edge, and stuck out a tiny, narrow pink tongue and started to lap up the milk. It seemed rather a painful business for him, and I found myself screwing up my face with pain as I watched. He gave quite a loud burp, paused momentarily, and then continued until the saucer was dry. Then he lurched away and crouched, staring up, eyes only half focused on me. I picked him up and the warmth of my body seemed to relax him. Again he pushed his face inside my jacket to escape the light. To find some sort of sanctuary in the darkness.

How had he found his way into my cottage? The front door had been locked. I found the kitchen back door was ajar, and I knew it was possible I might have forgotten to lock and bolt it when I went out early that evening. The storm could have blown the door open and blown the cub in. Robbie had then crawled under the sitting-room armchair. This seemed the likeliest thing to have happened. Stalker's Cottage was a quarter of a mile from the glen where Rufus and Frieda had lived with their cubs – until that night when the vandals, the local fox-haters, had done their work. Neither Don nor I had any idea what had become of Rufus and his family, whether they had been carted off or just clubbed to death and thrown away in the forest. We had searched for them for days all around the glen and the forest, and along the loch shore, Shuna, the Labrador, helping as best she could. But we had found no signs of them.

After several days we had given up hope, except that Don used to call for Rufus every night from his house which was just by the glen; and I used to do the same. I couldn't really believe Rufus was dead, that I would never see his wonderful face again, hear his excited greeting, and I called out to him in this way as a kind of act of faith.

But now Robbie had shown up. More dead than alive, maybe, but he had returned. How he had managed to escape and find his way to Stalker's Cottage was a miracle. It seemed unlikely that anyone had found him and dumped him on me. It was more likely that anyone hereabouts coming across a fox-cub would have quickly beaten its brains out. It would have been almost a reflex action; not much thought would have been given to it. Not in the Highlands.

It seemed to me as I stood there, the roof over my head gaping to the dark sky, and rain still spattering down, that this was no place for an injured, probably dying, fox-cub. The only place I could think of was the Fasganeoin Hotel. Robbie gave another muffled burp inside my coat, and I switched out the light, shut the front door behind me, locked up and got into the car.

Several times during the drive I felt convinced he was dead. Several times it seemed to me when I put my hand inside my coat, the tiny heart had ceased beating, the feeble spark extinguished. Once I was so certain that I stopped the car and took the small body out from my coat and scrutinised it. Then, the eyes flickered open, their vacant stare fixed on me for a few seconds before they closed once more. The heartbeats continued, and Robbie pushed his way back under my coat. I drove on.

I had to take the long way round, the last ferry had gone. The ferry from Portnacraig, the Ferry by the Rock. You would have thought that with those sort of injuries the cub would be suffering agony. But it is the same with birds. Mrs Turk's kestrel, which she had found injured, had never shown any pain, it had lain quietly in her hands while she had patched it up. It seems likely that a bird, though it may appear to be in no pain at the time of the injury, suffers a kind of shock, a form of delayed shock from which it may later die. I raced along the road by the loch-side, until I gained the road which speeded me towards the Fasganeoin Hotel.

It had originally been built as a private mansion of the local grey stone, slate-roofed. It stood several feet up from the main road, just outside the village at the end of a long drive. Its sharp Gothic-like gables were silhouetted against the storm-wracked sky, and lights glimmering from its windows welcomed the traveller. The Turk family had been there the past five years. A typical old-fashioned Highland summer hotel, it was, but with a terrific reputation for Mrs Turk's cooking. Across the main road from the drive-entrance stood the famed old distillery, its windows lit up, from which came long, heady wafts of whisky. If you wanted a closer sniff of the stuff you could linger outside the gates, glimpsing through the bright windows the night-employees proceeding about their enviable task. Beside you might be another onlooker, old Hughie Drummond, sitting there on his box, eyes closed, pausing for a while on his way home.

I went into the hall with the cub inside my coat. I didn't want any of the hotel-guests to see him, with their questions, and oohing and aahing, and fussing over him; I didn't want any stranger to know, I didn't want to give away to any human beings what had happened – human beings were the cub's enemies, from now on. Except one or two, like Mrs Turk.

But at the very moment I arrived, a little middle-aged woman hurried down the wide staircase and came straight at me. She looked dishevelled, her dressing-gown wrapped round her all awry. She was white-faced in the dim, pinkish light. In a choking whisper she said: "I–I'm afraid there's a ghost in my bedroom—"

She was obviously one of the guests. Perhaps a little dotty, I thought. "Oh?" was all I could say in reply. I was anxious to get past her to Mrs Turk. She reached out to cling on to me. "Don't worry," I said, "I'm sure it will be all right." She shook her head vigorously and gave a couple of gulps. But whatever she was about to utter was interrupted by "Boris Karloff" coming out of the sitting-room. "Tell Mr Klein," I said as he came towards us, eyes raised in his domed forehead. "Lady's got a ghost in her bedroom," I said to him.

Mr Klein was instantly charming and gracious, as if he was used to hotel-guests with little problems like supernatural visitations every hour of the day. He took the woman aside and while he asked her solicitously to tell him what it was all about, I headed for the sitting-room. The two youngsters had gone to bed, and Mrs Turk was about to follow them. She gave a sharp cry, as if she herself was suffering pain, the moment she saw the cub.

She and her family had been to see Rufus and Frieda and the cubs at the glen, and she was one of the few people who knew what the vandals had done to them – Don and I had good reasons for not wanting anyone to know what had happened. She handled the cub with gentle care.

She kept a kestrel, one wing shattered by a gun-shot, in the garden: as a result of her patience the wing had mended well enough for it to live a happy life. Fasganeoin is Gaelic for Sanctuary of the Birds, and Mrs Turk was pretty, a brunette with dark, bright eyes; she had lived in Hamburg during the war throughout the Allied bombing and as a result was rather deaf.

The cub's fore-paws had been crushed, there was no doubt about it – though he continued to show little sign of pain as Mrs Turk gently examined him. Probably caused by blows aimed at his head. The right paw seemed more damaged than the other. Only one thing to be done, and that was to get Robbie to a veterinary surgeon, quick. There wasn't anyone locally I knew who would be at all interested in saving the cub's life. The advice would be straightforward. Destroy him. It would be best for him, the most humane way to deal with him. Save yourself and everyone else a lot of trouble. Mrs Turk agreed that this was the sort of advice I would receive. And after all, you couldn't expect anything else. From Highlanders and fervent allies of the local farmers and game-keepers against foxes, you couldn't expect much else.

Already he had suffered what might yet turn out to be mortal injuries. There would be little if any sympathy for him from the folk round about. It was only the outsiders, like me and Mrs Turk, who wouldn't sooner see him dead. Wiped out. Exterminated. That was the way to deal with foxes. You could say I was a bit rattled. Robbie turning up the way he had, all but done for. Knowing as I did that there was no one to help. Looking back, you could say I had got myself into an emotional state; I over-reacted – "humanised" a wild creature's physical and mental agony. But I felt pretty desperate; more than that there was this feeling of guilt which had been over me ever since that night when Rufus and his family had been wiped out. It had all been my fault, if it hadn't been for me it wouldn't have happened. Added to this, I was in a neck of the woods where Rufus and his kind were regarded with such hatred, obsessional hatred, by so many people that I knew there was no safety for Robbie except far away. As far away as possible. I don't know, but I believe even if I'd given myself time to think rationally, I would have acted as I did. I couldn't have acted differently.

Mr Klein came in, eyes raised to Heaven. "Ghost in her bed-room," he snorted. "I will tell you what it was —" Neither of us were paying much attention, I had started to say to Mrs Turk what I was going to do. "I will tell you what it was," he went on. "It was the coat-hangers in her wardrobe, which rattled when she walked about the room. That was what it was, I tell you. Coat-hangers that rattled – what sort of skeleton in a cupboard is that?" He smiled at what he thought was a good joke, then broke off as he saw the cub. He listened gravely as Mrs Turk told him what had happened, then shook his head at what I planned to do. "You will never make it," he said. "Drive all the way to London—? It won't last the journey; it is kinder to put it out of its misery, now. Kinder that way. It is what we did in the war—"

Mrs Turk shut him up with a fierce flow of German. He shrugged his shoulders, spread his hands, and went out of the room, muttering to himself. No doubt he was putting me on the same level as the woman with the "ghost" in her bedroom, and I suppose you couldn't blame him. Only if you've owned a fox yourself, come to know it at first-hand, bringing it up from birth, can you have any idea what it means to your whole life. And Robbie was

Rufus's son. Only by keeping a fox yourself does any of the creature's imponderable mystery and fascination rub off on you – it's not like keeping a cat or a dog, it's different from that, although a fox does possess to a certain extent the physical characteristics of a dog or a cat. Half-cat, half-dog, is what a fox is. But the way its mind works, what makes it tick, isn't the same as either a cat or a dog.

Mrs Turk had found a basket, lined it with a blanket. I clutched a bottle of milk while she got me a flask of steaming coffee. Mr Klein was in the hall, his domed brow pinkish in the light, his eyes raised to Heaven once more as we came out of the sitting-room, Mrs Turk holding Robbie in his basket, me following with my coffee-flask and bottle of milk. He clasped his hands and peered at the inert little shape almost covered by the blanket, eyes closed, apparently lifeless, and he glanced at me, his face relaxed in a tender smile, his large, brown eyes luminous with sympathy. "Good luck," he said. He opened the front door for us and followed us out to the car.

With the cub beside me I drove off. I had done the trip often enough, by night as well as day. It was quicker at night, and I enjoyed night-driving more.

There must have been hundreds of people who, as a result of reading about Rufus, had wanted to own a fox of their own. Millions saw him on television, he made several appearances; thousands met him on his "personal appearance" tour all over the place – Glasgow and Edinburgh, down to Leeds and Birmingham, and London – to promote the book, giving his "autograph" with his paw-mark. It is for those who met Rufus and wanted a fox like him of their own that I started thinking of writing another book about him.

Like the young, fair-haired girl in Leeds Infirmary who stared at him in wonder and joyous disbelief at his beautiful, friendly face and hugged him to her so tightly. Who loved him so much – too ill to know that after he had nuzzled her in that loving way he had and had gone, she would never see him again, never again hold him in her arms. It was for her, and there were others, most of them children but some older people, to whom Rufus brought comfort and love, moments of happiness, that this second book was begun. That the story has turned out differently is because real life is like that. And this book is life, it is for real. Composed of living creatures, human and animal. Tamed and wild. I learned as best I could all the ways of Rufus, a once wild fox who had learned to love human beings, who learned the easy way, because for some strange reason that love was built into every nerve and fibre of his being.

When I came to write the first book about Rufus, I rejected any idea of becoming involved with him, of committing myself to him. Somewhere at the back of my mind, call it intuition – and this conviction strengthened as I got to know him better – I was aware that unhappiness threatened me; that to commit yourself to any animal was wrong, to love any animal, as a human being loves, was going against the imponderable riddle of Nature, the scheme of things. It brings its problems, lays a responsibility on the human being concerned. A wild creature brings with it a responsibility which becomes heavier the more you love it and it loves you. You shouldn't take such a responsibility upon yourself; you shouldn't be asked to bear it.

There was a stir in the basket beside me, a kind of whimpering noise, and then the cub vomited. I stopped the car and held Robbie close to me, to give him body-warmth, and he pushed his way inside my coat. Just as he used to do when I used to bring him, with the other cubs, up to the cottage, their bright blue eyes still not focusing properly, their tiny tails like dark, white-tipped carrots. And the way they used to burrow their way inside your jacket, into the safety of the dark.

After a few moments Robbie relaxed as if he was sleeping. I took him very carefully from under my coat. His eyes were tightly closed. I could feel the beat of his heart, the trembling of the pathetic little bundle of fur as I placed him back in the basket. I marvelled that he still appeared to be in no pain. Perhaps he was still suffering from shock. Perhaps when the effects of the shock wore off, that would be when his resistance would collapse and he would die. I reflected that what had happened to me was the last thing I had wanted. A wild fox-cub on my hands; and not only a cub, but a sick, injured thing that was likely to die on me.

When I began this second book I resolved again not to become involved, not to commit myself to any animal that it concerned. I was scared of what might happen to that animal, how it would end up. Yet in the end, as you will have read (I have begun by beginning with the end), I did become involved with Rufus's very life. Without realising this was what I was doing, I didn't listen to that inner voice. I ignored the promptings of intuition, which warned me to get out from under any responsibility, any commitment.

What followed is part of this story. A story that brought no happiness to Rufus, or to me. A story, if you like, of a betrayal. It begins on 22 April 1972, when the cubs were born. Or perhaps it began a few days earlier, for that was when I came on the scene, when I returned to Dunfuirich, the straggle of houses along the shore of Loch Fourich, with its pub, the *Fisherman's Rest*, and Stalker's Cottage, where I lived.

2

You turn off the road from Rannoch, the Road to the Isles, and drive down the ramp for the ferry. Other cars are in the queue ahead, six cars and two lorries. You take your place in the queue. Loch Fourich means the Lake by the Place of Watching, and the water lies quiet and still, pale grey beneath the evening sky. Across the loch your eyes are held by a cluster of white houses with grey feathers of smoke, the same grey colour as the sky, ascending from the houses straight up in the cool, still air.

The light caught the surface of the loch and struck shafts of iridescent gold from it, which merged with the pearly tints of the sky. It's a sea-loch, though the sea lies twenty miles away, and so seagulls swooped overhead and I fancied that the tang of salt-water was sharp in my nostrils, and my imagination filled with pictures of sails and boats.

The ferry-boat nosed against the jetty, low in the water, her red and white superstructure ringed with lifebelts, like those white, well-sucked mints with a hole they show on television ads. I drove aboard, led by a lorry. Clank . . . clank . . . Ten minutes later I was heading along the side of the loch towards the small, white circular lighthouse low against the darkening green of the shadowed hills. A dragon-fly that was an Ordinance Survey helicopter, its navigation light blinking like a bright red eye . . . bright-red . . .

bright-red ... came out of a cloud to the left, dipped, rose again and whirred off towards the head of the loch. You could think yourself into the tingling atmosphere of a spy-thriller of the sort written by John Buchan.

You turn off a half-mile past the lighthouse and the road wriggles up with forest on your right and the loch falling away below. The light was starting to fade, the shadows of the forest darkened, as the sunshine in the sky slipped away more quickly. I felt very lonesome, as lonely as any hill-runner.

A bend in the road showed for a brief glimpse a house lying back, with lights glinting in the downstairs windows. That was Tony Bailey's house – Captain E. A. S. Bailey, C.B.E., D.S.C., R.N. – energetic and enthusiastic leader of the local fox destruction pack, whose object was the total extermination of every fox in the vicinity. I had heard of him and his band of fox-haters, though I hadn't really believed he existed; I had comforted myself that he was the figment of Don MacCaskill's imagination.

I didn't know then, as I turned the car off on to a narrow winding lane, that I was to come face to face with Tony Bailey, and that he and his charming pretty wife, who was happy to lend a hand at killing foxes, were very much creatures of flesh and blood. "I regard foxes as I did U-Boats in the last spot of bother, my dear fellow. I respect 'em, but my God, I'm out to destroy 'em."

The road to Don MacCaskill's house was still winding up and Loch Fourich was still falling away below and growing more slatey in colour as the night took over the scene. It stays light an hour longer in the Highlands than down in the South, but the time was now pushing eight o'clock and I couldn't do more than 30 mph, the road twists and turns that much, and I seemed to be taking a long time to reach the house. Or perhaps it was because I was tired – I had driven up from London that day. Or was I recalling that on the other side of the forest was an ancient place where some enormous skulls were reputed to have been dug up, described by archaeologists as belonging to a prehistoric species of giant ox? Students of the occult had, it was said, thought them to be skulls of human monsters, to whom black magic sacrifices had been made. Human sacrifices. Certainly archaeologists had been interested in nearby mysterious stone circles, which might have been Pagan temples, scenes of strange ritual. And north-east was a wooded hill, where once had stood the Caisteal Dubh, or Black Castle, complete, it had been rumoured, with dark dungeons and a torture chamber where the bones of mangled victims had been discovered. Perhaps the air was beginning to grow heavy with the breathing of evil spirits already stirring abroad; perhaps their presence was the cause of my tiredness, the tension in my mind.

I had switched on my headlights, and as I rounded a bend for a fleeting moment I could have sworn there was a shape in the middle of the road, advancing towards me. I braked – was it a bearded figure, wearing sea-boots? Corpses of men drowned at sea were supposed to have been washed up on the loch-shore swept in by storms; and it was thought by those who believed in such things that whoever first found a corpse in this way should turn it over, otherwise its *tannasg*, spectre, would haunt the finder till death. There had been cases, understandably, when the corpse's appearance had been so horrible that anyone first coming upon it had screamed and rushed away, pursued by the *tannasg*. I peered ahead. Now the road was empty, and I shook my head to clear my vision, strained my eyes again at the still empty road, and drove on.

Then suddenly Don's home came into view, up there through the trees, and I recalled that was how it always happened. The house always did that. You keep looking for it to show, but it never does, until you begin to believe it never will. Then suddenly it is there, white and low-built, beyond a screen of birches on the edge of the forest. I swung the car off the road on to the track that leads up to it. There were no lights showing; no one was at home. Stalker's Cottage, which was almost next door to the old fishing-pub, the *Fisherman's Rest*, was a short distance down by the loch. You couldn't see it from here for the trees. I got out of the car and started off round the back of the house.

From here you could see the loch through a gap in the forest. It was at one of the times of the day – it could happen any time, early morning or just before darkness – when all around you was bathed in a strange light. As if you were looking at everything through double windows. The hills on the other side of the loch, and the mountains in their sombre mist beyond, you felt you could just by making a long arm lean across and touch them. I glanced down at the water, and the surface was curiously still, flat and leaden in colour. There were patches of tiny wavelets stirred by a faint breeze, but even they seemed not to move; you could have thought you were looking at a painting of the loch. Still, motionless. And that eerie, somehow scarey, light. And all the time you could hear the sound of the burns rushing down the hillsides. A steady, low-pitched roar that filled the air day and night. At times like this the sound also took on a different note; a curious murmuring. At other times, although the sound was still there, of course, you seemed less conscious of it. You seemed more conscious of the heavy silence. But at this moment, that weird murmur filled your ears.

Back of the house was the large old stone-built barn, and here was a secret place where a spare key was kept. The key was there, and I took it and went down the path. The opening to the glen was narrow with steep banks on either side. This opening was fenced in with wire-netting, the gate padlocked. The glen itself extended fifty yards, banked on either side and screened by tall bushes and trees opening out to an area in the middle, some forty yards wide, narrowing to the end of the glen.

Don MacCaskill had moved Rufus and Frieda to this place only a few months before; as a result of the publication of the book and publicity given to it locally, their old home had become too well-known to too many people; deliberate attempts had been made to release Rufus and Frieda by vandals, fox-haters, those who made attempts on their destruction. For Rufus's and Frieda's safety Don had converted this glen into a new, more secure home for them. It was some distance away from their previous place; it was sheltered from the road; it lay on the edge of the forest itself. No one would guess where it was located. That was Don's idea.

I reached the gate. I paused as a swift shape moved in the shadows. Frieda, slipping off to her den. She was in cub. She was shy anyway, when she moved she carried her body close to the ground. Not like Rufus who ran like a dog, upright and alert, unafraid. I turned the key in the padlock and opened the gate. I went in, closing the gate after me. I stood still. Behind me was the house, ahead and to my left was the loch. A seagull cried; somewhere in the forest an owl gave a long hoot. In response a wraith-like shape fluttered overhead in the gathering dusk. *Ke-wack . . . Ke-wack . . .* As I followed the owl's slow, steady flight I saw a star pierce the pale sky.

I called out Rufus's name. I was hoping he would remember my voice. We had enjoyed many conversations in the past; and I hoped, too, he would remember my scent. I hoped he would come to me. I recalled that previously I had always come to see him with Don; it was the first time I had come alone. And it was nearly three months since I had last seen him.

I called again. Suddenly he was there. Ten yards away. Once more I called, very, very quietly. He stood there. He saw me. His wonderful bushy tail began to wag, very slowly from side to side. He made a shadowy figure, but it was Rufus, all right. Straight and upright, a figure of strength and grace; the beautiful head slightly at an angle as he made a move forward, then paused. Then he scented me and he gave his strange little cry of recognition and ran towards me, still crying in that strange way, crying with pleasure and love. I bent down and as I stroked his head he nibbled my hand. My eyes were smarting, I had to swallow several times as I took him in my arms and his rough tongue was round my ear, and he was chattering at me, talking back at me in that extraordinary way of his. My own personal tension, my apprehensions for the future fell away; it was like throwing off a heavy coat. I knew everything was going to be all right.

I heard a movement behind me. Rufus struggled in my arms with excitement, chattering more loudly. I put him down, turning to see what it was had attracted his attention. He sped joyously to the gate which I realised I had left off the latch; I shouldn't have done so, and for a moment dismay filled me. I started after Rufus, then stopped. He had hooked a paw round the gate and was off, racing to a figure approaching out of the trees.

In the failing light the figure looked dimly grey, pale, almost luminous. "Hello?" It was a soft-spoken greeting, a girl's voice.

I knew I was scowling with a mixture of curiosity and apprehension. As she approached I could see she was wearing tight trousers, tapering to her ankles. She wore canvas slippers and a dark-coloured jersey up to her throat. She was very slim; she couldn't be aged more than sixteen, I guessed. As she approached, a bird flapped its wings in a tree-top and she turned her head. Her black hair fell to her shoulders and in profile I was suddenly reminded of a figure in one of those Graeco-Bhuddist friezes I had once seen in a mosque outside Bombay.

She was holding Rufus in her arms, while he chattered and

greeted her. They were obviously old friends. "Och, it's okay, all right," she said. I removed the scowl from my face and relaxed. She may have been Asian, but her accent was pure Glasgow. "Rufus," she said, "we are friends okay, all right." And she buried her olive-skinned face in his fur, crooning to him while he responded, licking her nose and chattering away happily. She looked up at me, and said quietly as if she didn't want Rufus to hear her: "Danger will come. But not now. Now, everything is okay, all right."

I suppose I wasn't listening to her properly. My mind was mixed up with a dozen images. This girl, appearing suddenly out of the forest. And seeing her with Rufus. And realising her affection for him, and his for her. And where the devil had she come from, and what was she doing there? Don had never mentioned her. And at the same time she was reminding me of someone – she might have been some phantom from the forest, some wild spirit manifesting herself in human shape – it was this, I suppose, that sparked off this sudden impression I had of her. I had been re-reading yet again W. H. Hudson's novel of the South American forest, *Green Mansions*, with the native girl, Rima, whose love for birds and animals and their love for her is the book's powerfully haunting theme.

All this milled around inside my head; and, of course, it was all mixed with the emotion stirred up by seeing Rufus again – and if you knew Rufus, you'd understand – and so when the girl spoke about danger I remembered how Rima had met her death at the end of the book, nothing had remained of her but the ashes of her flesh and bones, consumed by the terrible fire which had blackened the great tree in which she had sought sanctuary.

And I misunderstood this girl, holding Rufus in her arms. I thought she was talking about some danger she might be in herself.

2 The Heart of the Highlands

Frieda's cubs were expected any day now. That, the girl said, was why she was here. She wanted to be near when the cubs were born. It wasn't that she could do anything, she explained – Frieda was quite capable of managing without any human assistance; you mustn't think of a vixen as a human being, a woman, about to have a baby. It would all be quite natural, quite simple for Frieda. She most certainly wouldn't experience any birth-pangs, no pain at all – it would all be straightforward, no complications, just like it would be if Frieda was a wild vixen up in the hills. All the same, the girl said, she wanted to be there when it happened. She wanted to be there when the tiny cubs uttered their first squeaks in their blind, dark world. She spoke very quietly, in that Glasgow accent, holding Rufus in her arms.

I wasn't really taking in all that she was saying. I knew, anyway, that Frieda's cubs were expected any day; that was the main reason why I was there myself. You might say I had a vested interest in the cubs. So that part of what she was telling me didn't bother me. What did was that she knew about the expected cubs at all. It was supposed to be a close secret. I thought that outside Don and his wife I was the only one else who knew. I stared at the girl. In the evening light which was vanishing, ever faster, in the shadow of the tall, dark trees, she might have been someone from another world. I wonder, even now, if she was real. No evidence to remind me of her; no photograph, nothing tangible. A *tannasg*, or ghost or phantom or one of the "little people"; when you're in the Highlands, you soon get the feeling that strange things could happen.

They probably won't, you tell yourself – you whistle in the dark – but they could.

And she was from the East. And that was quite a combination to encounter, this slender creature, who reminded you of a figure sculpted on the wall of an ancient mosque, and around you the weird light of evening in the wild Highlands, the darkening forest, the muted roar of the rushing burns. Not that it seemed to worry Rufus. I noticed that. He was as happy as ever he was, chattering away – there was no doubt that they had known each other before. I would have started to ask her questions – how she knew about Frieda and the expected cubs – how she knew that Rufus was to be found here, in his new home, for that matter – who she was, and where she came from – when she was suddenly very still. Rufus knew that something had happened, he stopped his chatter, and stared, not at me, but beyond me, past my shoulder. I didn't have to turn my head to know that the light was on in the house. I saw the lighted window from the corner of my eye.

The girl put Rufus down. He came towards me slowly, his tail wagging. He loped past me, through the gate and into the shadows. There was a movement beyond him in the darkness. A low yap-yap to which he responded. Frieda was waiting for him by the den. There was a flickering movement of the white tip of his tail as he went off to join her. Instinctively, I moved to the gate and carefully padlocked it. I could hear Rufus and Frieda gossiping, and it was then that I thought I caught the sound of a bang, there was something familiar about it, but I couldn't place it. It seemed to come from the house. Perhaps it was the slam of a door; yes, Don was home. It was then I turned to speak to the girl. Of course, she wasn't there. It really could all have been a trick of the imagination. She could have been a spirit I would never see again.

I heard Shuna's familiar "wuff", and I started back to the house. Don would have seen my car, so he knew where I was. It was then that I remembered what the sound was that I had heard from the direction of the house. It had been Don banging with the flat of his hand on the back of my car, a trick he had whenever he saw me off in it, or welcomed me when I arrived. Shuna's "wuff", again, and she was lumbering down towards me, tail wagging away as ever. It occurred to me then – just a flash of puzzlement, Don called out to me, and I called back – that she hadn't barked on account of the girl. Shuna may have run to fat, just slightly (it was something you didn't mention within her hearing), but she was no slouch as a watch-dog. Any stranger – sometimes those she had met briefly before – would be received suspiciously, with loud barking. Either she had missed out on the girl, or they, too, had made friends already. I went indoors.

Arrangements for my return to Stalker's Cottage had been made a couple of weeks before, and I had kept the date and time of my expected arrival. Johnson, from the *Fisherman's Rest*, had looked in at the cottage that morning, and had put in a supply of milk, bread, groceries – even seen to it that the electric blanket had been switched on to have the bed warm for me. No burglars had broken in, no vandals set the place on fire. Shuna rubbed her plump body against me, inevitably leaving my trouser-legs covered with her hairs, and stared up at me with her soulful eyes. I commiserated with Don over Cassius's death less than a month ago.

Cassius had been a half-wild, half-domesticated tiny kitten which had been landed on Don when he had lived on Loch Aweside, Argyllshire. Before the flitting to Dunfuirich, Cassius had made a memorable impact on everyone, and that included Rufus, from the start. Not only did he grow up very like a wildcat to look at, with the characteristic stripes and short, ringed tail (his tail was short as the result of a bloodthirsty altercation with a dog who bit the end off it), he was of a wild, tigerish nature, always spoiling for a fight, though, strangely enough, since a fox and a wildcat are reputedly deadly enemies, he and Rufus had been the best of friends. It was the same when Shuna had arrived on the scene as a tiny puppy – which was difficult to imagine to look at her now as she lay stretched out before the sitting-room fire, very large and rather plump-looking – Cassius and the Labrador had instantly struck up a friendship, and more times than not the sitting-room hearth-rug was taken up by Cassius in the middle, with Rufus and Shuna on either side.

And there had been Cronk the raven, who had become an added member of the family, with her black, glittering eyes, always ready for teasing games with the other three; and who had taken a special delight in driving the very same dog that had chewed off Cassius's tail almost berserk with frustration by her imitation of a barking dog. Cronk would hop down from the garden-fence, the dog would charge at her, and she would promptly take off again just out of reach. Cronk, mischievous, exasperating, yet forever lovable, who had one day flown away with another raven appearing out of the sky over Loch Aweside, and hadn't been seen again.

And now Cassius had gone as well. Run over by a car one night only a short way along the road up which I had myself driven an hour ago. As undramatically as that had been his passing, not at all the way you would have expected him to go. In a furious scrap, going down before some equally fierce foe, with all claws tearing and scratching and the fur flying, fighting to the last.

Then Don was remembering Cronk again, the way she would disappear under the table at meal-times when friends had been invited and peck at the unsuspecting, and sometimes somewhat frightened, visitors' ankles – by now she was fully-grown, with a really powerful beak whose effect upon the recipients of her pecks she never realised. And, of course, of her never-endingly inventive games with Shuna – poor Shuna, how heartlessly she was given the run-around by her black, wickedly bright-eyed friend – in which Cassius and even Rufus joined, to their large, easy-going victim's discomfiture.

And then he was talking about Cassius again; that day of the removal from Loch Aweside to Dunfuirich, when he had been given this new job. The removal-men had loaded up everything in the van, they were ready for the off, when there was a cry for Cassius. Where was Cassius? All the animal "family" were making the journey in the Dormobile with Don and his wife, Catherine, who had handled and petted him for hours when he was a tiny kitten, so that he had grown up to become her shadow. Whenever he had involved himself in some scrape and, guiltily, refused to come when he was called, Catherine had only to appear on the scene and all was sweetness and light.

Now, once again, he was in trouble, he had gone missing, absent without leave. Of course, it was obvious that he was somewhere in the furniture-van, in a drawer or cupboard, calmly sleeping away the effects of some rumbustious activity in which he had been recently engaged. One of his predilections was for cat-napping in the broom-cupboard, at the back of a drawer left open, or in the cooker, especially when it was suitably warm. It meant the removal-men opening up the van and going through every piece of furniture in which Cassius might be taking his ease, all oblivious of the trouble he was causing. The removal-men, there were four of them, began wearily rolling up their sleeves and putting on their green aprons again, when Don's wife came out of the empty house, and called very quietly: "Cassius."

At once there was a familiar mew in reply – a muted mew, a very muted mew – from inside the house. Cassius had been in the house all the time. Everyone hurried inside. No sign of Cassius. Catherine called again, again that answering mew, nearer this time. It sounded as if it might be in the kitchen. At the same moment, one of the green-aproned men appeared. The eldest of the quartette, he had never removed his torn cap, worn with the peak at the back, reminiscent of the old-fashioned racing-motorist. He had forgotten to pack his table, he explained. His expression was a trifle anxious. He had left it in the kitchen. Don couldn't quite understand what the chap was doing bringing along his *own* table? It was for his porridge, he said, and went off to the kitchen. Porridge? Another removal-man explained to Don.

The old chap carried a small table with him on every job. Hadn't Don seen him when he first arrived, place it in the kitchen, and drawing up a chair for himself produce a knife and fork? They had horn-handles, he added, but Don asked him to get on with it; there was still Cassius to be accounted for. The other removal-man continued. His mate would sit down at the table, pull out the drawer and eat the porridge that he kept in it with his knife and fork. When he'd eaten all he wanted he'd shut the drawer, stick his knife and fork in his pocket and get on with his job. It was his breakfast; it would also be his lunch. And his tea. He liked porridge, the other removal-man had said.

Don went into the kitchen. There was the small table, with the man, cap back-to-front, about to carry it off. Don stopped him, and he put the table down. The unmistakable sound of mewing came from inside the drawer, and quickly he pulled it open. Cassius rose up from the back of the drawer, stretched himself luxuriously and jumped out. The man stared at him, mouth sagging. "That's where he was," he said. He glanced back at the open drawer. Don, Cassius forgotten for a moment, stared, fascinated at the huge piece of porridge. It was very thick, stiff porridge; like a large slab of very peculiar-looking cake. "Och, it's all right," the removal-man said, "he didn't eat onny of it." He closed the drawer and went off with the table, shouting out to the others that Cassius had been found, and they could be off.

I joined in Don's amusement as he recollected the scene; and then I broke off, and moved to the door. I had heard a badger. I stood in the doorway, a gentle wind soughing up from the loch and whispering under the eaves. I caught the shriek of a tawny owl. "*Kee-wick . . . Keee-wiicck . . .*" It rose into a yell – and there came a strident bark – the best way you could describe it – from the forest in reply. The harsh yap of a badger. I didn't hear the faintest rustle on the air as the owl swept overhead, but saw its phantom shape for a moment before it vanished into the trees above the glen where Rufus and Frieda were. Again it yelled at the badger in the forest. That nerve-grating, "*Keee-wi-icckk . . . Keee-wi-icckk . . .*" Long-drawn-out, rising to a knife-edge screech this time. And the badger's defiant response. That indescribable ba-arr-kk. For several moments I stood in the doorway, listening.

It was a boar badger. His sett, his earth, was down by the edge of the loch. Don thought his mate, the sow, had recently given birth to her young, below ground. He had seen the boar the previous evening; he had been watching for him to make his appearance from the sett. He had caught sight of him carefully scenting the night air before he had pushed his black and white striped face further out, feeling more confident. Slowly with his bear-like walk he had ambled on to the beaten-down earth platform, still sniffing.

"You make him sound like an actor making his entrance on to a stage," I said.

"You should have seen the way he began scratching himself," Don said. "I don't know if actors are supposed to do that."

He had watched the badger scratching himself first with the hind feet, then with his forefeet, scratching his chest and stomach, so that Don had difficulty in not laughing out loud and frightening him back into his sett.

Don and I walked to the edge of the forest. The trees reached up before us, dark and mysterious, and – as I thought, whenever I found myself in the forest at night – quite menacing. It was as if they were an army of giant monsters, their arms linked together, marching slowly, but inevitably, upon you, and you were trapped; you didn't stand a chance of getting away.

This part of the forest was known as Ennochdhu Wood, I knew. As if he had read my thoughts and wanted to reassure me, Don translated for me from the Gaelic: "The Dark Grove of the Birds." As if it would add to my comfort. All I could do was repress a shiver running up my spine. That horrific screeching from the owl, and the badger's grating barks, all of which added to the eerie, macabre atmosphere. I caught what I thought was another glimpse of that ghostly shape ahead. Again that piercing shriek. The badger's reply seemed further off, and as we stood there for several moments, the cries receded. Don would have liked to have gone further into the forest, but I turned and we went back into the house, talking about Frieda's expected cubs.

My mind went back to the girl, and I was seeing her again, holding Rufus, and I remembered noticing that she had surprisingly large hands, square and the fingers almost spatulate. I was reminded of Rima once more. The once-controversial sculpture of her in the bird sanctuary in Hyde Park, London. Epstein had depicted Rima with large hands, but they were full of feeling and tenderness, as if they could hold a bird, a sick or exhausted bird, and give it strength. And I recalled how when it had first been shown, it had been denigrated as monstrous, a scandalous misrepresentation of the character. It had been attacked by vandals, daubed with paint, and attempts made to disfigure it.

Then Don was asking me when the Rufus book was due to be published in America, and would it look the same as the English version; and I gave him the latest on that – the book was due out in the States, early summer; and the paperback was due in this country next November. And both versions would look different in format, I expected.

We talked about how dozens, scores, of people had written to Rufus, after reading the women's magazine in which his story had first appeared, prior to the book itself; then those who had seen him on television, had heard radio interviews about him (at which Rufus had joined in with his chattering noise), or who had actually met him at bookshops at publication-time, and at the big literary lunch when Rufus had caused pandemonium by yawning loudly and without any attempt at apologies during a very important speech.

There had been, too, the incident when Rufus had been invited to be interviewed by newspapermen at the North British Hotel, Edinburgh, and as he was being carried in, followed by press-photographers and press-men, we had all been stopped by the hall-porter. "Sae vurry sorry, but nae dogs allowed in the hotel – sae vurry, vurry sorry, but the directors have given strrrict instrrruc-tions—" "But it's not a dog," I'd interrupted him; and there was a chorus from behind me, "it's a fox . . ." The hall-porter's face had cleared. "Och, that's all right, then," and with Rufus chattering away, we had swept into the hotel. And that other time, the last time Rufus and Don travelled to London together – and he must have felt some premonition that it might be the last time of all, that the two of them weren't destined to be together for much longer – for, when they caught the night-train, Don felt anxious and had smuggled Rufus into his sleeper. The sleeping-car attendant had come along. "Och, sirrrr, ye're no rrrreally supposed to have a dog wi' ye – There arrre rrrules about that—" "He's no dog," Don said. "No dog; would he be a cat, then? There arrre rrrules about caats, too." "He's no cat," Don said. "Then what is he, then?" "A fox," Don said. Pause. "A fox – a fox, did ye say?" "Aye, a fox." "Och, a fox – that's all right, then. There arrre no rrrules about a fox."

What had become the cause for anxiety arising out of all this interest was that so many people had discovered where Rufus could be found. Men, women and children would telephone the house, or come straight up to the front door inquiring if they could meet him. At first Don had been mildly surprised and amused. Rufus had been kissed and cuddled and made a tremendous fuss of – and he as ever as good as gold, never objecting to having his tail pulled, always apparently enjoying every minute of it.

But then had come the threats, warnings of death to him. Don dragged out of bed in the early hours by some local fox-hater, promising him to expect a visit any time now from those determined to wipe out the fox-menace, to make an example of Rufus, who should have been destroyed anyway long before now, for the murderous vermin he was. There were other pieces of "advice" over the telephone at all hours; Don was stopped in the street and warned for "his own good" that it was wrong of him to keep a fox, to attempt to elevate an animal that preyed upon lambs and poultry, that notoriously killed for the love of killing.

There was Tony Bailey, for example. His views on the best ways of dealing with the fox "menace" had been headlined in the *Oban Times* and other Scottish newspapers – he had even got himself space in the London *Observer*; had received £3,000 backing from the local authorities (paid for out of the rates) to meet the expenses of exterminating foxes – and was enthusiastically backed up by farmers and sportsmen all around. It was unlikely that Captain Bailey felt any personal animosity against Don MacCaskill, or even Rufus, but to him, who had declared war on foxes even as he had once been at war with the Germans, the only good fox was a dead fox, just as the only good German had been a dead German.

Even if he himself wouldn't deliberately go out of his way to wipe out Rufus, there were many among those who supported him who only required the opportunity. Such as a farmer, also a contributor to the *Oban Times*, who had outlined what should be done to clean up these evil, murderous foxes that, according to him, took extra special delight in killing his lambs and his poultry. The farmer had even managed to talk over local BBC radio, urging that only total elimination of foxes would really settle the "problem". To chalk up Rufus's death would be rated a great score, and held as a warning example to those who felt compassion for hunted creatures.

There were those who took it upon themselves to draw Don aside and point out how ill-advised he was and that he was asking for trouble (there were a few who told him how much they had enjoyed reading about Rufus and how pleased they were to meet him – but these were almost all tourists, visitors to Dunfuirich, not local people). Don good-humouredly tried to brush off those who button-holed him with their views, and refused to join in any argument or be pushed on to the defensive. But then there had followed on several occasions the sound of footsteps in the night in the direction of the enclosure that Rufus and Frieda were occupying, and voices were heard – footsteps which receded quickly, voices which became whispers on the wind when Don went out to investigate.

He decided for their future safety to remove Rufus and Frieda to the glen by Ennochdhu Wood. It formed a natural enclosure, virtually only the entrance to it required to be fenced off with a wire-netting gate. Don fixed the gate, together with a short length of wire-netting fence on either side, with the help of a local gamekeeper. The upper part of the gate and the fencing was angled back, to forestall any attempts Rufus might make to run up the wire-netting and leap over to the other side. He was cat-like in his agility and ability to surmount high obstacles. It wasn't that he was anxious to escape and run free; it was only that he would be curious to know what lay on the other side of his territory.

He was very restless, and together with Frieda, to whom he communicated his restlessness, he remained in the corner of the old enclosure during all the time the gamekeeper was helping Don secure his new home-to-be. Don knew what the trouble was, but he didn't mention it to the gamekeeper, whom he knew wouldn't believe him if he explained what was going on in Rufus's mind. The gamekeeper knew all about Rufus, and was always anxious to meet this wonderful, friendly fox. But Rufus would have nothing to do with him. "How's old Rufus?" the gamekeeper would ask; and he'd try to entice him to leave his corner and act in his reputed friendly way. It was no good. Rufus never stirred from where he was until the gamekeeper had cleared off.

I knew the reason for Rufus's avoidance of the man, I'd witnessed the same sort of thing before. I was anxious that Don had asked the gamekeeper's help, as a matter of fact; the location of this new home for Rufus and Frieda was intended to be a close secret. The fewer who knew about it, the safer. Don explained that the man was a true Highlander. He knew the danger threatening Rufus, none better; given his word, he had, never to breathe a whisper of the secret of the glen. It had been good enough for Prince Charlie, Don said; it was good enough for him. And then explained how when Charlie was on the run after Culloden, he had had a price of £30,000 on his head, but of all the Highlanders who gave him sanctuary, or those who knew his hiding-places during those desperate days of pursuit and escape by the skin of his teeth, none betrayed him. "Ye could say," Don told me, "it was the only good thing ever came out of the '45 – not a Highlander played Judas. Not even for £30,000." It was the same, he assured me, with the gamekeeper. He wouldn't betray Rufus. I had to be duly impressed.

The glen ran deeply into the hillside, steeply banked on either side with a rock-face at the other end, providing no exit, no entrance from outside. Trees, rowan and young oaks, together with ferns and shrubs provided a natural background; and the higher banks of the glen were entirely shut off from the road, screened from the view of passers-by by the forest itself. From the bank on the other side, which ran precipitously down to the loch, the glen was almost inaccessible. Of course, anyone determined enough to break into the glen could do so, and there were those who were determined enough. But first they would have to know about it, where it was. All who knew, the very few, of the existence of Rufus's new home were sworn to secrecy. Inquiring visitors were put off. If they were genuine wild life enthusiasts, animal lovers, who had travelled a long way to see the celebrity, as in many cases they had, Don would bring Rufus up to the house to meet his admirers. Don felt he had provided Rufus, Frieda and their expected cubs with the best possible protection from their enemies. He could sleep soundly at nights – or at any rate with only half an ear open for intruders.

2

For some reason or another after I turned in that night I suddenly felt wide awake. It wasn't that I wasn't tired enough when I left Don and found myself at Stalker's Cottage, and my bed as promised welcomingly warm. The day had been a long enough haul, and I was looking forward to a good night's sleep. I had a thing or two on my mind admittedly. The girl. I hadn't mentioned her to Don. I didn't know why I hadn't. It had been on the tip of my tongue several times, but I'd held back. Perhaps because I'd only half-believed she had been there, that she hadn't been something I had imagined. Anyway, there would be plenty of opportunities to tell Don about her. He might have seen her himself, for that matter. He would probably be able to tell me who she was, what she was doing there.

I had lived in the Highlands at intervals for four years; the

intervals had been spent at Glencoe, and to-ing and fro-ing from
London. Whenever I went away to London I'd feel a lift of the
tension. Except for saying goodbye to Rufus; that used to give it
a down-beat, because I felt the chances were I might never see him
again. I was always very conscious that his life hung by a thread,
much more so than Don, who was something of a fatalist. You
could say there wasn't much else he could do about it except feel
fatalistic. He'd got Rufus, he couldn't rid himself of him – he had
tried it, in Rufus's interests; it hadn't worked – and there was no
more to be done to protect him than he had already done.

So going away from Dunfuirich was not such a sad goodbye for
me. And coming back, I didn't get the lift that most people feel
when they are in the Highlands. It may have been something to do
with the night-time. I spent a lot of time out at night, and the night-
sky in the Highlands was always remote, to me. When you're out
at night, you look at the sky a lot. You look for the stars, see the
moon, and your imagination takes off a little. But the sky at night
here isn't like the sky at night in the hills under Snowdon, where
I'd once lived, a village straggling on the hillside of Tregarth. Nor
was it like the night-sky in Sydney, where the stars above Rose
Bay always seemed close enough to touch, and there was a warm
intimacy about the Southern Cross night from the moment it fell
with that at first disconcerting suddenness.

Even having my own home near Dunfuirich didn't do much to
change the sense of loneliness, of being so alien, that was never far
away from me in the Highlands. There was this ever-brooding
wildness about the place, a savage wildness mingled with the haunting sadness that hung over the hills and lay along the loch-shore.
Perhaps if you didn't know about the murderous horrors of its
accumulated history, past and relatively recent, you would experience no such sense of desolation, of apprehension, when you were
in the forest, or the glen, you wouldn't feel the presence of those
ill-starred ghosts almost breathing down your neck. Here, along
this very road from nearby Moulin to Blair Castle, passed the
doomed Mary Queen of Scots. Resting at this house by the ford,
the strings of her harp found to be broken, a local harper restrung it
(it remains intact to this day), and the house was named Tigh-na-
teud, the House of the Harp-string. Nearby, in Coille-Brochain
Wood, Robert the Bruce and his few survivors took refuge after a

bloody skirmish prior to his even bloodier victory at Rannoch. Near here, too, was fought the Battle of Killiecrankie, where the English General Mackay's forces were cut to pieces by Viscount Dundee's (known as Claverhouse, who died in the battle) Highlanders' claymores. When those witnesses said "cut to pieces", they weren't fooling around. "General Mackay's officers and soldiers were cut down through the skull and neck to the very breast," the report says. "Others had skulls cut off above their ears, like night-caps; some soldiers had both their bodies and cross-belts cut through at one blow . . ." Their remains lie still under the battlefield, and a hundred years later, in a vault in the old Church of St Bride at Blair Atholl, Claverhouses's helmet and bloodstained breastplate were found. And can't you smell the blood on the howling wind across the moor, hear the thunder of '15 and even more strongly of '45? When exiled King James's Jacobites marched to defeat along the Kirkmichael road; and, later, Prince Charles Edward Stuart made Blair Castle his temporary headquarters on his fateful way south; his fleeing soldiers that following summer to be mercilessly hunted down by Government troops. And listening to old shepherds' tales and those of gipsies who wander the Highlands you could imagine that these events had happened within their life-times, as if they were personally affected, as if they still mourned their dead, even longed to revenge those whose apparitions might be met on midnight roads, or in mist-shrouded glens.

I had taken on Stalker's Cottage when I first came up to the Highlands to research on a book I wrote about an avalanche rescue-dog named Rangi. Rangi, who was in fact to die as a result of being caught in an avalanche, had been owned by the mountain-climber Hamish MacInnes and his wife, Catherine, a Glencoe doctor. The cottage belonged to McNab, the proprietor of the *Fisherman's Rest*. When he'd heard that I was needing a more permanent launching-pad he offered me Stalker's Cottage – if I cared to put it into some sort of shape, since the shape it was in wasn't all that welcoming. The price was ridiculously low, even though it was a ruin. But in any case I hadn't the courage to turn down his offer. He would never have spoken to me again, you knew that if you knew McNab. And I wanted to know more about him. I knew that he was an ex-Commando major, and had been suffering from Hodgkins Disease for the past ten years, which meant that he shouldn't really be alive at all. He certainly looked like some sort of pirate, who'd not only been at death's door but had crossed the threshold and come back, with his battered, hooked nose, fierce black moustache and one flashing, bloodshot eye; he'd left the other behind at Alamein.

It was a two-roomed cottage, with a lean-to scullery and a brick-built outhouse, which was also the lavatory, attached. The place had been unoccupied for more years than McNab could remember. No electric light or power or gas; and no telephone – but the pub was on the 'phone, and since it was only thirty yards away I could always use that and Johnson would take any messages for me any time of night or day and bring them to the cottage. Johnson was McNab's right-hand, barman, *maitre d'*, personal secretary, and knew where McNab hid all the takings. Neither he nor McNab trusted banks, and so the takings, which were always in cash – no cheques – were stashed away in various hiding-places all over the pub.

Johnson swore to me that McNab had a numbered account in a Geneva bank, but he'd lost the number and couldn't remember it. It sounded plausible enough, McNab couldn't always remember where the takings were hidden even, and there were often noisy rows when Johnson wanted his wages and McNab couldn't recall where they were. There must have been hundreds of pounds tucked away in odd places all over the pub – Johnson, in fact, swore the money amounted to several thousand pounds, but you may think he was inclined to exaggerate. I didn't see how the takings could add up to all that much, since the customers at the inn were few and far between: McNab only encouraged customers who were died-in-the-wool fishermen. Which made it all the more remarkable that he had been so kind to me, who hadn't fished since the end of the war and wasn't likely to now.

I had put in a tiny bathroom in the brick outhouse, joining it on to the cottage, and electricity so that I could have light and heating, and an imposing-looking copper immersion-heater for the hot water. It took all of three months; the less said about the punctuality of a very old man and his very young nephew who took on the job, the better. For some reason or other, which was never made clear to me, they had to blow up a rock-slab which was supposed to be in the way of the water-pipe from the main to the cottage.

It was Johnson, of course, who had recommended the pair to me in the first place and I did come to suspect that he had a secret cache of gelignite which he was anxious to put to use, and persuaded uncle and nephew that this was a most suitable occasion.

The explosion took place before McNab or I were warned to open our windows (mine only put in that week) against the blast. Result, neither Stalker's Cottage nor the *Fisherman's Rest* had a pane of glass left. And the glass of whisky in which McNab's dentures were resting was also shattered, much to McNab's anger. At the loss of the whisky, that is. He wasn't bothered about the dentures. He stepped on them, anyway, when he rushed to sop up the whisky with a sponge and squeeze it into his mouth, head held back, with his enormous Adam's apple shooting up and down. The effect on the rock-slab was less positive, and in the end the water-pipe had to be diverted round it anyway. Putting back the glass took the uncle and the nephew all of three weeks.

Despite this and several other mishaps, however, the cottage proved to be comfortable; walls thick and kept out the cold; the new roof-tiles remained in place, and the immersion-heater was a success. Always plenty of hot water when required. I covered the stone floors with heavy-duty linoleum, a warm red colour, which kept the damp out underfoot. I retained the fireplace with its huge mantelpiece. It was marble, so Johnson said, obtained from a Glen Tilt quarry, long disused. According to Johnson, it was really limestone – there are extensive deposits of it throughout the locality, but the process of aging it had purified it so that it had been quarried as marble. It was a strange pale green colour with dark veins running through it. I noticed that Johnson became somewhat reticent about it when I wanted to know where it had come from. It was a bit incongruous-looking for the cottage, but it was decorative and so it remained. In the winter the electric fires were supplemented with peat fires which if they didn't seem to provide much heat, nevertheless gave the place a picturesque aroma. I pannelled the walls floor to ceiling with white-painted matchboarding, which helped keep the rooms light; the windows weren't very large, and in the winter the rooms were pretty dark. The white walls helped. Heavy nylon net curtains over the windows (easy to wash, no ironing) and thick wooden shutters outside which I closed on winter nights. I cooked on the electric cooker quite a bit: bacon and eggs, omelettes (Mrs Turk taught me how to make them, and I began to fancy I was quite the expert: you use an iron frying-pan, of course; that's the trick), and there were summer salads, and plenty of milk. It's haunted. As I later found out. I don't believe in ghosts, I've never encountered one in my life, but, all the same, Stalker's Cottage is haunted.

Two or three times a week I went over to the Fasganeoin Hotel for dinner, and to talk to Mrs Turk and the family. Mr Klein and Mr Turk had been prisoners-of-war at a camp at Haxby, near York, before they had earned enough money working night and day in a restaurant to buy their own café at Berwick-on-Tweed; they had prospered and bought this hotel. Mr Klein was a cousin of Mr Turk; the two had been officers in the same Alpine regiment together, which had surrendered to the Americans in May 1945.

Sleep was beginning to catch up with me; I found myself trying to recall the names of the places I had come to know since I had lived at Dunfuirich. The names of the mountains, like Ben Vrackie, which is Gaelic for Speckled Mountain; like Ben Vuroch, the Hill of the Howling Wolves, the last wolf in the Highlands – after the fox, Scotland's most beautiful wild animal – had been destroyed 150 years ago; and there was Craigreach, the Raven's Crag – ravens were shot on sight, regarded as birds of ill-omen or predators who preyed on innocent game-birds. And rivers' names which sounded like the clang of war-like claymore against buckler – Aldrory, the Burn of the Sentinel, where robbers met to divide the spoils of their forays; Pool Dour, where otters were hunted; and names like Dunfallandy, the Fort by the Place of Blood; and Donavourd, the Fort by the Ford.

Sleep must have finally trapped me, caught me unawares, the way it sometimes does. At any rate I was suddenly awake. My bedside light was on. I looked at my wrist-watch. 3.13 am. I looked round the bedroom, at first not quite sure where I was, and then the fresh scent of the aired sheets told me. I switched off the light and lay in the semi-darkness; moonlight was seeping into the room through the curtains which I hadn't drawn-to properly. I realised what it was that had woken me; it was the wash-basin tap dripping in the bathroom. It was across the passage from my bedroom door, which was open. The bathroom door was open, too. I knew I would have to get up and turn the tap off more tightly. I didn't switch on the light again. My eyes were becoming used to the moonlight. I lay there for several moments, forcing myself to get out of bed. Finally, I jumped out; I could see my way without barging into the furniture, and went to the bathroom and turned the tap tightly. I waited for a moment or two to make sure the drip-drip had stopped. It had and I came back into the bedroom, and drew back the curtain.

The moon was a pale sickle, veiled now by mist that lay above a deep, dark curve of the distant hills across the loch. Streaks of black cloud moved across the sky. My mind went to the glen by the Dark Grove of the Birds, and Rufus and Frieda. The darkness that could not be so dark to them as it would be to human beings, because surely the mechanism of their eyes enabled them to see what they saw in a kind of daylight. The night was illuminated for them, because their eyes were like cat's eyes. I hoped that no damned poacher, no damned fox-hater had discovered their secret glen. My heart constricted at the image of some ruffian in the dark creeping upon Rufus and Frieda, and blasting out their lives with a shotgun. I shook off my fears. Did Rufus love the night-time best of all? It was the time that was most natural to him, the time for which he was most suited, with his cat's eyes which enabled him to search the darkness.

Rufus had committed himself to Don and had changed the pattern of his life, becoming an animal of the day in order to share the company of the man he loved. This had been at the beginning, when Rufus had spent a lot of his time in the house, sharing the hearth with Cassius and Shuna – and there had been the time when he had been ill, when he'd nearly died, and the sitting-room had been his hospital-ward.

When he recovered, Don had come to the decision that he should be returned to the wild, where he belonged; he had tried to send him back, but without success. Rufus had returned, and Don had reached a compromise by finding him a mate. Frieda. This had entailed providing the pair of them with a home which would give them as near as possible a life in the wild. And Rufus had spent more time there, with Frieda, which was how it should be. Did Rufus now live a life more closely approximating to the life he was meant to live? At night did he move about the glen, alert for a rat, vole, or rabbit, on which to pounce? Don had never observed him kill a single creature; but at night did he revert to his true, predatory self?

As always whenever I thought about him, I pictured his sharp, yet gentle features, those extraordinary round, innocent eyes; that slim, tapering body and great, white-tipped brush, and my heart warmed towards him. A freight-train chuffed in the distance, on its way to Inverness. I wondered what sounds Rufus heard in the night; that knife-edge bark of the badger down by the loch and the screech of the tawny owl, what did they convey to him? Would he move quickly to Frieda's side, in case that blood-curdling noise gave her cause for alarm – she was in a jumpy, nervous state, she was carrying his cubs.

The slivet of moon had disappeared behind a mass of black cloud. I heard the high note of a gust of wind from the loch, and my thoughts began to drift, my eyelids felt heavy and I got back to bed. I think I was wondering if perhaps the girl was out there, like some wraith, watching and waiting, talking in low whispers to Rufus – Frieda would be lying deep down in the den, restless and secretive, waiting for the birth of the cubs – when I fell asleep once more.

3 The Scent of Fear

Don was telling me how, six weeks before, he had thought he had lost Frieda. We were in the glen in the afternoon two days after my return to Dunfuirich. Don was saying that it had happened just prior to Rufus and Frieda being removed from their old enclosure to their present home. One night she had got out, vanished. Don didn't understand how she had managed to escape. There were no apparent signs of her having made a hole in the wire-netting, nor that had she tunnelled a way out. It wasn't until two days later that he came across a corner of the wire-netting near the padlocked gate which had been carefully cut and pulled back to provide a gap large enough to invite Rufus or Frieda to slip through. The wire had then been pushed back and held in position with some thin wire. A vandal or fox-hater had been at work.

What had happened to Frieda? It depended upon the vandal's purpose. It might have been to set her free, so that she would be hunted to her death. Or she might have been killed there and then, and the body minus the brush, which was worth £1 reward, left hanging nearby as "warning" evidence of what was in store for Rufus. In fact, it was more than likely that the escape-hole was intended for him to use, he had been deliberately let loose on a previous occasion; instead it was Frieda who had escaped.

She stayed away for twelve days, but Don had felt convinced that she would return, calculating that she would wait until late afternoon, when the daylight was beginning to fade, before she would condescend to come home. He left the enclosure-gate open from 4.30 until last thing at night. He trusted Rufus not to seize the opportunity to take himself off, on the basis that he too was anxious for his mate's return, and would remain behind to help lure her back.

On the thirteenth day, at 4.00 in the afternoon, Catherine was reading a letter from Meg Allan, who during Loch Aweside days had been a devoted friend of Rufus – then she had married and with her husband left the Highlands. Meg was asking after Rufus, when Catherine thought she heard him give a yowl, and looking out of the bedroom window she saw Frieda at the enclosure-gate, with Rufus on the other side, scratching at the wire-netting, trying to let her in. Catherine hurried down to catch her, but Frieda had slipped away.

Don could hardly credit it; it seemed to him that Frieda had returned before at about the same time. Next day at 4.00 he was waiting. Frieda duly showed up, and after a game of hide-and-seek which he eventually won, he took her back to the enclosure. She replied to Rufus's warm greeting with a nonchalance that suggested she had been out doing the afternoon's shopping.

When Don and I had first gone into the glen Frieda hadn't come rushing forward with Rufus to greet us, she remained out of sight. But presently she appeared, her manner somewhat abstracted, and came to Don, wagging her tail tentatively. She looked very pretty, the fur pale gold, her face and breast a startling white. At first wary of me, she then approached me slowly. She made little bites at my heels. It was her way of "defending" her cubs in advance, so to speak. And she made bites at my outstretched hand. Not to hurt, just as a sort of warning not to make any move which might harm her unborn young.

Rufus had wandered off, to stretch himself full-length in a patch of sunlight. He was inclined to give the impression at this time of being thoroughly exhausted, as if being a father was a monumental task almost beyond his strength. His appearance at this time was also, regretful as it is to have to mention it, not what it might have been. This was nothing to do with his having been made a father; it was simply his natural moult. But he didn't shed his fur in a neat uniform manner; instead it seemed to take place in haphazard patches, and bits of fur which hadn't quite released themselves clung to him in various parts of his anatomy, giving him the look of a rather worn, moth-eaten rug; or perhaps, better, an old out-of-work actor, for despite his world-weariness, every now and then he would sparkle into life, his eyes would brighten, his teeth would glisten in that laughing grimace, he would leap and chatter and give his inimitable performance. Frieda was only a little plump round her belly; you wouldn't think she was shortly to give birth to five cubs.

Don had dug out her earth for her, because he wanted to construct it so that the roof would be removable, enabling him to observe her with her cubs from the start. It hadn't been as easy as it may seem. Frieda, aided by Rufus, much preferred to dig a den for herself. She and Rufus worked extraordinarily fast; they would burrow three or four feet deep in a night, and Don had to fill in the earth with chunks of rock in order to prevent them continuing with their self-imposed task. Next morning there would be a new earth dug out. Don had to fill in half a dozen half-begun earths before Frieda finally agreed to take on the one he had provided. In the wild, a vixen in cub and her mate would move around a wide area, testing various locations for their den, and at the slightest sign of human beings, any hint of danger, would slip away to find another home, undisturbed.

Don removed the wooden roof to the den which Frieda had decided to occupy, and I looked down on the smoothed-out earth below, an area of one square foot, with pieces of rock providing the walls of her home. The cubs' "cradle" was nothing more than hard, smooth earth. I had imagined that Frieda would have lined it with the fur she had pulled out with her teeth from around her teats, but, no, the cubs would rely on her body-warmth and that from each other.

Frieda stood "on guard", biting at my heels and my hands, while I knelt to look down into her home. Don calmed her with gentle fondling and murmurs of comfort. Frieda wouldn't leave until Don had replaced the roof, whereupon she shot down, a flash of pale gold and white, into the den. We could hear her muttering – a kind of purring growl – until we turned away and left her, a mother-to-be, to enjoy privacy and quiet. Don thought the cubs would be born either that night, or the next. He picked up Rufus in his arms, and went out of the glen. I followed him, locking up after me. We went up to the house, Rufus chattering away in Don's arms, nibbling at his ear, then at my ear as I walked beside him.

There was a short, sharp shower, and then from the window Rufus watched a patch of blue push the dark clouds aside. Even before the shower had stopped, a rainbow arched the sky from the mountains across the loch to descend in a mist of colour into the roof-tops of Dunfuirich.

A teacher from a local school was bringing her class over for a nature talk. Don enjoyed interesting visitors in the forest, nature-trail walks, and talks about wild-life conservation. Some 150,000 visitors, mostly tourists, made their way up the winding road to the forest every year, and Don found that school-children were his best audiences. At any rate, he enjoyed talking to them best. Naturally, they all wanted to meet Rufus.

The school-mistress and the children, boys and girls of eight to twelve years' age-group, were just arriving; they grouped round a fallen tree-trunk near the house. There were cries of delight at the sight of Rufus, a burst of spontaneous applause, which Rufus acknowledged with much wagging of his magnificent tail. As the children crowded round, the school-teacher turned to me with an incredulous expression on her face. She had been reading the Rufus book, she explained, though she had been sceptical of some parts of it. (Don hadn't had a chance to introduce me, she took me for a passing friend.) Yet here was this fox, the children clamouring to cuddle him – they soon took him over, passing him from one to the other – burying their faces in his fur, pulling his tail, and all the time Rufus chattering at them, entering into the spirit of it all. "Frankly," the young woman said to me, "I thought the book was rather exaggerated. But they believed it." She stared at the children – you couldn't see Rufus. "They knew he was true."

She and her class had gone, and Don was in the house. I had gone to the garage, I'd parked my car outside it, and was thinking about returning home. An affable-looking man, wearing a deerstalker cap appeared. "How's old Rufus?" he said. He was carrying a stick under his arm as if it was a double-barrelled gun, it seemed to me. He was a gamekeeper from an estate the other side of Dunfuirich. I'd met him once before with Don. Had I any news of the cubs, he wanted to know. "I'd heard Rufus's vixen was expecting."

At that moment, Don came out. He had heard the man's voice. Asked the same question I had been asked, Don gave the man the same reply I'd given him. The gamekeeper nodded, and said that he must have heard wrongly. When Don asked him where he'd heard about the cubs, he couldn't recall where or how. "How's old Rufus getting on," he said. Don almost stiffened, then he glanced at me and gave me a conspiratorial wink. I followed him and the gamekeeper to the house, where Rufus and Shuna were enjoying a snooze together in her basket in the kitchen. The basket, which was really on the small side for Shuna, had once been used by Rufus when he'd lain ill from German distemper; after his recovery Shuna had taken it on, but Rufus liked to renew acquaintanceship with his old sick-bed, and Shuna gladly allowed him to share it. Don called to Rufus, who came to the back door, paused, looked at him, and advanced slowly towards him. Then he stopped. Don talked to him as if to calm him. The gamekeeper was a dozen yards away. By now Rufus's nose was tilted, he was getting the man's scent. Suddenly he turned and dashed away, his brush waving to give him balance, and he was hidden behind the corner of the house. I knew then what Don's conspiratorial wink had been about. The gamekeeper had foxes' blood on his hands. Rufus would have nothing to do with him. Rufus knew he had killed foxes.

"You'll never convince him," Don said, after the gamekeeper had gone, frowning to himself in disbelief. "I've explained to him before that Rufus won't have anything to do with him."

It was difficult to explain; if you hadn't witnessed Rufus's reaction to anyone who had foxes' blood on his hands you wouldn't believe it. When I had first met Rufus four years ago, I had waited in Don MacCaskill's sitting-room one morning while he went out to fetch him. He was enjoying a meal with Shuna and Cassius in the kitchen. Outside the warm room the sky looked grey and chilly, gusts of wind off the loch rattled the windows and I felt a stranger in a strange land. A hostile land, even; the same feeling I had experienced when I had been there before. A savage, wild place it had seemed to me to be. I had been made very welcome at this house on the forest-edge, all snug and cheerful, but somehow the heart of the Highlands still didn't beat for me. True, I've never holidayed here. I've never been free in my mind of work, of meeting people, of getting to know human beings, some of whom didn't want me to get to know them. Not too well, at any rate. And getting to know the place where the events I needed to learn occurred, where the action was. And so anxiety, tensions build up, and the day's work doesn't go well. You wonder sometimes if there aren't influences in the atmosphere which aren't on your side. You feel this especially in the Highlands, when you're here to work, to research, to write. I'm sure it would be different if you were on a vacation. Feeling free, running away, escaping.

I was certainly feeling some anxiety about this first meeting with Rufus. I had already built up a picture of what he would be like from what MacCaskill himself had written and had told me over the telephone during the past several weeks. I had never seen a fox at close quarters before. I had glimpsed one once or twice as a boy when I'd stayed with relatives who lived outside Worcester; I had watched one race across a field one typical Sussex summer's evening, when I was driving down to Lewes. Supposing he took an instant, instinctive dislike to me? I had no special feeling for animals, so far as I knew, or they for me. There had been the inevitable boyhood rabbits, white mice, but I couldn't recall that I'd shared any special empathy with them. I had once exchanged a rabbit, which had won prizes at local shows, but had bitten me – I bear the scar to this day – for a pair of pigeons, whose owner omitted to mention that they were of a variety which resulted in their flying back to him after the briefest stay in the loft I'd built for them, and I never saw them, or my rabbit, again.

I heard Don's voice outside the door and I tensed as it opened. He came in with Rufus in his arms and made straight for me. I stared entranced at this beautiful creature, his round, hazel eyes shining with friendliness, mouth wide open as if he was laughing with pleasure at meeting me. "Take him," and Don pushed him into my arms. I held him to me, my throat constricted, my eyes wet as Rufus chattered at me, nibbled my ear and licked my face. "You've never killed a fox," Don MacCaskill had said. I knew that I had passed the test. The acid test. Don went on to explain, his face very serious, that if I had ever killed a fox, Rufus would have acted very differently towards me. He would have rushed out of the room, out of the house if he could have got away, at the first scent of me. "He can tell, you see – don't ask me how – but he won't have anything to do with a fox-killer." I stared at him disbelievingly, while Rufus's warm, musky smell filled my nostrils. I hadn't really believed him, but I felt it was as well to humour his little idio-syncrasies. I was to learn that it was the truth he was telling me.

It was at the *Yorkshire Post* Literary Lunch, at Harrogate. A tall, rugged-looking man had come up to Don, Rufus and me, anxious to meet this wonderful animal that everyone was crowding round, and flashbulbs were popping. Instantly Rufus gave an agonised yelp and ran for it. I went after him and grabbed him. He was shivering as if he was bitterly cold, cold as death. The tall man was smiling, more than puzzled by Rufus's reaction. What was the matter, he wanted to know. Don told him that Rufus didn't like him. The other glanced round the crowd – the children had surged towards me, jostling each other to get close to Rufus. "He seems to like everyone else, why pick on me?" Don replied that the only reason must be that he had killed foxes. Which wiped the smile clean off the man's face. "Well," he said, "I do happen to be a Master of Fox-Hounds," mentioning the name of a famous hunt. He still couldn't see what that had to do with Rufus not wanting to know him. It wasn't as if, he said, he hated foxes; he thought they were rather jolly, sporting little chaps, as a matter of fact. Don had turned his back on him.

Referring to the gamekeeper who had just gone, Don was saying: "He hasn't got it in for foxes, no particular hatred for them, but it's a fact that it happens to be his job to kill them." And Rufus was aware of it? Some kind of vibrations, whatever you like to call them, that he picked up? But how did he pick them up? I don't know that I'd had a lot of time for human beings who are supposed to possess psychic powers, second sight, let alone animals. Even Rufus. Don was recalling the first dog he'd ever owned, named Queenie, a black-and-tan Scottish collie; she was an example of a dog's second sight. At that time, Don's father ran the village-store and post-office. A local woman who was supposed to be strange in the head called regularly every Friday to collect her pension-money. Every Friday Queenie would post herself at the window just when the woman was due to appear down the glen at the other end of the village on her bicycle. The moment she showed up, Queenie would start growling, her hackles would rise. Don, or whoever was about at the time, would have to grab her, otherwise she would have gone for the woman. It was the only occasion in all her life when Queenie's behaviour was other than most friendly. But Queenie knew there was something off-key about that woman on Friday, and she didn't like it.

I was thinking about Rangi, the Glencoe search-and-rescue dog. As I mention in the book I wrote about him, it had never been explained to me how Rangi, an Alsatian, had learned to search out a lost climber avalanched, buried several feet deep in ice and snow, in the blackest night in the middle of a howling blizzard. It wasn't a case of giving him the man's slipper and saying, "Good dog, go find." Rangi had never met him before. Yet though there might be a thousand other scents in the vicinity – rescue-parties, other climbers, police, RAF helicopter personnel – Rangi would unerringly nose out the lost man. The most convincing explanation of his scenting powers was really a chemical one, that the buried individual was under tremendous stress and consequently giving off a perspiration-odour totally different from that given off under normal conditions. It was this that Rangi's remarkable scenting apparatus was able to pick up and sort out from all other scents around.

In fact, though Rufus runs like a dog, has scenting powers as phenomenal as those of a dog if not more so, there exists some uncertainty concerning what precisely are a fox's antecedents. Rufus wags his tail, barks in a dog-like manner, but he also jumps and climbs trees like a cat; he is a nocturnal animal with typical cat's eyes. The evolutionary history of the horse begins with the Eohippus, "dawn horse", of the Eocine period, fifty million years ago, which is described as a four-toed, fox-like creature. But whatever Rufus's most distant origins, however far back his genes may reach, while horse, dog and cat have become the most domesticated of animals, with the closest relationship to man, the fox rarely becomes friends with a human being (perhaps because the hand of friendship has been rarely extended to him). Possibly, therefore, as a consequence of this human contact, dog, cat and horse are most of all credited with second sight, clairvoyance, or however you prefer to name it.

Perhaps if you started to think about the fox, or, for that matter, other animals that have never had the luck to be domesticated and protected, the same as you think of the accepted "friends of man", if you were less anxious to destroy Rufus's kind, you might be able to ascribe to the fox even more impressive powers of seeing round the corner of the future than those of the dog, horse, or cat. And, also, of course, Rufus was Highland born and bred; he weighed more, he was bigger, tougher, with thicker, more reddish-coloured fur than an English fox. Rufus's ancestors raced through the hills and glens when local Pictish Druids, tonsured from ear to ear, were priests of the Sun Worship and Nature Worship religions before the advent of Christianity, times of witchcraft and "magic", the festivals of Hallowe'en and Beltane fires; when the rugged mountains and wild moors were peopled with supernatural beings, when the very air must have vibrated to the scalp-prickling presence of *uruisgeans*, goblins – water-witches, *glaistegs*, rose from the depths of the lochs (such apparitions, according to some, may still be seen at certain times of the year, when the moon is in some particular phase) – and it is not difficult to believe that vibrations such as these must have been picked up by, rubbed off on, the wild creatures such as the fox. Even lately, the neighbourhood boasted strange people possessed of occult powers. Wandering tinkers; an aged widow in a hillside croft; a loner living in a tent in some dark glen; many were supposed to be wizards who could transform themselves into animal shape, though I hadn't come across anyone ever having been turned into a fox. None of which could explain Rufus's uncanny ability to scent a fox-killer out of the thousands he encountered. There is a dramatic story, as it happens, concerning a husband whose wife turns into a vixen, and what happened to him – and her. How it came to be written, and how Rufus came to be involved in it had something to do with my motives for being back here. And there was that rather odd twist to the story of Rufus and the gamekeeper.

The cubs weren't born that night.

Or the next.

2

Friday morning was bright, the loch lay quiet, ranging in colour from various shades of blue to that slatey grey, and white cotton-wool clouds were festooned low over those dark, plum-coloured hills in the distant haze. I could sniff the tang of the faraway sea and my imagination filled with some tiny harbour on a loch-side, with white cottages clustering round it, and a ferry-boat heading away from the quay – this was the gentle, wistful magic of the country that the proximity of the sea gave it; at least it always felt like that to me. A skein of Greylag geese – I counted seven of them in perfect, characteristic V formation – flew overhead, beginning their long journey across the Atlantic to Iceland. They made for the hills beyond the loch, where lay the moor where they would rest on their way north. Their passage above was silent, only in the imagination could you hear the whirr of their wings, and then as they sped away, there came back the sound of their wild honking, musical and thrilling, unforgettable.

Hughie Drummond and I came past the farm, and the blind sheepdog appeared from the derelict barn and came up, sniffed at Hughie's hand, and got into step beside him; as well, that is, as you could expect a four-footed animal to get into step with a two-footed animal. Hughie observed that it was the wrong way round, a sighted man leading a blind dog, it should be a sighted dog leading a blind man. He went on about the intelligence of dogs. Did I realise how extraordinarily intelligent they were? That before attaching themselves to man dogs had run in packs, led by a boss-dog, and they had followed him because he led them to food. Then dogs had found food more easily outside the caves where cave-men threw the bones and remains of their meals. Where man was there was food – accordingly the dog had stopped running in packs and started to run with man. Man was their leader from then on, man gave them food. The dog relied on man; man trained it. "Dog became man's best friend," Hughie said; he had a rather unctuous manner and came out with utterances as if they had never been said before. "Yet," he went on, "although a dog has been trained to obey man, to follow him as his leader, it's been found that he is so intelligent he can be trained to act in reverse – to lead a man. That's what your guide-dog does." He grinned at me triumphantly and, inevitably, added: "Elementary, Dr Watson."

Hughie had been born in Fife 73 years ago. He had served in the Scots Guards in the First World War, after which he had led a rover's life up and down the country. It was his daily routine to trudge from his tent on the loch-side to the public library to pore over books concerned with local history, folk-lore and legends; and gossip with cronies – tinkers and gipsies. Somehow, he always managed to acquire an unwanted box, or a broken chair – once, it had been a child's pram – upon which he could rest on his return journey and then convert into kindling for his fire, which he kept

going daily. To rest his legs was a necessity, you see, owing to his
having been badly wounded, both legs, on the Somme (or it might
have been Mons, or Ypres – after all, it was a few years ago, now,
and an old soldier couldn't be expected to remember details).
"Wanted to amputate, them sawbones did. But I wouldn't let 'em.
If ma legs go, then ma body goes with 'em, was how I put it to the
quacks. And d'ye ken what? Got up off ma stretcher and walked
away, I did – God gave me the power – and back to the mud and
blood of Flanders." He would show you the scars to prove it – in
fact, you would have difficulty in preventing him from doing so –
for the price of a dram. A dram for each leg. And, lowering his
voice, he would add that he could also show you scars of other
wounds in other parts of his anatomy, which, of course, a natural
modesty made it quite impossible to display to your fascinated, if
sympathetic, gaze.

The last nine years he had lived, summer and winter, in a patched
old army tent that looked like a First War relic itself. You could
wish him good-morning as you passed; you could always tell
when he was at home – he wasn't an early riser, anyway – by his
huge army-type boots, toes turned up, which stood on an impro-
vised table, beside which bacon-and-eggs sizzled in the frying-pan
over the fire. When the weather became too fearful for even his
hardy nature Johnson had let him sleep in Stalker's Cottage – this
was before I had taken it over. Now, I suspected, he sheltered, if
ever the need arose, at Blind Dog's Farm, as it was known locally.

Many years before, according to Hughie Drummond this was,
the owner of the farm had met and married a girl from Edinburgh.
The girl had been sick and ailing, and her mother had insisted on
coming to live with her and her husband. Over ten years she had
lived with them, dominating her daughter, who remained ill, and
causing trouble between her and her husband. He had tried to
persuade the mother to leave, but, strangely enough, the daughter
had always prevented it. There was nothing he could do about it.
There came a development. The wife's sister arrived at the farm for
a holiday. To the husband's delight – premature as it transpired –
she did manage to persuade the mother to go away on a protracted
visit to relatives. The farmer was full of gratitude to his sister-in-
law; at last it looked as if after all these years he and his wife would
get a chance to make their marriage work. Within three weeks,

Hughie continued, shaking his head, the sister had taken over where the mother-in-law had left off. She was dominating the marriage of the farmer and his wife. Now, he failed to persuade *her* to go; his wife insisted on her remaining. In a last effort to prevail upon her that this was no sort of marriage, he went off. He would return, he said, when the sister-in-law left. The mother-in-law promptly came back from visiting relatives, and she and both her daughters took over the farm. The husband was never heard of again.

I wanted to know what happened to the three women and the farm. Why had it stood empty? Hughie replied that the wife was still there, though no one ever saw her, and the farm was falling about her ears. Her mother died. The wife, who was now convinced that her husband was dead, and her sister had quarrelled over a young sheepdog that turned up out of the blue. The wife and the dog became firm friends, but it took an instant dislike to the sister, who wanted it destroyed. The wife refused and in the end the sister left. Soon afterwards the dog became blind. "And that," said Hughie, "is why it's known as Blind Dog's Farm." He nodded at the sheepdog at his side. I looked at him questioningly. "Elementary, Dr Watson," he said, and I felt a prickling under my scalp. "He's the husband, come back to the farm again."

The blind dog had hesitated, now it stopped. As we paused, he turned and began to make his way slowly back to the farm. He held his nose close to the ground along the side of the road. A man in a long black coat and wearing a flat cap over his long nose approached us, walking very quickly, passing the blind dog, who didn't appear to take any notice of him. I knew the man by sight, and after he had passed us as if we weren't there, Hughie explained that he was a "tink", a tinker, who spent his life walking from one end of the Highlands to the other. He had never been known to speak to a soul. He never answered if spoken to, just walked on, eyes fixed ahead of him, oblivious to the world. You couldn't help wondering who he was, where he came from, what calamity in his life had impelled him to turn away from any human contact, to prefer an existence unknown, unwanted, and unwanting. "Even the dogs don't bark at him," Hughie said.

The tinkers are still a feature of Highland life, though they usually prefer to form a group remaining in one place, instead of wandering about as individuals. Some claim to be descendants of the victims of the infamous Highland Clearances of the 1780s, driven from their homes by their own chiefs; whole families drifted about the neighbourhood of their burned and destroyed homes, hoping against desperate hope that they might yet return. They never did. Some of these joined up with gipsies, to wander further afield. It was the gipsies who used to make the wooden whistles which Highland watchmen used as warnings when the hated evicters approached to throw them out of their homes. Other tinkers had originally found their way up from the Lowlands, because they found the people there much less generous than the reports that had been passed on to them about Highlanders. It's the poor who help the poor, according to the saying. Certainly Highlanders were much worse off economically than those of the Lowlands and the Border.

Three families of tinkers were well known locally. The Stewarts, who claimed they were descended from Scottish royalty, which accounts for another saying: The Stewarts are akin to kings and tinkers. There were the Reids and the MacArthurs, who equally claimed descent from the great clans. The tinkers had lived together as "tribes", with an elected chief – the last was the venerable Elijah Stewart with his long white hair – who performed his tribe's marriage ceremonies. There was "Gentleman" Duncan MacArthur, who attended bible-study, went regularly to church and was all for his tribe's strict moral discipline. The tinkers in more recent years seemed to have joined up with the gipsies and other free souls, one of the most famous being Black Donald, poacher, who, emulating the style of other sportsmen, used to have his own gillie and pony. Once, when returning from a successful foray, his pony laden with game, he chanced upon the aristocratic owner of the shoot over which he had been poaching, entertaining his party of guests to lunch. Undetected and undismayed, he coolly halted behind the wall of a sheep-fold and together with his gillie sat down to a more frugal lunch, over which they proceeded to take their time until the other party moved on, enabling Black Donald to proceed in peace.

"Mind ye," Hughie insisted, "I'm no tink, though I dinna follow any particular calling. I never carried me meal poke." This was a reference to the sort of beggar's bowl carried by the tinks, who

(*previous page*) "Wooh-wooh-hoo" – Rufus practising one of his famous love-calls, of which he possessed an extensive repertoire.

Family group – or part of it, two have dodged out of the picture. It's becoming increasingly difficult to keep them together.

(*below*) Robbie has found a comfortable corner with Shuna.

Robbie, with two of the other cubs. But not for long,
he's about to take off again.

(*below*) Robbie's gone, another's come back, but another has also gone –
still only three cubs together.

Robbie putting up his usual performance on the scales.

(*left*) Robbie, blind to the world and its wickedness. Note the characteristic white tip to his "sausage" tail.

(*left*) Shuna, looking maternal, with never a child to call her own.

(*above*) Cronk, putting on a dignified pose against the back-drop of the loch.

(*below*) One of his play-mates; Rufus takes it easy for a time.

A week or two before he was killed, Cassius had brought home a baby roebuck as a friend.

(*below*) Shuna pays a call on Rufus down in the glen.

usually received gifts rather than money. Hughie sang (if you can
call it that) to an accompaniment of sly winks and nudges, to ensure
that I got all the points of the old ditty, all of which totally escaped
me:

A bag for his oatmeal, another for his salt,
And a pair of crutches to show that he could halt;
A bag for his corn, another for his rye,
A little bottle by his side to drink when he is dry.

What trade he ever had followed he kept wrapt in mystery. He
had apparently reached a kind of identification with Saint
Columba, born A.D. 521, belonging to the powerful O'Donnell
clan of Ireland, who were of royal blood. "Scots fra Ireland had
already invaded this part of the worrrld," he explained, "and in
A.D. 563, Saint C., he was an Irish monk, sailed for Iona, that's off
the Isle of Mull, as ye ken, with twelve apostles, just like Jesus
Christ himself had. This was before this land was ever known as
Scotland, and the Highlands were shrouded in Pagan darkness,
governed by Druids, and Saint Columba came here to win the
souls of the people for that same Jesus Christ I've just mentioned —"

An RAF Phantom suddenly screamed up the loch, its ear-
splitting noise deepening into a horrendous roar as it hurtled
towards us. I was calculating that it must be flying lower than
Don's house, it kept so close to the surface of the water. Hughie
moved his mouth against my ear. "Och, Saint Columba believed
that evil spirits existed in the very skies of the Highlands," he yelled.
"The *Sidhe*, they were called, who lived in the green hills and in the
waterfalls, the clouds, the earth, the trees – the force of Fire, the
flash of Lightning —" The rest of what he was shouting was lost
in the roar of the jet as it went past. I watched it; it seemed it must
fly straight into the great wall of mountain at the end of the loch.
But at the crucial moment, it suddenly peeled off upwards, to the
right in a breath-taking arc and vanished from sight. It was
probably practising avoiding radar interception; and then it
occurred to me that I must ask Don if there was any danger of the
shock of its tremendous noise causing Frieda to abort.

Hughie continued on his way towards the public library, I went
up the drive to the Fasganeoin Hotel. Mrs Turk used to allow me to
telephone from her office instead of using the coin-box in the hall.

Sometimes I felt I didn't want to risk being overheard. The *Fisherman's Rest* had only one telephone, in the tiny passage with no door between it and the bar. It was pretty public.

I called London. I called Edinburgh. Then I went into the Turk family's private sitting-room. Mrs Turk and Mr Klein were discussing how they could accommodate an American married couple writing from Boston. "We are full up," Mr Klein was saying, "and the hotel wasn't built with rubber walls." Mrs Turk pointed out that the husband and wife had stayed at the hotel last summer, and that they were such nice people. "But they slept with the electric light on all night," Mr Klein said. He turned to me. "It is true. Every night – for a week they stayed – they kept the light on all the time –" Mrs Turk said to me that they were a middle-aged couple, and Mr Klein wanted to know what that had got to do with it. Mrs Turk explained to him carefully that if they had been young, probably on their honeymoon, they wouldn't have wanted the light on all through the night. Mr Klein had no answer except to raise his eyes upwards as if seeking guidance from Heaven. Mrs Turk added that the Boston married couple had notified her that they'd kept the light burning, and expected to be charged extra. "Only we didn't charge them," Mr Klein pointed out. "In any case we still can't accommodate them this time." He shook his head. "Very regretfully, we can't accommodate them – I'm sure they were very nice people."

He went to the office to type out a letter accordingly. I gave Mrs Turk the latest news about Frieda, that the cubs were expected any time; and she wanted to know when she and Norbert and Sabrina would be able to come and see them. I thought about a week after the cubs had been born; it depended on Frieda's mood, and what Don felt about disturbing her and the new arrivals. Previously, he had always left her well alone with her newly-born until several days after birth. This time he planned to observe them as soon as he thought he could reasonably expect Frieda not to be upset, weigh the cubs, learn all he could about them from their earliest moment. Norbert and Sabrina came in to hear my news, and Mr Klein poked his head round the door. "By the way," he asked. "Why did they want the light on all night."

"They never said," Mrs Turk replied. "And I didn't ask."

"Oh," Mr Klein said, and withdrew.

Norbert and Sabrina looked blankly at their mother, who explained what the brief exchange was all about. "It's happened several times with American visitors," Norbert said. And they didn't all let her know about the extra use of light, Mrs Turk said. "You wouldn't have charged them if they had," Norbert told her. Mrs Turk agreed she wouldn't have done so, but she still liked to know. Mr Klein put his head round the door again, this time to know about the young man with the candle in the wash-basin all night. Norbert and Sabrina laughed and their mother explained to me that a young man and his mother from Glasgow were staying at the hotel. The first morning after their arrival Mr Klein had gone into the young man's room with early morning tea, and there had been a candle alight in the wash-basin. By the look of it Mr Klein deduced it had been burning all night. The mother didn't have a lighted candle in her bedroom all night, he said to me. But every morning – and mother and son had been at the hotel nearly a week, they were leaving tomorrow, Saturday – the candle had been burning in the young man's wash-basin. "I really would like to know why," Mrs Turk said.

"I will ask him tomorrow," Mr Klein told Mrs Turk, who said on no account was he to do so, and so did the others. He appealed to me. Why did I think the young man went to sleep with a lighted candle in his bedroom? Obviously, I thought, the chap was afraid of the dark. But he was a grown man, Mr Klein said: "Though I did think," he added, "he was very much under his mother's thumb." He shrugged his shoulders, spread his hands. "Very well, if you don't think I should ask him why does he sleep with a lighted candle in the wash-basin, I won't. It will just have to stay a mystery, that is all."

"We have plenty of mysteries at this hotel," Mr Turk called after him as he went out, Norbert and Sabrina following him to get on with their jobs. "But so long as we are kept busy," Mrs Turk said to me, "then we are happy. Our mysterious guests help to make hotel-life interesting, don't you agree?" I agreed, and she went on to tell me about an intriguing offer she'd recently received from a husband and wife who stayed with her the previous summer. It was to convert the Hotel Fasganeoin into a health-farm. The wife and husband knew all about it, how to set the place up with all appropriate amenities to attract an overweight, jaded rich clientele seeking rejuvenation. Mrs Turk, and the husband and wife, would make a fortune. The wife was large and fat, the husband a little weedy man. He claimed to have been a one-time physical-culture instructor, and it was he who would supervise the exercises for weight-reducing and slimming – "a less likely-looking person you couldn't imagine," Mrs Turk said.

No doubt to impress her, he arranged for parallel-bars to be set up in a more secluded part of the hotel garden. The morning following the installation of the apparatus, Mrs Turk watched from her bedroom window. The physical culturist appeared in singlet and white trousers, still not too impressive, none the less, an opinion which was shared by her family and Mr Klein. However, he set about the apparatus with supreme confidence, Mrs Turk watching him from her bedroom window. He advanced swiftly upon the parallel-bars, both hands outstretched – and completely missed. Falling, he caught his nose a frightful bang and sprawled on the grass. Mrs Turk had to turn away and choke back her laughter, before she hurried down. He was on his feet when she reached him. "Must have been the morning dew on the grass," he muttered. "Caused me to slip." No more was said by him or his wife about converting the hotel into a health-farm.

Apart from being a superb cook, Mrs Turk is a remarkable woman. She refuses to let her deafness worry her; those war-time years of death and devastation at close quarters might have toughened her, instead she reacts with immediate compassion to anyone, or any creature, in trouble – like the kestrel with its shattered wing. She loves the Highlands. "I had seen a postcard of Loch Fourich – during the war my husband found it after a battle, and sent it me. From that moment I longed to come here. I knew I would. Somehow. It took a long time, and hard work – it made my husband ill, he'd been ill while a prisoner-of-war, and he overworked to earn money to get us started – but I am here." Every penny that she and the family could save would pay for her husband to return to Germany to receive special treatment for his illness.

Mr Klein came in and sat down at the piano. He stared at the score of Rachmaninoff's Second Symphony. "I've finished the first," he had earlier told me with a wink and a smile, when I asked him how his music was progressing – he had a sense of humour, all

right, even though he was passionately fond of music, and prac-
tised as much as he could find time for. He was preparing for the
"concert" which he gave to family and friends every Christmas.
He played a few notes – he had a nice, gentle touch which contrasted with his military bearing, his family had for generations
been officers of the Austro-Hungarian Empire's armies. "No time
for practise," he said, leaving the piano abruptly and heading for
the door. "Practise – discipline, that is what is necessary." He
paused, the door open. "Do you know, that was what saved my
life. Discipline. When we were captured by trigger-happy
Americans, in the Alps, my section maintained discipline. We
obeyed orders. We stayed put. But others, who felt uncomfortable
the way the Americans kept looking at them and then looking at
their guns, they deserted. Besides, they wanted to get back home,
quickly. They were caught by the Italian Resistance, who were
even trigger-happier than the Americans, and shot. They didn't
get home." Again that smile. "I didn't get home, either, as it
happened. I got here. But I wasn't shot. Discipline. That is what is
necessary." And he went out.

But he was back again in a moment. "It is the lady who knows
Rufus," he said. "She is here with her nephew." Mrs Turk quickly
explained that she intended to tell me that the aunt and her nephew
had arrived that morning. They had come to see Rufus. I recognised their names, the previous day I'd read a letter from the aunt
which Don had received. It was in fact written to Rufus.

"Dear Rufus,
I want to thank you for the marvellous sense of peace you brought
to me when I was all knotted up with worry and you came to the
Manchester bookshop for a signing session. When I gave my nephew
the copy of *Rufus* that you signed specially for him, I heard a note of
warmth and interest in his voice that had been missing for 10 days –
and that was the start of a slow thaw. Last evening he came to me and
asked me to tell him about you! So, thank you for the wonderful
therapy.
"(Mr MacCaskill – the pictures in the book do not do Rufus
justice – he is such a beautiful creature – this is not a criticism of the
photography, because I expect he is quite a difficult subject – it's just
that he is too beautiful for even the camera to portray. I can still feel
his beautiful, silky coat and ears in my finger-tips, and I shall never

forget my first glimpse of his face – friendly and intelligent and not a bit as I always imagined a fox would look. In fact I don't really think he is a fox, but some faëry creature that has wandered into your life from the forests and adopted the appearance of a fox! !)"

The aunt went on to say that she was coming up to Dunfuirich with her nephew, giving the date, and hoped she would be allowed to bring him to see Rufus – to continue the "therapy". She would telephone, she said, to find out when it would be all right to come along.

She and her nephew, aged about twelve, were in the hall, and I remembered them from the bookshop. It was midday, and I said I would take them up to the glen; Don, I knew, would welcome them. And so would Rufus, of course. When we got to the house, Don fetched Rufus, and found the old tennis-ball which he used to enjoy playing his "hunting-the-mouse" game with. The aunt watched entranced while her nephew, face glowing with joy, threw the ball in the air for Rufus to chase after, waiting for it to roll to a stop: then he would walk past it with a great show of nonchalance, pretending he hadn't seen it. Suddenly he would pounce sideways, leaping high and coming down on the ball with his fore-paws.

The Phantom went roaring past once again, low along the loch; this time I could make out its camouflage livery. Rufus and the boy went on playing with the tennis-ball unconcernedly. The aunt put her clenched fists tight against her ears. It was a Rolls-Royce Spey-engined job – two supersonic by-pass turbo-jets each of 12,250 lbs thrust – 20,515 lbs with re-heat – skating along at 420 knots at 250 feet; it could carry, in various permutations, eleven 1,000 lb free-fall or retarded bombs, 234 SNEB 68 mm armour-piercing rockets; it was armed with four Sparrow air-to-air radar-guided missiles, four Sidewinder air-to-air infra-red missiles, plus a reconnaissance pod with cameras and radar equipment. "In the Highlands," the aunt cried, fists still over her ears, "of all places. Fancy a thing like that." It didn't seem to me to be all that much out of keeping with the surroundings. You could say that its savage destructiveness might match the savagery in the jagged outline of the mountains to the north, the snow-edged crags of Glencoe, themselves a result, aeons ago, of some of the most colossally explosive eruptions of the earth's crust our world has ever known. If you let your imagination over-heat you could compare the Phantom's roar reverberating among the hills with the echoes of battle-yells of phantom warriors, berserk at Glencoe's massacre, or the shrieks of their victims, or the murderous crescendo of war-cries at Culloden; it was only a matter of degree, you might think. In your imagination you could replace the picture of the Phantom in its war-livery as it pulled out of its bullet-like trajectory, twisting upwards to vanish out of sight to the right of the hill-side, with images of sword-brandishing men, bearded, in their befeathered bonnets and bloodstained tartans hurtling down to drive their adversaries into the loch itself; and as the aircraft's shadow lifted above the loch you could imagine instead a crimson stain spreading across the water from the dying on the shore.

Don was staring in the direction of the glen, where Frieda was. Was there any risk of the row of the Phantom causing her to abort? He shook his head, with a wry smile. He didn't think so. He nodded towards Rufus and the boy. It didn't seem to have bothered them. But had there been any complaints from the shepherds and farmers? Not in the Highlands so far as he knew. Down in the south, where farms were numerous, there had been a bit of a fuss; but where farmers had suffered on account of stock aborting due to aircraft noise, they had been compensated. Anyhow, it had been discovered that farm-animals had quickly become used to it, and soon took the roar of jets for granted. The only hazard, and that was probably greater in the Highlands than elsewhere in the country, was from wild birds flying into the aircraft. The impact of the smallest bird against the cockpit cowling could cause bad trouble, the effect could prove disastrous; if a bird hit against the wing-edge it could cause handicapping damage; if it was caught in the jet-mechanism it could cause total power-failure. The miracle was that almost always any bird encountered seemed at the last split second to be caught in the airflow and pass safely either above or beneath the aircraft.

No, Don was positive, if there were any complaints from shepherds or farmers of any of their ewes having aborted, it wouldn't be the Phantoms they would blame, it would be a fox.

It was the approach of a human being on foot that was to interrupt the game between Rufus and the nephew. He was giving his fourth encore to the delight of the boy and his aunt, when suddenly he stopped and spun round. The man was walking on the grass; none of us heard him – except Rufus. Or he sniffed his scent. For a moment, I mistook the man for the gamekeeper whom Rufus the previous day had bolted away from on sight. The stranger wasn't wearing the deerstalker or carrying a stick, and he called out that he was the other's brother, and there was a very strong resemblance. He added that he'd heard about Rufus, and he would very much like to meet him. But before he was a step nearer, Rufus gave an odd yelp and disappeared behind the house. It was almost a repetition of his reaction to the gamekeeper. Rufus wouldn't have anything to do with him. While the nephew dashed off after him, Don told the man, who was staring open-mouthed at the rest of us, that it was no good. Rufus knew he'd got foxes' blood on his hands.

"But I've never killed a fox in my life," was the pained reply. "I couldn't shoot a rabbit." He sounded almost affronted and explained that he worked in Stirling, that he'd never had anything to do with the country. He was a townie, he visited this part of the world only occasionally. Don was looking at him. The nephew appeared from round the corner, holding a struggling Rufus, who was looking the other way, in his arms. The boy shouted that Rufus was all right and went back round the corner once more.

"You must be identical twins," Don said, and the man nodded. He and his brother were identical twins. "Then you and he have got the same scent. And that's what Rufus has gone by," and he went off round the corner after Rufus. The chap appealed to me. Was that a fact? I could only try to look knowledgeable. When you were dealing with animals, I said, especially wild animals, it was difficult enough to sort out fact from myths and misinformation. But with Rufus, it made it even more difficult. He didn't seem to fit the facts, or they him. Rules didn't apply to him. He was unique. After the man had gone, Don reappeared with the aunt and her nephew, clutching Rufus, who was chattering away and nibbling his ear, tickling him so that he couldn't help laughing. The boy was still smiling to himself when he and his aunt left.

The cubs were born in the early hours of Saturday, 22 April.

4 The Ropes of Love

It was still dark. Heavy cloud obscured the moon. It was the safe hour for Frieda, when instinctively – she knew it in her blood and just as her cubs already had the knowledge deep in their blood, tissue, and tiny brains – she knew she was safest from her age-old enemy, man. There is no one else the fox has to fear but human beings. She went quietly down into the den. She turned round a couple of times as if smoothing the already smooth earth and then lay down. She experienced no fear, no foreboding for the future. She felt secure in the warm darkness. There was nothing to worry about, she felt no concern for the outcome of what was happening within her body. This was the inevitable phase of the yearly cycle; this was the scheme of things. She could feel the automatic tension of her muscles. Very soon she began straining. She made no sound; she relaxed, then strained a little, then relaxed. It was almost a reflex action.

The cubs were born head first, with only a few moments' interval between the first four; the interval before the fifth and last cub was longer – nearly two minutes. They looked like five plump, three-inch long sausages, almost black in colour; their tiny paws very pink, like a baby's hands and feet. Their coats were in fact a dark chocolate colour, very woolly, which provided their only bedding on the hard, smooth floor. This explains why Frieda hadn't used any of her own fur in the den. They were blind: this way they would be discouraged from straying from their mother's teats – foxes are especially curious; baby foxes most curious of all – what the eye couldn't see they wouldn't be curious about. This way nature had, as is her meticulous rule, put priorities first and completed all the most important work on the senses they had to rely on for the present, their hearing, so that they could hear any warning note in their mother's mewing, and most important their scent, so that they knew the smell of her body's warmth. Frieda licked each cub carefully, thoroughly removing the afterbirth fluid. This was before she began suckling them.

There was a time when Don had experienced some doubt that Frieda would in fact give birth to cubs at all; that she had missed the boat for this year. Foxes mate virtually only a few days every twelve-month; Frieda had been ready to conceive and Rufus ready to fertilise her during the last few days of February and the first day or two of March. For the rest of the year they would remain just good friends. During the significant nights – foxes mate at night – Rufus was away from home, appearing at Edinburgh and Glasgow book-shops and those in the North of England. He was provided with an ink-pad (very wet) on to which he stuck his fore-paw, right or left, it didn't matter which, and this was then applied to the fly-leaf of the book to the delight of the purchaser (even adults insisted on "autographed" copies) and the accompaniment of applause from the onlookers.

Rufus never seemed to mind whether blue ink or red ink was used for the purpose – perhaps because he is colour-blind – though I used to think sometimes that when his paw was covered in red ink he would regard it with more interest than when it was blue; he always seemed to splosh it on the book with an eye for a bloodily dramatic effect. No doubt he was encouraged by the children's squeals of delight. "Do a red one for *me*, Rufus ... Oh, can't you ask him to do a red paw in *my* book – oh, please." And Rufus would oblige, with what appeared to be appropriate enthusiasm. But perhaps his thoughts weren't really concentrated on his task; not all the time. Perhaps they were mostly with Frieda, at home.

He, Don and I were kept on the go, often making two or three appearances at different places every day. Early one evening Don introduced Rufus to an audience of children and their parents at Edinburgh University Chaplain's Hall, and spoke to them about Rufus's life and forest wild life. From the start Rufus was restless, and I had a job to hold him – I was on the platform with him and Don – he kept turning to me inquiringly as if to say wasn't it time to go home? Soon he began yawning, very loudly, and the children were delighted (no reflection on Don's talk). It was a bit off-putting, Don had continually to break off and admonish Rufus for display of bad manners. Soon, his yawns were turning into howls; with his jaws wide and ears flattened back, he yelled and "wooh-wooh-hooed" away, to the audience's ecstatic delight. Don was determined not to be put off, and went right on to the end. You could have thought by the applause that it had been one of his most successful talks.

I didn't realise what Rufus's contribution to the entertainment was all about. That night when he was in his pen at the local RSPCA kennels, the late hours and early morning hours echoed and re-echoed to the sounds of his howling. Howling for Frieda. It was reported to Don later that she had demonstrated similarly her longing for her lost one's return. Both she and he were capable of an impressive repertoire of what might be described as love-calls; none of them, it must be admitted, as attractive as the Indian Love-Call from *Rose Marie*, for example, or popular renditions from other famous scores. There is some controversy among Don and those of his friends who have studied Rufus's and Frieda's musical accomplishments – which is the better performer of the two? – but that between them they can contribute a fascinating variety of shrieks, screams, yaps and yells isn't questioned. "Wooooowoooo-wooogh," was one of Frieda's more musical offerings to the absent Rufus, intermingled with a "wo-wo" here and a "wo-wo-wough", on a distinctly more piercing note, there. (More critical, perhaps, than the others, I, when I heard Frieda at her loudest, inclined to the view that the utterances resembled nothing less than those emitted by a goat strongly resisting various unorthodox attempts at strangulation.)

As for Rufus, a dog in the next-door pen at the kennels in one city joined in the love-lorn one's yells and "woo-woo" barks – Rufus was putting his heart and soul into a hoarse, hollow-sounding howl which ran on, up the scale, culminating in a really frightening bark – and needless to say every dog in the immediate neighbourhood joined in with enthusiasm. According to the kennel-manager, Rufus, distinctly flattered by the response, there-upon obliged with variations. "O-oo-ooh," was one offering, resembling very much the row given off by a band of tom-cats waltzing on an area of red-hot coals from which they found it impossible to remove themselves. Another successful solo, which defied the kennel-manager's description and also the attempts of any dog to emulate, was a kind of "Qwoo-qwoo-qwoo-ahhh", culminating in a high-pitched whistle. Then Rufus fell asleep.

Frieda's appearance when she might be expected to show that she was in cub had during the last two previous pregnancies become deceptive. She held her belly high up in her slim frame, as if she didn't want her condition to be known, which might have been instinctive; she had probably realised that she appeared more vulnerable in motherhood, and the less it was advertised the safer for her cubs and herself. At any rate, at the beginning of April, with only an estimated three weeks to go, her slim line didn't appear to have altered – though it was true that her vocalisations had diminished, as had Rufus's, which was typical if they had, in fact, mated – and Don thought it as well to learn if she was in cub or not. I watched him pick her up and place her on the roof of the den. Rufus stood up on his hind legs and also watched with interest as Don gently felt her warm belly. Five embryo in the uterus, two in one branch, and three in the other branch. I looked at Rufus.

"You're going to be a father, all right," I told him. He sat back on his haunches, looking up at Don with his usual round-eyed, innocent expression, before trotting off round the glen, nose to the ground, as if his head was bowed in deep thought.

Someone was banging on my front door. My watch said it was just 5.30. It was the girl. "It's the fox's cubs," she said. "They just been born okay, all right," It didn't seem so very strange to me that she should be standing there. Her face was pale in the grey early morning light. Her eyes looked very luminous, and I noticed how their upper and lower lids met in a sharp point in the inner corners, so that she had an almost feline expression. I left the door open and went and dressed quickly.

She was waiting along the road. I caught up with her and as we hurried in the direction of Ennochdhu Wood, I tried to find out what she had been doing there at this hour of the morning. She just wanted to be there when the cubs were born, that was all. But who was she? Where did she come from? She was living in Glasgow, she said. (She meant she had been living there.) She was with relatives in Moulin, she said. (Moulin was a nearby village.) They were going to Stornoway. (Stornoway, Isle of Lewis in the Hebrides.) She was going with them. I remembered that I'd heard of a Pakistani community who had settled in Stornoway. She would be happier there than in Glasgow, she said. She didn't say so much as before. She seemed very reticent. Nervous. We reached Don's house. She stopped suddenly, and pointed to the glen. "The fox's cubs, I kept watch on them," she said. "They are okay, all right." I heard Shuna give a bark from the house, Don wouldn't have taken her with him to the glen. When I turned back to ask the girl why she was so interested in the cubs – I was still concerned that she knew anything at all about them and their secret home – she wasn't there. It was the same as the time before. Another trick of the imagination; but, no, I knew she was real enough.

Don was at the gate of the glen as I arrived. He didn't say anything. We went in and he closed the gate behind him carefully, as Rufus rushed up. We stood, listening. We could hear a faint squeaking from the den – I couldn't hear anything at first, except the low roar of the burns tumbling down – but Don has extra good hearing. It was the cubs.

In the east it was palest yellow shot through with pink and banners of black cloud zig-zagged across the sky. The air was flat and still, only the tip-tops of the trees above the glen rustled. Rufus had rushed back to the den and sprawled in a small clump of primroses nearby. He wagged his tail in a rather automatic manner at Don and I, as if he didn't really understand what the fuss was all about. He got to his feet and chattered at Don as he fondled him and stood between him and me at the side of the den. Don had the roof off. The den was dark with shadow and in the light of his flash-lamp Frieda's white breast seemed almost luminous. The five dark "sausages" were huddled tightly together, their tiny mouths burrowing into their mother's body. The tips of their minute tails were bright white. Frieda lay there almost nonchalantly, her expression pensive, if not disinterested in what had happened. She uttered a kind of mew at Don and me, a whimper of frustration, it might have been; she was slightly nervous, wanting to warn us not to trespass too far on her magnanimity in allowing us to observe her in such intimate circumstances, while at the same time not wishing to appear antagonistic towards Don. As for me, I think she would have given me a warning-off nip had I been there on my own. Her trust in Don, her complete lack of fear, were miraculous. It was the first time so far as I knew of a person being allowed so close to a vixen a few minutes after her cubs were born.

Frieda shifted her position – it seemed to me without very much regard for her new-born babes, who looked in imminent danger of being trodden on, squashed by her paws. She hardly seemed to bother, let alone notice, where she was placing them. She was much more interested in keeping an eye on Don. She was murmuring at him, a sort of low purr, you might call it. But the cubs seemed to come to no harm. Their ears were very low on the side of their heads, on a level with their closely shut eyes, and it occurred to me that the babies didn't look in the slightest as if they would grow into foxes. More like otters, I thought.

I noticed that Frieda had pulled the fur away from only five of her eight teats. The other three were half-hidden by belly fur. So she had known she was going to give birth to five cubs only? There were only occasional flickers of wariness in her eyes; she appeared to be relaxed and reasonably well pleased with herself. Every now and then, however, a flash of fear would show in her face. Instinctively, she was frightened. Instinctively, she was prepared at any moment to up with her cubs and remove them one after another to a more secret place. Then, you would see that frightened look change to a more relaxed attitude as she glanced up at Don. Despite her instinctive fear for her young, she placed her trust in him. It was oddly moving to watch.

It was difficult not to humanise the scene; not to observe Frieda and her new-born in terms of a human mother and newly born babies. To imagine what were her emotions, what heights of happiness she was experiencing at this hour, as a woman is supposed to feel at the birth of her child. I glanced at Don, who didn't appear to be emotionally moved, and I took my cue from him. He had witnessed similar scenes before, I recalled, though several days following the birth; Frieda had cubbed at Loch Aweside three times. He viewed it in terms of zoology, as a naturalist.

Frieda herself? Apparantly she was feeling no elation, no emotional reaction whatsoever. She had merely undergone the natural and inevitable result of her coupling with Rufus. The entire experience had taken place almost mechanically, you might say. The result of an instinctive urge, the birth of her cubs had followed with the inevitability of the night following the day, the dawn following the night. The natural consequences of a biological drive.

This was what she herself had been born for, why she was here: to perpetuate the species. This was what, in the wild, was the motive for her living at all, what activated her unceasing hunt for food. This was what the mystery of life was all about. This miraculous combination of sinew, nerves and muscle, of hearing, sight and scent and other senses, perhaps "sixth sense", of which we are only dimly aware; the power of instinct, of communication in subtlest forms – all this simply in order that the species might continue.

Later that morning I produced the bottle of champagne I'd brought up from London in anticipation of celebrating the cub's birth. During his illness in the summer of 1969 from German distemper, when Rufus had been prescribed a magical herbal remedy which had saved his life, he had much enjoyed another prescription. Raw egg and Amontillado sherry. That winter, when he had fully recovered, Don introduced him to an occasional nip of malt whisky, which he took to with relish. On his visit to London to appear on television and at a National Book League exhibition, he had met newspapermen and photographers at a Fleet Street reception, at which there happened to be the sales representative of a famous champagne firm, who was so enraptured by Rufus that he felt impelled to open up a sample he had with him. Rufus knocked back a glass with enthusiasm. Bulbs flashed, loud applause.

Don and I went down to the glen. I saw that he was clutching some kitchen-scales. He was full of assurances that he wouldn't break them, they were made of plastic – the cubs wouldn't weigh enough for that. His methods were inclined to be somewhat unorthodox on occasion; borrowing the kitchen-scales to weigh the cubs in was an example of his preference for making do with what he found to hand, rather than equip himself with special gear.

I filled a glass, Rufus almost climbing up me to get at the champagne. We managed to quiet him down sufficiently so that he could partake of the celebration with some show of decorum, lapping up the stuff with noisy enjoyment. I poured him another glass, but he wasn't to be allowed to finish it. Before any of us, including Rufus, had realised what was happening, there was a flash of pale gold and white. Frieda had appeared from the den, ignoring the plaintive mewlings of her cubs, and shoving Rufus aside, finished off the champagne herself. Without so much as a look at any of us, and licking her whiskers, she dashed back down into the earth.

Don lifted off the roof of the den, and while I held the scales with one hand and clutched a notebook with the other, he picked up one of the cubs and weighed it. "Four ounces. And it's a boy," he added. I wrote it down in the notebook. Don weighed the next cub. "Three ounces. And it's a girl." Frieda grumbled under her breath; the five tiny creatures squeaked, but Don continued gently but firmly, to weigh the remaining three. Another cub, a male, also weighed four ounces. The two others, both females, weighed three ounces each. They ran true to pattern. Male foxes are normally heavier than females at birth, and remain so throughout their lives.

I noticed that each cub's fine furry coat was full of sandy soil, accumulated already from the den-floor. Don noticed it, too, and as he returned each tiny shape to Frieda he tipped the plastic bowl up as I gripped it so that the residue of sand was thrown away. "Och," noting my expression, and reassuring me, "the wee bairns are clean as new pins." He stared down at Frieda with a little smile. After a few moments: "All the same," he said, "I shouldn't be using them. There must be another pair somewhere – what did I use last time?" He replaced the roof on the den. He nodded absently, he wasn't really thinking about the scales; his thoughts were pre-occupied with Frieda, as he listened to her purring, more softly now, on a less tense note. She was in the dark again, and the darkness was her friend, the light her enemy.

He muttered to me that he would look out another pair of scales with which to weigh the babies in a week's time. Rufus accompanied us to the gate, circling ahead of us, his marvellous tail wagging, and then jumping up at me, asking to have his chest scratched. Don turned suddenly – you might be forgiven for thinking he had eyes in the back of his head – with an exclamation, just as Frieda emerged from the den. She was carrying a tiny, sausage shape in her mouth.

We stopped and watched her. Rufus ran a few yards towards her, then he paused and turned aside. As if it was no business of his. Frieda saw him out of the corner of her eye. But her attention was fixed on Don, though she pretended not to notice him. Involuntarily I had made a move towards her, but Don stopped me. "She's all right." It seemed to me that Frieda was biting the cub so hard you would think she'd bite it in half, but there was not the faintest squeak of protest from it. She was making up her mind whether or not to remove the cub to a fresh hiding-place. She had been disturbed by all the attention she'd been given. It was an instinct embedded deep inside her to fear for her cubs' safety and to want to hide them for protection.

We watched her move her head from side to side as if making certain no enemy was about. It was almost a reflex action. It was as if what she was doing was purely automatic. She was confused. In the wild, had she been disturbed even slightly by the sight or sound of human beings near her den, she would have whipped her family off to another place to hide them without hesitation. Now she had been disturbed by human beings who hadn't acted as her instincts warned her they would; she hadn't felt fearful of Don, or even of me, because I was with him. Instinct battled with her confidence in him. Her trust in him won the upper hand.

But when he had gone, instinctive pressure had impelled her to act out her rôle, to obey the maternal, protective instinct. She was really looking at Don as she moved her head, first to one side, then the other. She stood tense and motionless for a moment, her face tilted up, the cub limp in her jaws. You could tell she was getting a good scent of Don, you could see her shiny black nostrils quiver. Reassured, tension relaxed, she turned and went back into her den.

The cub would have been wriggling and squeaking with fright if it could see. That's another reason for their being born blind. Sight triggers off fear instinct. So, on the principle that what you can't see you can't be scared by, it makes them easier to handle. Don couldn't recall the colour of the cubs. I felt sure that they were chocolate, he was certain they were black. But he couldn't remember for sure. "As bad a memory as Frieda's," he said. "She could take a cub off and hide it, and then forget where she'd hidden it." It was true, a fox, like plenty of other animals, has a bad memory. You could take a couple of the cubs away from Frieda and she wouldn't remember there'd been five in the first place. The same as with a cat and her kittens; she can't remember how many she's given birth to. So long as you left her one, you could remove the rest and she wouldn't feel bothered.

Anyway, the main thing was that they had been born, and got over the first hours of birth. They looked healthy enough; they weighed the right amount, and in a week's time we'd tell if they were making progress by their weight-increase. Just the same as with a human baby.

Don had already hinted to me when there had been some doubt about Frieda's pregnancy that he hoped it would prove to be a phantom one. No problem, then, about releasing the cubs when they were old enough. Always before they had gone to wild life reserves; the idea of their being penned in zoos, or worse still, made "pets" of, was to Don totally abhorrent. He had tried to return Rufus to the forest, but failed: Rufus had insisted on remaining with him. In order to keep him happy, he needed to be provided with a mate. Frieda was an RSPCA rescue-case from Lanark. Because they had lived together in semi-wild conditions (otherwise Frieda might never have given birth to them), cubs had followed. Accommodating them when they became full-grown was becoming more difficult, and Don had no plans for the present cubs. Which was why he had hoped there wouldn't be any; why he had entertained the wishful notion that Rufus was becoming past it.

My feelings then had been equivocal. But now that the cubs were safely born my feelings were positive enough; I was filled with elation. I had not yet divulged to Don my vested interest in the cubs and their future. But the time when I would have to tell him what was in my mind, the real reason for my return to Dunfuirich was now. It was what my telephone call from Mrs Turk's office to London had been about.

2

All of us live behind our own masks, masks of our own making. Some of us never drop the mask, even to ourselves. Only animals show a face to the world which hides no secrets. They have no secrets to hide. But, for all that, the naturalist-philosopher, Konrad Lorenz, thinks for a writer dealing with animals to tell the exact truth about them is virtually impossible. Nevertheless, he should do his homework, stick to the facts he's learned, set them down accordingly, and as entertainingly as possible. Which, it seems to me, applies equally to writing about human beings. The best you can do is set down the truth as you have observed it, and as entertainingly as you can make it. Best you could do was to write directly from experience. Put down what you witnessed: the wild creatures you encountered and were permitted to know and understand, some better than others; the human beings you knew and understood, some better than others; the strange, wild places you saw, and where you had made a home, if only a temporary one. With one proviso, which doesn't apply to animals: be careful about naming names. It can hurt people – those you wouldn't think could be hurt, and whom you wouldn't want to be hurt. I'd learned that, and I'd learned to be careful about naming places. Places where someone, or some creature, like a wild thing you loved, might be vulnerable. Vulnerable to those who hate, those out to destroy; vandals and their like.

Which is why you may search any map of the Highlands, but you won't find Loch Fourich, or the village named Dunfuirich, or Stalker's Cottage, though it's there (it's locked and shuttered, except when Johnson allows Hughie Drummond to sleep there when his old tent gets blown down in a really bad storm); or the *Fisherman's Rest* – McNab isn't his real name, and in any case I swore him a solemn oath I wouldn't give away the pub's whereabouts. Not to anyone, he said. This was before he knew I was writing this book. This was when (as I became certain was the case) he guessed, or you might say he knew, somehow, don't ask me how – I've said that in the Highlands you come to expect this sort of thing, you almost take it for granted – that I knew Iris.

He and Rufus had become great friends. He entertained no illusions about the motive behind Rufus's affection for him. It was the malt whisky. McNab realised how deeply Don loved Rufus; and the way I felt about him. He was a strange chap; it was strange for a start that though he'd hunted and killed plenty of men, he'd never killed a fox. And I suppose you might think it a bit out of the ordinary the way he had come by the *Fisherman's Rest*.

It was when he was aged sixteen, walking along the promenade of a little seaside town above Oban, that he saw the yacht *Penelope* wrecked. It was a stormy autumn evening, he was with his father, and their heads were bent into the gale which blew off the headland. Suddenly the clouds were illuminated by a distress-signal out to sea. His father couldn't make out the sinking vessel, but young McNab was able to sight the mast like a needle against the black horizon. He and his father stood in the crowd which had collected on the promenade and watched the lifeboat put out, marvelling at the way she thrust through the waves, every line of her seeming to be tense with urgency, her crew oil-skinned silhouettes, one moment dark against the sky, the next vanishing as if totally submerged by the devouring sea.

The lifeboat rescued the *Penelope*'s crew of half a dozen only a few minutes before McNab saw the needle-like mast snap in half and the yacht was gone. At that time McNab was taken up with sailing. He owned a dinghy, becoming expert at handling her in the rough weathers that seemed continually to buffet the bay. His reading was entirely made up of sea-adventure stories, tales of shipwrecks and treasure at the bottom of the ocean. He made a mental note of the spot where the *Penelope* had sunk, marking her position against the headland, and then lining it up with some installations which marked the other side of the bay. When he got home that night, he noted the yacht's position as he'd memorised it on a local map.

It was later that autumn that he nearly died from tetanus poisoning. He was the accident-prone sort, forever in trouble with his boat, or smashing up a bicycle – it was the same in the Western Desert; he managed to turn jeep after jeep into complete write-offs with no trouble at all – and he trod on a rusty nail one day when he was working on his dinghy, wearing canvas shoes. Typically, he neglected the wound and tetanus set in, and you would have thought his number was up. But, miraculously, he survived. His growth, however, was permanently halted. The effect of tetanus poisoning had been to fuse the ephiphyses, the growing ends of his long bones. ("Like that chap who did all those girls at the Moulin Rouge, Toulouse Lautrec," was the way McNab described his appearance.)

In fact, he was runty-looking, squat, but with shoulders as wide as a door, and his muscular development hadn't been affected. And despite his fearsome appearance there was something very attractive about him. Probably it was his voice, its soft, beguiling lilt. It had beguiled Iris. Despite being so accident-prone, he had managed to come through the war pretty well all of a piece – there had been the eye gouged out by a bit of shrapnel, the chipped spine and broken limbs, and the collar-bone broken twice, as a result of his misadventures with the jeeps, but the rest of him held together. It was six months after he came home from the war that he was told he had Hodgkinson's Disease. With a bit of luck, he had six months to go.

To get hold of a boat and sail away. Sail up the West Coast of Scotland to Skye; he'd always dreamed of doing that when he was a boy – his family came from Skye, he had always longed to sail there himself, in his own boat, instead of by ferry. Now, it was all he could think of. He hadn't much money, certainly not enough to buy the boat he wanted. And he had in his mind's eye the very yacht. It was then, going through some old papers, it was a kind of tidying up, you might suppose, before he took his final departure, that he came across some of his boyhood books about sailing, and tales of sea-adventure; and the local map on which he marked the wreck of the *Penelope*. She was a yacht, with a wooden hull, which would have rotted away by now. But she would have had a lead keel. A lead keel worth several thousand pounds. All he had to do was raise the *Penelope*, and he'd have the money for his own boat he so dearly longed to sail home to Skye.

He hurried down to London and made all the right noises at Lloyds, confirmed that the wreck had a lead keel, and laid claim to salvage her. (Out of curiosity, if you like, or just for the record, when I was at Lloyds later in the year I checked this out for myself.) He managed to scrape together enough money to hire a tug and a diving-crew, enough to pay them for six days. No more. Accident-prone as ever, everything that could go wrong for him, did. Every day a storm blew, making it impossible to dive – the men weren't geared for the job as divers are today: they used the old-fashioned round helmets with air-pipes to the surface – and it wasn't until the sixth day, his last day before his money ran out, that the *Penelope* was located. She was rotten and half-submerged in sand, but for once Fate was kind to McNab to the extent that the yacht had tilted over to one side, the keel – the lead keel – resting on rock so that it was relatively easy to get at and haul up to the surface. The rest of the hull was left where it was. McNab had the money for his yacht.

He and Iris met while he was buying the boat. She had done sailing and crewing while she was a medical student, and she crewed for McNab. They shared the skipper's double-berth cabin, and their first night together she could feel the growths in his arms and shoulder muscles. She knew what they meant, you didn't have to be very experienced as a doctor to know that he was a doomed man. She began crying and he held her very close. She was never to think of it again. Understand? Never to speak of it.

They didn't make Skye, after all. McNab was growing weaker. The yacht was tuned in on a loop, a navigational instrument which enabled him to set a course for the port he was aiming for – the vessel merely bleep-bleeped her way to her destination – but she needed more than a sick skipper and crew of one to sail her. It ended with McNab in hospital and Iris returning to Edinburgh, and then on to a job in London. McNab made another attempt to reach Skye. He discharged himself from hospital, and sailed off in his yacht alone. He was wrecked in a storm. Miraculously, rescued. Despite the doctor's prognostications he hadn't given up life, but knew he would have to give up the sea. Later, back in Edinburgh – Iris had gone to New York, where she married – he ran up against Johnson, who had served with him in the Commandos. Johnson happened to know that the *Fisherman's Rest* could be bought cheaply. McNab had always enjoyed fishing; and it was the nearest thing to the sea he was ever likely to know – and he hadn't got long to know it, anyway – so he bought the pub. That had been twelve years ago.

It so happened that I had known the *Fisherman's Rest* before he had taken it over; I had been there before it had fallen into neglect. In the old days when the Highlands were a seasonal must for sportsmen, shooting-types and fishermen, there were a number of tiny fishing-pubs tucked away in the glens, or up in the hills, or alongside a loch where salmon and trout rose invitingly in the evening mist, leaving behind echoes of that unmistakable "plop", and widening ripples on the dark water. John Buchan's tales use these pubs as a background for pulse-stirring drama; and other writers relied on them as a warm, comforting refuge from the storms and menace of an outside world, where counter-spies or arch-criminals stalked the glen and the remote rain-lashed heather-clad moor, or manoeuvred muffled oars over a loch crowded in by louring mountain-crags. The proprietor was inevitably some pawkily humorous retired deer-stalker, gillie or poacher, or the ex-butler from the neighbouring crumbling castle; his heartily masculine clientele equally inevitably composed solely of dedicated fishermen, or keen-eyed expert shots, who would turn up every seasonable time of the year from various parts of the world. The whereabouts, even the existence of these pubs was a closely guarded secret, this was the most important part of their appeal (in the fiction versions, the hero invariably stumbled on it by chance, usually in the nick of time when on the run from villainy, or well-intentioned but wrongly suspecting law). They were virtually lodges of a world-wide freemasonry whose members, in real life, dutifully obeyed its first and only rule. Keep it to yourself; keep your mouth shut about it.

I'd first heard of this particular pub from a Canadian tycoon who annually brought his fishing-rods to the *Fisherman's Rest* to enjoy the fishing, the like of which there was to be found nowhere else in the world – in every other way he was perfectly normal. Then I came to know it better in my mind's eye through Sam Campbell, editor of *The People* and the last of Fleet Street's "crusading" editors, who described it to me often in detail. He had got to know it when he was working on a Glasgow newspaper before he came to London, but he had refused to give me its location; even then the owner, like McNab, had been a dedicated fisherman who wanted it to retain its atmosphere of an old fishing-pub. Sam had always promised me he would take me for a holiday to his secret pub one of these days, but it was about the only promise he made to me he failed to keep. Then, when I was working on the Rangi book in Glencoe, I'd picked up a story about a strange little pub over on Loch Fourich, and I'd been reminded of the one Sam Campbell had talked about. I hadn't been so very interested at first. Sam was dead, anyway, and the pub had a new owner and was likely to have changed out of recognition itself.

I had met this woman doctor in Edinburgh. Iris. You could say it was Rufus brought us together. It was at a children's party where he was the guest of honour, as usual. She was there with some doctor friends who were concerned with this particular charity bun-fight. You could say, with only a small amount of exaggeration, that she never took her eyes off Rufus. She was over here from New York on family business – some tangle about property left her by her mother – and we found we had mutual friends other than Rufus, in Edinburgh and New York. As well as our mutual love for Rufus, Iris and I shared an interest in medicine; her father had been a doctor, as had mine and my grandfather – had things been different for me when setting out to steer what proved to be a somewhat erratic course upon life's tempestuous sea, I would have been a doctor myself. Instead of which I was to become a life-long, enthusiastic hypochondriac, which you could reasonably say was compensatory, and apart from my father, and a doctor who had saved my life and consequently suffered the penalty of becoming a close friend, conceived an obsessive admiration for Nostradamus, whose contribution to medical science has it seems to me been overshadowed by his reputation for sorcery. Iris was intrigued by the careers of seers and prophets (she referred me to Jung, who explains Nostradamus's occult powers with some conviction); when she had been working as an anaesthetist at a London hospital, one of the surgeons with whom she was enjoying a passing romance frequently expressed his admiration for a colleague, a surgeon who was fast making a name for himself. Iris's friend described how he had once followed his hero out walking with a woman-friend on Brighton front, fascinated by his elegant suit and charm of manner. He had also happened to notice the pattern of the woman's head-scarf.

Later Iris (inevitably) attracted the brilliant surgeon's attention, and this gave her an opportunity to practise on him her own brand of sorcery. One night she told him with a duly intense expression, how she had always known that he and she would meet, it was predestined. She had seen him in a dream, she explained – it must have been a dream, or perhaps she had undergone some kind of clairvoyance; her maternal grandmother had she felt sure come from the Isle of Skye – at any rate, she went on to describe, to his wonder and fascination, how she had seen him walking beside the sea, accompanied by a woman, describing the pattern of the woman's head-scarf. The surgeon had been totally convinced and, of course, flattered out of his mind. By now he had become the proud owner of a smart yacht, and since Iris loved the sea she was delighted to accompany him sailing, a consequence which in this case she hadn't entirely failed to predict, though she didn't foresee that her addiction for sailing was to grip her increasingly, and that as one result of it she would meet McNab.

I had told her about my father, who had worked as an assistant to a doctor outside Glasgow when he was a fourth-year student. In those days it was an accepted practice for doctors who were so hard worked that they felt in need of assistance to employ hard-up unqualified students in need of money, who would work during the vacations to earn money to pay their fees. My father was a student at Birmingham University, and for his first vacation went to work for a nearby country doctor, where, so he said, he had been preceded by a student as hard-up as he himself was, who had come from Edinburgh. His name was Arthur Conan Doyle, and he was to become less famous as a doctor than as the creator of Sherlock Holmes. My father was not one for name-dropping or bathing in the reflected glory of the famous, and only trotted out the information, inconsequentially, many years after I'd set out to become a writer. His job as assistant to this doctor was almost entirely concerned with dispensing, bottling, and carefully labelling prescriptions for patients, a hundred or more every evening.

For his next vacation he went as assistant to a doctor near Glasgow. From the first day he realised that he was going to do more than deal with prescriptions. He was to be required to learn how to treat serious cases and midwifery; he delivered an average of three babies a night during his first week – it was a poor, heavily populated neighbourhood. The patients weren't very speedy payers, either. One woman hadn't paid any bills for five years, during which time she had been delivered of a bairn annually. My father was informed by his employer, in one of his more coherent moments, that she would be giving birth again any day. My father would be dealing with it, and would he, this time, collect? He must be insistent. Two nights later, the night-bell rang. It was the woman's husband, very harassed – you'd think he'd never fathered a child before; would the doctor come at once? My father, young, eager, enthusiastic, night-shirt tucked into trousers, hurriedly accompanied the other back and duly delivered the child. He interrupted the husband's heartfelt expressions of gratitude – the mother, rather to his surprise, had promptly got up to go out to clean the front-door steps – to ask politely for something slightly more concrete in the shape of a coin or two, reminding the other of the several sums long outstanding. The reply was that there wasn't a penny in the house to buy any milk, let alone pay the bluidy doc. And the happy mother returning from washing the steps, added cheerfully: "Och, weel, ye canna put the wee thing back, noo, can ye?"

The reference to the incoherence of my father's employer was not entirely irrelevant to a further event – every morning, announcing that he was away on his rounds, he would set off in his pony and trap, but get no further than the pub up the road. From the surgery window, late every afternoon, my father would observe him, with assistance from the publican and a number of friends – he was a large, florid-faced man – crawling back into the trap. The pony knew his way back home, it hadn't far to travel anyway. This state of affairs continued for two weeks. Daily, the doctor would go off in the pony and trap, get no further than the pub, and return in the afternoon, paralytic. What puzzled and concerned my father, amongst other things, was that once a month the doctor, being health officer for the neighbourhood, was obliged to make his report to the local authorities. How could he stand up and utter in the condition he would apparently be in? My father waited, with anxious curiosity, to see what would occur.

The meeting the doctor was due to attend was at four o'clock in the afternoon. The day dawned. Pony and trap and occupant set off as before; as before, getting no further than the pub. My father had, of course, reminded the doctor of his important meeting, but it didn't appear to have sounded any warning. Sweating on the top line, but getting on with his work, my father waited. As before pony and trap returned, its occupant, speechless and all but dead to the world, fell out and managed to make the surgery. It wanted less than an hour before he had to be at the meeting. This time, however, he didn't struggle upstairs to collapse on his bed. As my father, desperately worried, held him up, he fumbled in his pocket and produced a key. He pointed shakily to the poison cupboard, and gave slurred instructions for it to be unlocked. At first,

understandably fearing he meant to do himself some harm, my
father refused, urging the other to go to bed. To no avail, incoherent and incapable as he was the doctor insisted on the poison
cupboard being opened. My father could do nothing but obey.
Now, take out the cyanide, he was ordered. With trembling hand
and perspiring with apprehension, my father obeyed. He was
instructed to measure out precisely a few drops into a glass. He
couldn't help the neck of the bottle rattling against the glass as he
obeyed. Just a drop was all you needed on the tongue and you were
dead as a doornail. As fast as that, cyanide is. The doctor clutched
the glass and as my father watched in horror he knocked back its
contents – and dropped like a felled bullock.

With a shout of alarm my father knelt beside him, undid his
collar, slapped his face, although he knew it was hopeless. After a
minute or two, to his astonished gaze, the doctor suddenly sat up,
got to his feet, stone cold sober. He fixed his collar and tie, brushed
himself down, picked up the notes for his report and went off
smartly to the meeting.

As my father explained to me, the doctor was saturated with
alcohol to such a degree that the cyanide where it would normally
have killed him outright merely rendered him unconscious. The
alcohol in the system acted as a buffer warding off the poison's
deadly effect. The doctor took this carefully calculated risk; took
it, with the help of his assistant, every month on the afternoon of
his report to the meeting.

Then, one night, Iris was telling me about how the sea and
sailing was in her blood, and it was through it that she had met up
with this ex-Commando chap, with whom she had fallen in love.
She had sailed with him up the West Coast of Scotland and found
out he was dying. She didn't need to say his name. I knew who it
was. I obeyed the first and only rule of my lodge. I don't know why.
Sometimes you come out with things, sometimes you don't come
out with things. It was what my telephone call from Mrs Turk's
office to Edinburgh had been about. Iris was still in Edinburgh,
still tying up the family business-matter, and she had asked me,
should I find out anything about McNab, would I let her know.
I had telephoned to ask her when she planned to leave to return to
New York. In a week or two, she thought. No, I said, I hadn't any

news for her. I thought to myself I could think it over and decide what good it would do for her to know that McNab was alive. She thought he had died. He must be dead, she thought. What purpose would it serve to tell her he wasn't? What good would it do either of them? I'd give it some thought.

One night, a week after the cubs' birth, Rufus, Don and I were in the *Fisherman's Rest*. We had been weighing the cubs that afternoon. I'd been right about their colour. They were chocolate, though by now you could make out a tinge of reddish-brown showing through. There was no one in the bar except ourselves and McNab and Johnson, so we felt safe talking about Frieda's new family; McNab and Johnson were on their side. With the exception of Johnson's cronies, local people never came to the pub, anyway. As for McNab, he only welcomed fishermen whom he put up in the four bedrooms available, during the fishing season. Personal friends, old army pals, and *aficionados* from Canada and America, came over regularly every year to fish and talk about nothing else but salmon and trout, about a new fly they'd discovered, or a new-type rod or piece of gear, the place a shambles of waders and creels; the heavy smell of wet tweeds of customers caught yet again in a rainstorm, or dripping from the mist off the loch; and talk about another of the pub's attractions apart from its atmosphere so congenial, McNab's malt whisky, and Johnson's culinary gifts when cooking the fish. Salmon or trout as dished up by Johnson was a gastronomic experience not to be missed.

Don had found another pair of scales with which to weigh the cubs, finally unearthed in a deep cupboard after much rummaging. The cubs' weights had more than doubled in a week. The three females weighed eight ounces each; one male weighed ten and the other nine ounces. They were doing well, taking their nourishment. I tried to make notes and hold the scales while Rufus would grab them and run off with them; at the same time Frieda went off with each cub as we tried to weigh it, not to return it to the den, but to hide it. Between the pair of them they gave us quite an afternoon. The cubs took their usual inactive part, squeaking in protest when Frieda picked them up, squeaking more when she dumped them in various parts of the glen, and squeaking again when Don and I dashed after them and returned them to the den. They were still blind, their tightly closed eyes wouldn't open for another three or four days. Not being able to see helped Don and I find them; they simply lay supine, wriggling aimlessly in the direction in which their tiny noses were pointed. They felt no fear of Don or me, no fear of human beings yet.

I noticed that their woolly fur was still full of sand from the floor of the den. It probably helped to keep them clean, the same as birds used dust to clean themselves, enjoying frequent dust-baths in the summer. I noticed, too, that their minute ears had moved up the sides of their heads, so they were now above eye-level. They were suckling strongly and noisily, while Frieda lay there, wearing her abstracted expression, glancing up at us as we looked down. She would suckle them for another three weeks before they would tackle solid food. Rufus was carrying out his rôle of provider, bringing Frieda the food that Don put into the glen. Don would bring to the mouth of the den, every evening, rabbits, hares, rats and mice, voles and birds, all found dead in the forest, or wild life killed on the roads; as the summer approached you could come across any amount of dead birds and animals on the roadside, from pheasants to lambs, victims of speeding cars. Venison – deer died in the forest, especially weakly babies abandoned by their mothers – fresh meat, and dried meat were added to the menu.

I was saying to Don that Rufus never as much put his nose in the den when Frieda was there with her cubs. Sometimes, when she was out on a quick foray for any food tit-bits that might have been left outside, he would nip up to the den's entrance, take a sniff at his children down below, listen for their squeaks, and, apparently satisfied that all was well, push off again before their mother's return. Shelter under a bending tree or some tree-roots was home for Rufus. He didn't ask for anything more luxurious. Often he would sleep in the open, his eyes covered with his brush. He'd sleep so soundly you could walk on him almost before you would disturb him. It's what has helped the fox to survive; he's always been mobile, kept on the move, never to be found in the same place twice.

Johnson was scratching Rufus under the jaw. "Glad to see you're looking fit," he said. "Aye, ye're a good advert for my whisky" – Rufus enjoyed his usual tot whenever Don brought him here – "I always say it's the best medicine for man or beast." Rufus looked ready for another spoonful of the prescription, but Don didn't want him to get the habit. "Ye're a handsome feller," Johnson said. "Ye want to watch out ye don't end up as a present in a glass case for some tourist to take back to America."

He was referring to local gift-shops who did a growing trade in wild birds – eagles and hawks – and animals – wildcats, otters, badgers and foxes – mounted in glass cases, a revival of interest in what was once a popular Victorian eccentricity, the preservation of wild creatures or beloved domestic pets, mounted and glass-eyed, ornamenting the parlour. I didn't think that Johnson's observation was in the best of taste. Waving a hand at some specimens of stuffed fish in glass cases around the walls, bought at a Glasgow auction to give "atmosphere" to the bar, Johnson was giving an account of how the taxidermists went about their handiwork. According to him, several retired gamekeepers round about had picked up the knack of mounting wild birds and animals, of which there were always plenty available, or made available. The specimens had to be in good shape, not damaged by shot or as the result of having been trapped, with a mangled leg, for example. Birds were the most difficult. The thinness of their skins required the greatest care in removing the flesh and bones without a tear and without losing any feathers. There were all manner of trade-secrets which each of these practitioners kept to themselves. Johnson had once tried it himself, he had tried practically every job in his fifty years all over the globe, but you needed a lot of patience; and he found it pretty repulsive, anyway. Then, the money hadn't been so much, either. Nowadays, the local taxidermists were asking and being paid so much for the job that the gift-shop owners felt they were pricing themselves out of the business. They were even learning to mount the birds and animals themselves, Johnson said. They were in the market for wildcats and foxes, especially.

McNab leaned across the bar. "Ye'll do well to take another drop," he said to Rufus, giving him a scratch under the chin, "after listening to all that." And with a grin at Don that looked as if it had been made with a can-opener, he reached for the whisky. Rufus's large pink tongue was soon licking the glass clean, not wasting a drop. Johnson was now on about illicit whisky-distilling in the Highlands before the war, and which – according to Johnson – continued to flourish. Stills built of stone and turf, hidden in the remote glens and hillsides beside rippling burns. The caves and mountain fastnesses of Rannoch and the Black Wood have provided innumerable hiding-places for those who made the illicit hard stuff, and those who smuggled it away. The hidden caves were used by many previous fugitives, from Robert the Bruce to harassed Jacobite supporters after Culloden. Inevitably there's a hide-out called Prince Charlie's Cave, in the Black Wood – black, by the way, means the dark wood of the pine which is lighter in colour than birch or oak – and many outlaws and men on the run have found their way to these parts of the Highlands seeking escape.

Whisky smuggling had been a profitable business during the nineteenth century, when the duty on legitimately manufactured stuff was ever on the increase. Johnson's father and grandfather had been engaged in smuggling illicit whisky down to the towns of the Lowlands and the Border at various times. Even up to the last war, Johnson claimed he had on sporadic occasions carried on the family tradition. "Part-time, you understand; I had other trades as well."

He and his companions would deliberately utter strange calls at night in the woods and cause lights to flicker on the hills and in the glens – following in his father's and grandfather's footsteps – to spread abroad the idea that the places were haunted and so frighten local folk away. The *Fisherman's Rest*, he boasted, was a favourite whisky-smuggler's inn in the early 1900s. Johnson's grandfather had made it a stopping-place many times on his way down to Glasgow with his illicit spirits concealed under straw in a cart. Sometimes, to allay suspicion, Grandfather Johnson would pretend to be bed-ridden, lying on his bed of straw. Anyone, police or excisemen, stopping the cart would be told by the driver, Grandmother Johnson, in suitably ominous tones, beshawled, and with baskets filled with various wares, lace and ribbons, which she was supposed to be taking to market, that her husband, groaning realistically, was suffering from the *duibh-leisg*. This, of course, was taken to be some dread malady, at which the suspicious officers of the law would hastily wave the cart on. *Duibh-leisg* is Gaelic for black laziness.

By now the tiny bar was beginning to look crowded. Three Americans who were staying at the pub, each wearing peat-redolent tweeds, Palm Beach tans, and one smoking a cigar, had come in. Don and I knew them from previous visits; they'd been

coming to Loch Fourich for several years. This was the first time
they had met Rufus, however, and after they had mistaken him for
a dog, and then were convinced that he wouldn't bite, they made a
great fuss of him. But Don wouldn't let them treat him to any more
whisky. Rufus didn't seem to mind, so long as he was surrounded
by friends he was content. The cigar-smoking American asked me
if I could explain the reason for him being so tame. "Gee, I always
imagined foxes were really wild – savage, I mean – and would tear
out your jugular."

"It is man who has the instinct for the jugular," McNab said,
"not foxes." Don emphasised that he had made no attempt to tame
Rufus, he hadn't tried to teach him any tricks; it was simply that he
had been brought up from the tiniest cub by and with human
beings, and through Don he had given them his trust. No fox,
unless he's suffering from a brain injury, or some injury to his
central nervous system, was "savage". He was just behaving
naturally. Fear of human beings had been inculcated in him over
the centuries and when confronted by one he reacted instinctively
with fear-aggression.

Rufus was lying at one end of the bar-counter, his tail hanging
over the edge, giving it an occasional wag of pleasure whenever he
glanced round at the company. He chattered at McNab who was
scratching the side of his jaw. I advised McNab to watch out, any
minute now Rufus would turn over to have his chest scratched,
and he might send the glasses within reach of his tail flying. Even
as I spoke, Rufus flopped over. McNab was just in time to push a
couple of glasses filled with whisky out of reach of his tail. He bent
his black eye-patch alongside that flat wedge-shaped head, and
Rufus responded by licking his ear.

"Some day, perhaps," I heard McNab say, "I'll be a man not too
hard to find," and he turned away to serve a customer. I went to
the door. I stood outside, the babble and laughter behind me. I
stared out across the loch. The burns, white and creaming in the
distance, as they careered down the hillsides, seemed blurred. It
seemed to me there was a touch of rain or mist in the air. Love is
supposed to be an inspiring chemistry, to love another human
being is supposed to nerve you to endure suffering. Requited love,
that is; what unrequited love does for you, the record-books don't
have much to show. And that's the nice thing about loving an

animal, it never goes unrequited; once an animal – a dog, say, or a fox – commits itself to you, you can kick it to death, it'll never go back on you. Of course, it may not really be love (what can an animal know about love, as a human being knows it?) but whatever chemistry it is, it's what makes animal pets so popular with human beings.

The blurred mountains beyond the hills were black round the edges of the silhouette they made against the pale light, the afterlight of the dying evening; that pale pink, which as I watched turned to red, blood-red. If you love a human being there are supposed to be unbreakable ropes, hawsers of steel, that will forever hold you to your loved one; if your love is requited, that is. If it's rebuffed or exploited, then those steel hawsers can turn to ropes of sand. Not with an animal, say, a fox, though. The mist or rain on my face. But as I touched my face with my fingers, I knew it wasn't the mist or rain.

5 Red Thief and Black Devil

Two days later. What, I got round to asking Don, did he think about Rufus appearing in a film? What did he think of it? Not much, was his reply, as I had anticipated. We were in the glen with Rufus and we had the roof of the den off, and were talking to Frieda with her cubs. They were looking fine; already we could note one dog-fox slightly bigger than his brother, the pair of them each bigger than their three sisters, who all weighed the same. Frieda would "mew" at Don and me – less at Don than at me – when we came down to the glen. A kind of frustrated whimper. She was a little nervous, anxious that Don was allowing human beings to trespass too far on her generosity in permitting us so close to her family.

She was, of course, confused; she should be signalling her cubs of the presence of an age-old enemy, man. They hadn't been born with this built-in information, they weren't aware that our scent which they were receiving really meant menace, because Frieda couldn't signal them accordingly. Don and I were their friends. But other human beings outside the den could be enemies, fox-haters out to exterminate them. And it was up to the cubs to know the scent of man, to identify it, to store it in their memory and to act upon it sharply. Man was the only predator the cubs had to fear. Centuries of harassment by human beings, armed with snares and traps, poison and gas, dogs and guns, had inculcated in the fox an instinctive fear of man. It was a development of a natural evolution, warning the fox to hide from man, to escape from man's sight. This was the reason for the fox's survival, its built-in intelligence,

its instinct which taught him that man was his mortal enemy and
that he must adapt himself to the world in which man was not only
his enemy but the master of all other living creatures.

Don was reiterating how totally he was against attempting to
tame wild creatures. As for teaching animals to perform, to do
tricks, that was even worse. I knew this, he said, and I said, yes,
I knew it, but this was something different. And, anyway, I added,
this was in a good cause. He didn't think there could be any cause
that justified treating an animal as if it was a puppet, something to
be manipulated by human beings, to be exploited.

Don was concerned for Frieda: he realised that she was confused
as well as anxious. He replaced the den roof, and she rewarded him
with a little grumble of relief; you could imagine her relaxing and
wrapping her body more closely round her family in the warm
darkness, communicating to them that now, at any rate, any
danger was past. Probably she had decided to warn the cubs that it
was the scent of menace they had been sniffing with their tiny
noses, even though in this case it was only Don and me. When the
time came for them to meet us, to get to know us, then they would
have to make up their own minds that despite our scent we were
friends, to be trusted. Frieda would prefer to be on the safe side;
every instinct warned her that human beings, no matter who they
were, meant danger to the cubs. Don was reminding me how we
had both experienced a certain amount of guilt over the way Rufus
had been used to promote the book, and we'd agreed that there had
been enough of it. The only exception would be in the case of
children, where they might learn and understand from meeting
Rufus that foxes weren't "red thieves", "scarlet outlaws", as they
were so virulently described in human terms, but that they were
wild animals, part of nature, of life itself, and therefore the concern
of man as much as was any other wild animal. You had a chance of
putting this across to children, Don felt; you couldn't put it across
to adults – they wouldn't learn.

I explained that the film was to be based on a novel called
Lady Into Fox, by David Garnett, which had made quite a hit in the
early 1920s; it had won the Hawthornden Prize and the Tait Black
Memorial Prize, which meant that it must have possessed considerable literary merit as well as making money. I'd read it, but had
forgotten it, and had read it again, now, and it was a light,

fantastic story, a "biological fantasy", Garnett called it, about a man whose wife turns into a fox. A vixen, that is.

One definition of man is that he is a story-telling animal; from his earliest beginnings he must have spun tales round his cave-dwelling fire. His stories handed down, embellished, enlarged upon, modified, through thousands of years, were to emerge as folk-tales. Folk-tales ultimately became written down, to become folk-lore. Then men began to write down stories from their own imagination, they became known as authors and fruit of their authorship was described as literature. Where the folk-tale became a literary work was the subject of considerable controversy among those erudite scholars who considered this differentiation a matter of importance. For example, those allegorical poems, or bestiaries, which were popularised in the fifth century, and depicted animals, birds and fishes behaving and talking like human beings, were thought by some to have been originated by folk-storytellers. Others concluded that the tales, which were written in Latin, were composed by monks, and a certain Peter Alfonsi was credited with being their author. *Reynard the Fox*, however, seems to have earned, together with *Aesop's Fables*, the distinction of being a folk-tale elevated to literature.

This may be due to the fact that it was brought to this country from Cologne, about 1475, this would be, by William Caxton, who was not only the first English printer, but also something of a translator, *Reynard* being originally *Raginhard*, a German name, meaning "strong in counsel" – the French having already changed the name to *Renard*. There was a Flemish *Reinaert* in 1230; before that a Latin poem *Ysengrimus*, while parts of *Reynard's* adventures have been attributed to Aesop. At any rate, as a folk-lore and literary character the fox has been going for a very long time; and you may think it significant that *Reynard*, though his appearance is that of a fox, acts and talks as a human being; which suggests that even that far back in history, human beings were concerned with the mystery of animals communicating with one another, even though the best they could do about a solution was to depict animals using human speech. Today, we know that animals do have a power of communication of their own which, in the case of whales and dolphins, for example, we are hoping to translate and fully comprehend. Perhaps we may learn that animals do, in fact, possess their own languages, as lucid, as beautiful, as poetic as those of men.

The stories feature various animals as well as *Reynard* – *Lion the King, Bruin the Bear, Curtois the Hound, Isegrim the Wolf and his Wife, Tibert the Cat, Grimbard the Brock*, and others. But *Reynard* always proved to have the widest popular appeal. His adventurous character, the shrewd, wily nature by which he outwits his enemies attracted mass-admiration; when brute force – power at the top, if you like – rules tyrannically, your only recourse seems to be cunning and guile. And in some ways *Reynard* has much the same attraction as David against Goliath; in the tales he often turns the tables on figures larger and more fearsome than he. Also he is adept at duping the Establishment, sometimes even going to the extent of disguising himself as a monk, confessing his sins, and when scarcely absolved, not in the least hesitant about repeating his crimes.

So when Garnett made the main character in his projected novel a vixen, of a very feminine and wild nature, he had whether he realised it or not made a best-selling choice for a heroine. One spring day in 1922 when he and his young wife, who was pregnant, were on holiday near Westerham, in Kent, they kept watch, hoping to see fox-cubs in a larch wood. But the cubs failed to show up, and Garnett remarked to his wife: "There's no hope of seeing a fox – unless you were to turn into one. You might. I should not really be much surprised if you did." He had the notion that she was like a wild animal in her ways, but thought how easily his intense love for her would overcome any difficulty if she should become transformed into a wild creature. Like a fox. Later that evening, she said he must turn the idea into a story. A one-time botanist, he had just opened a Soho bookshop; but he wrote every night after the day's work in the shop, encouraged by his wife (she illustrated the book herself). He wrote it quickly, called it *Lady Into Fox*, and took it to the publishers of a current freak best-seller, *The Young Visiters*. "How many copies did you sell of *The Young Visiters*? 100,000? I believe *Lady Into Fox* may do as well." They published it and its world sales in fact ran into 500,000 copies.

After I had started to become involved in the film-version of the novel, I learned that W. H. Hudson and Garnett had been friends, and that Hudson had looked forward tremendously to reading

Lady Into Fox, but had died without even seeing the manuscript. Another coincidence at this time, at least that's how it seemed to me, was that at a party I was introduced to a man who began talking about *Lady Into Fox*, and explained that he was a friend of Garnett and had that very day returned from staying with him at his farmhouse in the South of France.

I told Don about my meetings with the film-producer who wanted to make the book into a film. Bernard Smith was from Hollywood, now living in London. He had read Garnett's novel some time back, and had been attracted by it and felt that it could make a good motion picture. Then, he had been producing films for Metro-Goldwyn-Mayer and no opportunity had come up for him to work on *Lady Into Fox*. There were difficulties about it as a film subject. First, it was a fantasy and Hollywood financiers had found that fantasy was less than a spell-binder at the box-office. The other problem was finding a vixen that could play the title rôle.

Coincidentally, Smith read my Rufus book, and saw a film version of Paul Gallico's *The Snow Goose*, directed by a young up-and-coming director, Patrick Garland. It proved to be a hit in Europe and America, and received a best television film award for 1971. A feature of the film was of course the snow goose itself, and Garland had done marvellously well with the wild geese he had used in this vital rôle. Smith knew from bitter experience what problems there are when directing animals to act in films. Knowledge of Garland's handling of the geese actors in the film, and then reading about Rufus, his friendliness and loving disposition, suggested to Smith that here might be an ideal combination for putting together a film version of *Lady Into Fox*. A further coincidence was that I had seen *The Snow Goose* film and got in touch with Garland at the same time as Smith had told him that he wanted to make *Lady Into Fox*: if he were interested, would he read the story. Garland's reply was (a) he was interested, and (b) he would read the story. Smith went on to say would he (c) also read a real-life story about a fox named Rufus? He was sure he would be ideal to play the rôle of the vixen in the film. Garland said (c) he would read this book about Rufus. Which was the beginning of my involvement in the project.

The idea of Rufus playing a vixen was quite amusing, Don thought. I explained to him that the making of animal films involved all sorts of trickery and faking. For example, the star part in the famous *Lassie* films had always been played by a male dog, named Rags, and later by one of Rag's sons. But from the start Don was never really enthusiastic about the idea. He felt it was just another way of exploiting animals for financial gain. I knew I would have my work cut out to persuade him that Rufus's appearance in a film would be of positive value; the more publicity he earned as a fox that was unusually friendly towards human beings the better for all foxes, all wild life. It seemed to me that here was living proof that the centuries-old ruthless harassment of foxes, because they were regarded as murderous, evil, thieving pests, was totally unfounded, and a horrible example of human ignorance and cruelty. My view was that foxes should be protected, together with other wild animals – otters, badgers, hares, wildcat, pine marten – all condemned out of hand as deserving no better fate than to be hunted down, shot, gassed, poisoned or cruelly trapped. I thought that these creatures could be protected by law, as are wild birds, so that there was no danger of their being exterminated.

But Don knew I was on a loser. I would never obtain protection for the fox, any more than I would for any other threatened British wild animal. No top-level action would ever be taken, no legislation set up which would ensure the safety and preservation of many wild life species which were in danger of extinction at the hands of man. As for the fox, beautiful, intelligent creature he might be, but in the eyes of most people he was a red thief who should be exterminated. What was so special about foxes, anyway? I had to remember that Rufus was special, he was unique; but there was no reason to suppose that I would ever find another like him. It would be a lucky chance. Generally, foxes were like any other wild animal, who should be left alone to live their own lives in the wild, keeping as far a distance as possible between themselves and human beings.

What about his environmental rôle? He slotted neatly enough, didn't he, into his particular area of the environment which nature had provided for him? He'd never stepped out of line; he was a member of the animal kingdom, an integral part of life, he'd carried out his appointed rôle, hadn't he, which was to survive and procreate his species? Where had he failed, why should man have it in for him so implacably? Didn't he, in pursuing his rôle, help control the rodent population, which menaced forest and food-crops? (If you let a couple of foxes have the run of a farm, wouldn't the rat-problem disappear overnight – a fox was a better ratter than any dog – and the loss of poultry, if properly secured, negligible?) He would clean up carcasses, wouldn't he, left rotting on the hills or on the roadside, such as sheep, deer, poultry, dead from natural causes or killed by motor-traffic?

Don shook his head. Farmers, shepherds, poultry-keepers in the Highlands were convinced that the fox lived solely on sheep – especially lambs – or poultry, which he murderously slaughtered. I recalled a Glencoe shepherd I knew, a delightful, typical "character", who had assured me perfectly seriously that foxes were that cruelly cunning they would wait especially until lambing-time, when they would attack only the ewes, because they would be full of mother's milk for their offspring. "Och, it wad be the puir mither's belly the fox wad go for, ye ken, and rip it open for the milk – just for the milk – a fox is vurry partial to ewe's milk." What the ewe was supposed to be doing while the fox was attacking it and slitting up its belly – a sheep is twice the size of a fox and, unless sick or injured, could see it off any day – wasn't vouchsafed.

Why didn't I go and have a talk, Don was saying, with Captain Bailey, c.b.e., d.s.c., r.n.? He was making a name for himself, leading local farmers into battle against the wily, murderous fox. He wasn't a Highlander himself, perhaps he merely wanted to ingratiate himself with his neighbours by siding with them against their traditional foe. Talk to him about the fox's place in the scheme of things, and see where it got you. Or the fox. No, man would be interested in the fox's preservation only if he got something out of it. Like the dog, which had been disciplined to keep watch, sniff out cannabis for police, guard property, lead the blind, act as companions for old ladies (who had to rely on dogs, because their fellow humans were too busy to care for them). A lucrative industry had been built up around the dog and its exploitation – to man's benefit; not the dog's, of course. But if you set about treating the fox in the same way – and you could do this, it was just as intelligent as a dog, probably more intelligent – selective breeding, training, taming, you would throw a spanner in the works of the dog-industry, for a start. What would happen to fox-hounds?

They'd be unemployed. Same with horses, used for fox-hunting. What about the manufacturers of guns, traps, gases, poisons for killing foxes? (Wasn't there a powerful "gun lobby" that saw to it that no government banned the use of the sporting-gun? Understandably, come to think of it; sporting-guns could cost £1,000 each, or more, and the gun-industry was flourishing.) Besides, if you protected the fox, inevitably you would have to do likewise for the otter, wildcat, badger, hare, pine marten – pretty soon there wouldn't be anything that moved left for human beings to kill; instead of wild things being outlawed as vermin and pests, it would be man who'd be outlawed. Good God, carry it on too far and you'd put a stop to human beings trying to exterminate their own species. Which wouldn't do at all.

There was more involved in attempting to gain protection for wild life than there appeared, more considerations to be taken into account. Where would you start? To whom would you appeal? Who was there who wasn't blinded by prejudice, or by vested interests? Whom did I know who would subscribe a penny to finance a campaign to effect the preservation of foxes, for example – or otters, or badgers – what private body, what authority, or Government department? I'd have no trouble obtaining money to further the destruction of foxes, or otters – fox-hunts, otter-hunts, hare-coursing were maintained by private subscription, but public money was used to try to exterminate the fox species.

Stop bashing your head against a brick wall. Best thing to hope for was that because he was intelligent, and, above all, because he kept moving, the fox would survive.

I got Don to agree, however, that my proposition, if it did no good, did no harm, and might help people to have more insight into the life of wild creatures, while at the same time it could be hoped to entertain them. Rufus would achieve a new image. As a performer, instead of a denigrated wild creature hated and hunted to death.

Looking back, I don't know how I did finally convince Don that the proposition had merit, that it was worthwhile. I didn't manage to do so there and then, but I felt confident that he would agree to fall in with me, perhaps because I had such belief in it myself, because I visualised only the good that would come of it; I couldn't or didn't realise that the means to the end could result in something that was less than loving to Rufus and Frieda and their family. What did help me put the idea over was my promise that Rufus wouldn't be required to learn any tricks, nor would Frieda, or any of the cubs. They wouldn't have to be "tamed", Rufus taught to jump through the hoop, as you might say; there would be nothing of the circus element about preparing him to appear in the film. In fact, how he and Frieda and the cubs would be taught to "act" was the fascinating part of it.

Teaching an animal to act isn't the same thing as teaching it to do tricks. A dog, for example, can learn to "count" – that is to say, bark the appropriate number of times when you show it a numbered card – simply by its powers of observation, which at close quarters are acute. (This applies to a "counting" horse, which bangs out with its hoof the appropriate number of times corresponding to the number you show it on the card; or the bird, which "counts" by pecking out the number it is shown.) Although your dog may not see you so well at fifty yards (it relies on its power of scent for identifying you at that sort of distance, which it does immediately) when close it can virtually see you think, while every inflection of your voice registers, for a dog's power of hearing is phenomenal. Every conscious or sub-conscious movement of your hand, turn of your shoulder, flicker of your eyelid or the faintest shade of expression on your face is correctly interpreted by your dog. When you hold up a numbered card for it to see (the numbers go up to six usually) and ask it to bark the correct number of times, you, of course, know the number. You know the answer. You know that one and one are two, and twice two are four. When you wait for him to bark the answer, unconsciously you tell him. The dog watching you closely, observes you mouth it, or unconsciously move your head that number of times. It barks accordingly. If you yourself were unaware of the correct number the dog – as has been carefully tested – would be totally unable to give the correct answer.

But an animal as an actor is something different; teaching it to play a part, express an emotion that isn't inherent in its nature, of which it has no knowledge, has no possible means, so far as is known, of knowing, or of communicating in terms understandable to human beings – love, jealousy, sadness, horror, greed, for example – is, of course, impossible. These emotions are human, known only to human beings, and recognised only by human beings. A dog or a horse does not cry if it is sad, or if it is happy it does not laugh – two of man's most universally experienced emotions, expressed in graphic and dramatic terms most universally understood – a dog or horse does not go insane with jealousy and murder another dog or horse on that account. The secret of an animal's ability to "act" lies in the ability of the human actors concerned in the particular scene with the animal. It is their reaction to what it is supposed to be expressing that conveys the impression that the animal is portraying the required emotion. The way the scene is written, the words spoken by the human actors, the skill of the director and of the camera-man, and that of the effects (or "tricks") department is what persuades the audience sufficiently to suspend belief to accept that the animal is giving a performance. The audience, of course, is conditioned by the action, the drama, or humour of the situation presented so that they themselves contribute to the skilfully built up illusion.

The cubs would be fully grown by the time the film was in production, which was scheduled for the coming late winter. The purpose of training them, together with their parents, was so that they could substitute in the event of Rufus or Frieda being ill at the crucial time; they would provide a pool of "understudies" on which to draw. It was anticipated that Rufus and Frieda, plus cubs, would be required for the entire film for no more than two and a half weeks. Another eventuality to be taken into account is that an animal isn't always able to portray a rôle entirely on its own throughout a film. It becomes tired, loses the necessary concentration, and another animal, similar in appearance, has to take over. For *The Snow Goose* film the part of the goose was acted by a dozen different geese, all similar in appearance, and brought in to play the rôle if the previous goose had become tired and less manageable, and wasn't responding as required.

I felt that Don was beginning to feel a bit edgy about it all, and I didn't push it too far at that time. Bernard Smith's offer wasn't down on paper yet; numerous clauses, sub-clauses and other snags would require ironing-out before we had a tight contract between us. But I knew that bar the signatures we had a deal. I knew that when the gears were meshed, Don would make Rufus and Frieda available. And the cubs.

Later, on my way back to Stalker's Cottage, my mind full of optimistic excitement which quite over-rode any feelings of guilt or chime of any warning bell at the back of my mind, I caught a flash of movement in a group of trees ahead. At first I took it to be the Asian girl; perhaps now I would see her in daylight, instead of in the darkness of night, or half-light of the dawn. Again the flash of movement. It was a wildcat. It was thirty yards away. A shaft of sunlight spot-lighted it against the darkening green of the forest behind it; trees and foliage were starting to show their summer hues, greens of varying intensity, from the colour of the bracken to the darker oak-leaves. The wildcat's eyes glowed momentarily. It stared at me, tensed and motionless. It was so unusual for it to stay there, not to turn tail and bolt for it, that I wondered if I wasn't mistaken, if it wasn't a feral cat. While a wildcat is rarely seen by human beings – it takes care not to be seen, for man is its hated foe – feral cats are frequently encountered in the Highlands, where folk are no less inclined than anywhere else to throw out unwanted cats to fend for themselves. A family going on holiday would drive up to the forest with an unwanted cat which, for example, had grown up to be too much of a nuisance to take with them, and dump it with as little compunction as they would a load of rubbish.

A cat that survived, though most died, would turn feral within a matter of a few days of desperate existence in the wild, the veneer of domestication sloughed off like a snake's skin. These cats would quite often mate with wildcats (which are said to be of a species quite distinct from the domestic cat). Cassius had been the result of such a union. But I knew I hadn't been mistaken, this was a wildcat. I could make out its flat, broad skull; its legs were longer. My heart went out to it, and I called to it. A flicker of slackening tension across its face, and for a moment I thought it would come towards me. Then its whole body became taut, and it swung away and vanished like a puff of smoke into the birches which were intermixed with rowan trees, the birches golden by contrast with the rowans in the sunlight. Deeper into the forest, where you could glimpse the grey-green upper branches of elders against a misty purple of glens and hills beyond, the wildcat disappeared.

Next morning, the tenth day after their birth, each of the cubs' eyes were open. They had looked as if they were about to open the past couple of days. I had been asking Don when their blindness would end, as I was able to see the tiny slits beginning to show: the cubs were just starting to get their first glimmer of what it was like, the daytime brightness that lay beyond the blindness of the world in which they had lived. Now their eyes were open, widening every hour. They were a bright, brilliant blue, just like a normal human baby's eyes at birth, which are invariably blue, changing colour when it grows older. So with the cubs. Just now, they weren't able to focus properly; it was as if the brightness of the world with its mounting hopes and impelling promise of life, joyous and overspilling with adventure, was too much for them at first.

2

The raven sped above Loch Aweside towards Ben Cruachan, her ultimate destination Loch Fourich, her glossy black wings – though they weren't really black: there's a lot of purplish-blue mixed up with their black colour – moving almost ponderously. But this clumsiness was only apparent, her flight was purposeful, she was answering a call from the past, and she knew where she was going all right, in fact she possessed considerable acrobatic ability. In the spring she and her mate had tumbled high about the sky, and half-closing their wings, would roll sideways to peel off in sudden nose-dives. Her flight seemed effortless enough when she rested on the thermals – rising columns of warm air expanding bubble-like, which are cut off by uprushes of cold air, thus creating revolving warm air rings that are constantly driven upwards, and on which the raven could soar.

She weighed three pounds, she was built compactly and robustly, yet she was comparatively marvellously light in weight. Most of her major bones were hollow, but honeycombed with strengthening criss-cross struts; her upper wing-bones provided a good example of this lightness combined with tremendous strength. Her wings spanned three feet, very much out of proportion to the rest of her body which was 25 inches from beak-tip to tail. She hadn't built her nest that spring; but neither had she died, as a female raven who fails to nest is supposed to do, according to the Gaelic rhyme:

A nest on St Bridget's day,
An egg at Shrove-tide,
And a bird at Easter;
If the raven have not these,
Then it dies.

In fact, it was her mate who had died, as the result of feeding on a sheep he had found dead on a hillside near Loch Awe. Farmers and shepherds make a practice of filling a dead sheep or fowl with strychnine, as deadly bait for foxes, hooded crows or ravens, all of which they fervently believe prey on their sheep and lambs. The male raven, unsuspecting, had opened up the dead sheep's stomach, eaten the poison and had died an agonising death. Ravens pair for life, and with her mate gone the female had no reason to remain on Loch Aweside, which had been her home territory for over three years. But solitary and insecure, she had roamed the forest and shore alongside the loch aimlessly for several weeks, until some memory had reached out, some pull of recollection had set her nerves tingling, beckoning her to fly eastwards, beyond Rannoch, beyond Cruachan and Buchaille Etive, the Shepherd. Beyond Schiehallion's beautiful tip to the south.

That dawn, when Loch Awe reflected the lemon sky, streaked with pink, with its black and purple banners of the night still unfurled, she had set off. The forest was dark green below, the loch lay flat and shining as she gained 4,000 feet. Her eyes bright and forever searching the skies about her, she flew against the wind which brought a taste of the snow that still clung to the peak of the Shepherd. Cruachan, one of Argyllshire's highest mountains has two crests, the eastern one at 3,689 feet, the western at 3,611 feet. The raven winged across the ridge connecting the crests, flew onwards to halt on a crag just below the snow-line of the Shepherd.

She looked straight across the Moor of Rannoch, that vast undulating waste of peat-marsh, of heather hills and lochs, stretching from the Black Mount towards the east to wedge itself between the towering groups of Ben Alder and Beinn Udlamain to the north, and the Glen Lyon range which is dominated by Cairn Mairg and, of course, beautiful Schiehallion's rocky spire. The result of cataclysmic upheavals beyond the mists of ancient history, Rannoch had in glacial ages become a sea of ice, fed by glacier streams proceeding from surrounding ice-caps, thence to overflow its sea and spread its waves as far north as Badenoch's core and Loch Ericht – as they were to become named. This sea of ice pushed into what are now Loch Rannoch and Dunalastair and Tummel to the east, and to the west, through Glen Etive and savagely sinister Glencoe.

The raven observed the red deer moving slowly below, where once, following the ice, extensive forests had ranged, whose fragments may still be seen in the Black Wood and whose roots are still to be found embedded in the peaty marshes of the Moor itself. A gust of wind brought a flurry of snow from above. The raven ruffled her feathers against the snow-flakes, poised for a moment, spread her wings and took off, her huge beak pointed at Schiehallion. She performed two or three acrobatics as she flew, forgetting for a moment that she was alone, that her mate was no longer flying with her. Together they had always enjoyed performing aerial tricks, diving at each other out of the sky, or flying upside-down – this she was especially fond of; she found she was able to fly like this for longer distances than her mate. Somehow, it wasn't so enjoyable without him, and she righted herself and rested on the first crag she reached. Here were no trees, only a wilderness of rock and scree. A low shriek of wind shifted some of the looser scree which began slipping down the slope and over a gully's edge. The sharp clatter of the falling pebbles and small rock fragments caused the raven to take off with a hurried flap of wings.

Her eyes glittered watchfully. No danger showing itself in the immediate vicinity, she flew on to rest on another jutting piece of rock. Her pointed throat feathers stood out beneath her grey, formidable-looking beak, fashioned to deal with the bones of dead sheep and any other carrion that could be found. Often described as vultures of the Highlands, because of their propensity for hunting for carrion, sick sheep or lambs left to die, young deer neglected by their parents, hares and rabbits, ravens once scavenged London's streets, where their appetites became famous – hence the word, "ravenous" – feeding from gutters stinking with dead cats and dogs, rats and butchers' offal, but civilisation has driven them out of cities and northwards to the mountains or the sea-coasts' rugged cliffs.

She flicked her wedge-shaped tail as her eye caught sight of a golden eagle which suddenly appeared silhouetted against the dark cloud above a craggy mountain-top. It made a black shadow as it soared up, its flight feathers spread, its wing-tips beating to a measured rhythm, but as it turned its plumage gleamed, the gold of its head and back of the neck showing clearly.

It was out hunting, soaring majestically above the surrounding mountain pinnacles, its brown piercing eyes alert for the faintest flutter in the gorse or heather below which might betray the movement of a blue hare or grouse. Then its soaring flight would switch to an earthwards plunge at fantastic speed; up to 90 mph, it has been calculated. It killed unerringly, its great, hooked bill tearing its prey to pieces in a few seconds. It wasn't really golden in colour, a dark, shimmering brown colour it was – except for that glint of gold round its head.

It came at the raven, changing gear to a powerful flapping. It separated its massive wings so that each primary flight feather became an individual wing, adjusting itself to each change in the air-currents, while its pectoral sinews and muscles took the increased strain. Then its wings half closed as it dived with terrific speed. Grey-tipped yellow beak gaped, talons spread wide. The raven was trespassing on the eagle's territory; somewhere nearby would be its eyrie, a mass of sticks and heather, perhaps lined with woodrush, with the young guarded by the mother. Its territory ranged over some twenty-five to thirty square miles, and it did not need like most birds to fight for this living-space, the fact that it was there was sufficient to stake its claim. The same distinction applied to the raven, also; her presence was sufficient to announce her territorial claims. In this case, however, she had no intention of sticking around. She was on her way.

The golden eagle was no mind-reader, it was giving nothing away to this brazen intruder. Its wings, spanning seven feet, whistled overhead, but the raven hadn't been taken unawares, her reflexes were as sharp as those of her adversary. She slipped sideways off her perch, and as the other bird plunged past, she barked at it. A harsh, grating bark that brought the eagle's head round with a jerk of surprise, and its beak snapped shut, its talons clenched tight on the empty air. The raven had alighted on another crag twenty yards off, as the golden eagle climbed upwards to prepare to attack again. Its yellow eyes glinted beneath the grey hooded lids as it poised on the thermals, its gigantic wings spread so that their shadow fell across the raven. Then it swooped again with a remorseless thrust of wing-power, its beak wide, huge tongue curled, and talons extended.

This time the raven stood her ground until the last tick of a second, stretching out the sliver of moment to its uttermost limit with typical audacity. Then, with adroit coolness, she slipped aside, but instead of descending in her flight, she swung up above the plunging eagle. Again she barked, that harsh uncanny sound, and again her opponent's head jerked round in surprise. Its heavily flapping wings took it upwards, now, circling and gaining height, so that the raven was once more below it. The tremendous force of the golden eagle's wings had disturbed some scree, so that there was another clatter of small rocks and pebbles rushing downwards. This time their fall was broken by a wide ledge of rock below and the falling scree came to rest, with only a trickle running on over the ledge to continue downwards, the clatter growing fainter. The raven had ignored this distraction; a thin finger of sunlight had poked hesitantly through the cloud touching her feathers so that they became an iridescent blue-black as she spiralled up. Now she wheeled and soared, while the eagle waited, resting on the thermals, before coming in again to attack.

The raven continued upwards, she, too, separating her flight feathers to give them increased manoeuvrability and power. Then suddenly she side-slipped and plunged down at the other hovering bird, barking harshly at it. The eagle's wings were motionless, it watched the raven shoot past, then it swung away as if with astonishment at this noisy display. The raven's bark turned into a triumphant screech, she was quite obviously enjoying her foe's discomfiture. She went into a series of acrobatics which shot her all over the sky immediately surrounding the golden eagle, turning, twisting, rolling and diving to hurtle herself upwards again. The raven pulled every acrobatic trick out of the hat. And all the time she barked and screeched.

Her behaviour was instinctive, part of her genetic inheritance. She had no choice but to follow her instincts. You could say it was something passed on from generation to generation as a sort of memory. Even if she had been reared isolated from other ravens, her behaviour patterns would still have been prompted by instinct;

she would have needed no one to teach her how to perform her acrobatics. And if she was not capable of deciding to stand on one foot, for example, in order to rest the other; even if she wasn't capable of working such a relatively simple matter out for herself, because this was not instinctive, nevertheless she could be taught . tricks. Her intelligence wasn't as limited as might be supposed. Under laboratory conditions, in a controlled situation, she could be taught to "count" up to about six. (Whether she would learn to count, as understood by human beings, or whether she would really learn to read her teacher's mind, as dogs and other animals are able to do under similar conditions, is something else again.)

Now the raven observed her enemy change its attitude: the great wings flapped, the flight feathers seemed to claw at the very sky itself. As the greyish-golden silhouette soared high above and then hung there for a brief moment preparatory to its downward plunge, the raven knew she must concede. Her wings beat a retreat, she uttered that dreadful bark and took her leave. It was a bark of defiance, as if to inform the other bird that she knew she was the trespasser, and she was on her way, that she wouldn't want to stay where she wasn't wanted, anyhow.

Once well clear of the golden eagle's territory, her flight became less purposeful; the acrobatic display had tired her and she planed effortlessly on the thermals, taking her time, pausing at intervals to alight on the mountain-slopes in search of food. She talked to herself continually, uttering little cries and coughs, interspersed with harsh yelps, even letting out with that bark, that nerve-stretching bark. Then she would croon quite musically, softly and gently, as if communing with herself, enjoying a pleasant reverie. Or she would give a little chuckle – it really seemed as if an amusing thought had occurred to her, some whimsical notion had been recalled. All this was to reassure herself; ever since her mate's death she had felt insecure, this was what her journey was all about. She was seeking security. The security of friends.

She grabbed insects and seeds wherever she could find them; flying on, she caught sight of some sheep grazing with their lambs on the sparse grass. She circled one ewe and then dropped upon its back, where she proceeded to probe the thick matted wool for juicy, blood-filled ticks that infested the animal. They are insects with a simple life-cycle; picked up from the grass by the sheep, whose blood they suck until bloated, when they fall off, they cling to the grass to lay their eggs, which themselves become ticks which are picked up by the sheep. The sheep continued its nibbling at the thin grass stubble, unperturbed. To speak again of instinctive behaviour, you could also say that it is derived from long processes of learning which is gained by experience, plus insight sometimes, but mostly the ability to size up a situation and deal with it successfully. The raven is one of the bird-species which has learned to live close to man, by this experience adding to its intelligence. It had realised that sheep's wool, which it often found lying about, was most suitable for lining its nest; and it soon had no compunction in removing some from the sheep itself if there was none handy lying about. This way it had discovered that a sheep carries parasites on it. Further investigation had added to this knowledge, that these parasites, ticks, were good to eat.

Her appetite was stimulated, for as she continued her journey a movement on the edge of a fringe of pines caused her to hover with a flapping of wings. It was a baby deer born too sickly and weak and consequently left by its mother to die. The raven slipped down out of the sky, which had begun to lighten, a pale blue spreading upwards from the lemon and pink, purple and black of the east. She landed only a few feet from the deer, as its round eyes rolling upwards, its tiny hooves jerking convulsively, it breathed its final gasp. The raven approached it cautiously, glancing round all the time. Then she ran at the feebly twitching form and plunged her powerful beak into its entrails. She would leave little work for the blowflies to do before she finished; and gorged with food, she lurched up into the sky once more.

Ravens figure prominently in Celtic folk-lore and myths. Even to this day it is readily believed that a raven will attack you, deliberately attempting to peck out your eyes with its powerful, all-purpose beak, its special victim being a baby left alone in its pram. In fact, like all birds, a raven is instinctively aware of the danger its beak may be to its fellow-chick's eyes, and their beaks to its own eyes, while they are being brought up together in the crowded nest. From hatching out of the egg this inhibition restrains a bird throughout its life from deliberately attempting to blind another creature, however grim the fight. Its miraculous eyesight is to a bird as important as its feathers; for either to be damaged or destroyed is a matter of life or death. Which is why a bird rarely seeks to fight another whose superior strength might result in the weaker aggressor's feathers getting broken or injured. It would be tantamount to committing suicide.

There was the myth that warriors of old were supposed to be able to renew their strength for battle by eating a raven's heart; the myth that ravens drop stones in their nests to induce the hen-birds to lay, and that an expectant mother obtaining such a stone would be assured of easy childbirth. There are many age-old tales of stones being laid by ravens in place of eggs, and whoever came by one of these stones could make themselves invisible. Or to find a stone laid by a raven would bring you a longer life, or even resuscitate the dead. To Highland children ravens were known as Birds of Satan, because they were believed to be in league with the Devil, and to smash their eggs or kill their young was to place you decidedly on the side of God and his angels.

As she flew onwards, the raven's eye, half a dozen times more acute than a man's, caught a flash of light from below. She peeled off in a plummeting dive and alighted on a broken wall that had once formed part of a crofter's home. Not much else remained to show what it had once been, the roof had long fallen in and the lichen-covered rafters together with the rest of the woodwork were almost entirely obliterated by brambles and nettles. What had attracted her was a piece of shattered mirror which pointed up a dagger of reflecting light from its rotted frame amidst a whole load of rubbish that had been dumped nearby beside the track leading from a road. It was an all too common sight in the Highlands – roadside rubbish dumps, where someone moving house or clearing out an attic had loaded up a van or car and dumped the lot. She hopped around, from an old iron bedstead to a frigidaire, to perch for a moment on a broken-down cooker. There were several other items which took her glittering eyes. Several large household paint-containers, a broken step-ladder, and a large framed picture of *The Stag at Bay*, the glass shattered, the engraving itself not very sales-worthy. She finally settled for a large kettle, where she perched, head on one side.

She began to preen herself. Fluffing up her body feathers, she passed individual flight feathers between the ends of her beak, removing tiny bits of irritating matter from the feathers and her skin, together with lice and mites, blood-sucking and feather-eating parasites which endangered the feathers and her health. She applied oil with her beak from the preen gland immediately above her tail, rubbing it well into the plumage. She began drawing a feather from her tail, pulling on it steadily with her beak. She stopped suddenly, and released the feather as she stared down inside the kettle. Through a hole in its base scurried scores of ants.

The raven pushed her head inside the kettle, picked up a beakful of ants and began applying them to the underpart of her primary feathers. She balanced herself carefully on the kettle-handle, while she rubbed the ants vigorously into the feathers. She was spreading the ants' formic acid, together with their other body fluids, plus her own saliva over her plumage. Methodically, she applied beakful after beakful of ants to both wing-tips, rubbing them vigorously into the feathers. She paused. Head on one side she eyed the ants which she had disturbed, now streaming over the side of the kettle. With a jerk of her beak on the handle she tipped the kettle over on its side, so that the ants could escape more easily. Shaking flakes of rust from her beak, she hopped to the ground in the path of the ants. She leaned back on her tail and spread out her wings in front of her, fluttering them agitatedly so that the ants as they swarmed over her were encouraged to retaliate by squirting their formic acid all over her plumage. She ruffled her feathers so that the parasite-killing acid reached down to her skin. Now, she lay spread out, beak to the ground, body and wings continuing to flutter agitatedly while the ants obliged by scurrying over her, shooting out their formic acid as they went. She crooned contentedly to herself; the jagged dagger of mirror nearby caught the ever-changing early light and glinted and winked conspiratorially. She lay there for fifteen minutes, wallowing in ants before she hopped on to the side of the kettle, vigorously flapping her wings, to shake the ants out of her. She took off once more, heading eastwards.

The raven sighted Loch Fourich ten miles distant to the east as she came over a high ridge of cliffs. Below, the heather was stunted and thin, giving way to tough grass and moss among the rocks and loose scree. She glimpsed a covey of ptarmigan, on their way down the mountainside to feed on seeds and sparse green shoots above the tree line, their brown and pepper-and-salt colouring providing them with a marvellous camouflage against the moss-patched rocks. She sensed rather than saw the covey freeze to the ground as her shadow passed them, and knew that they would sit as quiet and motionless as the stones about them. She would need to fly virtually on top of them before they would break cover and give themselves away. She soared above some crags that stuck out like a giant's jagged teeth and headed purposefully towards Loch Fourich.

Don MacCaskill heard her raucous bark down the chimney as he came downstairs to the kitchen to put the kettle on for the early morning cup of tea. Shuna, who was dozing in her basket, was instantly awake. She stood up and gave a "wuff" in reply. She stared at Don, who was like a statue, listening. He was tingling all over with excitement. It came again, that dreadful, familiar, unmistake-able bark. He was out of the house in a flash, Shuna right beside him, her tail wagging and barking with excitement herself. Three days previously she had trod on a piece of glass and gashed the pad in her right fore-paw. It wasn't such a terrible wound, and was quickly attended, swabbed with antiseptic; it didn't even require bandaging. But Shuna was out for sympathy, and made a great to-do of walking around on three legs, wounded paw held well off the ground, while she gazed up at you with such a soulful expression, you could almost see the tears of self-pity beginning to brim over. She duly received sympathetic pats on the back, and although she delighted in the notice her wounded-soldier-from-the-wars-returned performance was earning, by the third day the whole thing was beginning to become a slight embarrassment – the paw had healed very quickly – she was caught once or twice using all four legs quite normally, and had to go into her three-legged act, "injured" paw held aloft once more, soulful expression renewed.

Don was staring up at the chimney, his eyes shining, his heart racing. There she was, that blue-black crouching shape, her great beak half-open pointing down at him, those brilliant eyes fixed on him. "Cronk," he called. "Cronk." She answered him with a soft crooning, "*Cronk-cronk . . . Cronk-cronk . . .*" and flapped her wings to drop on to his shoulder. Don turned his face to her and she rubbed herself against him, still crooning softly, happily, convey-ing as best she could her thankfulness to be back home.

She sat on his shoulder while she rubbed herself against his chin, the familiarly rank smell of her feathers filling his nostrils, and they talked to each other. Shuna followed them back to the kitchen, Cronk clinging to his shoulder while Don put the kettle on the cooker, and he fed her pieces of sugar, which she crunched noisily in his ear, so that he winced and screwed up his face painfully. The kettle boiled and he reached for the teapot. Shuna, whose tail had never stopped wagging since Cronk's arrival, and whose eyes continued to shine and bulge, gave a bark. Cronk took off from Don and landed on Shuna's broad back. Don suddenly laughed out loud. Cronk's dramatic return had come in the nature of a godsend for Shuna. In the excitement she could now safely walk on all four legs, without losing face. Which she proceeded to do, with Cronk on her back. And safe in the knowledge that no one would notice the sudden healing of her paw; that she was walking normally once more.

It was just like it had been at Loch Aweside, before Cronk had met her mate in the sky. She might never have flown away. So Don felt as he opened the door for Shuna and Cronk, crooning to herself and contriving to maintain her balance as she preened her flight feathers, to go out. He still read Shuna's mind as if she was speaking out loud. She was taking Cronk to see Rufus. He turned away to make the tea, and Cronk looked at him over her wide extended wing. Caught by a sudden flash of sunlight the plumage gleamed with blues and purple, with a greenish iridescent effect which made him think of a pantomime demon. She fixed him with a bright eye and he could have sworn she winked.

6 The Villain of the Piece

When Highlanders get together and the whisky circulates and tongues loosen, conversation centres round themselves and their condition; really what they talk about is the sense of guilt they feel in the gut. Guilt which may lie beneath the level of consciousness, or rises to the light like a corpse surfacing in the loch, to float and stare at them with its accusing eyes. They are not alone among those who suffer from tribal guilt: the English experience it to a greater or lesser degree, though they are slow to stretch out on the confessional couch; Americans, who are faster off the mark than anyone to fill you in with traumatic detail, even more. But Highlanders seem to suffer with an Old Testament intensity, with a less than sophisticated acceptance of the inevitability of the punishment to be meted out to them. Once a passionate faith was put in their chiefs and lairds; to them they were irrevocably committed. But Culloden changed all that. McNab put it this way: "Our history finished after '45."

McNab had been a professional soldier, typical product of Sandhurst, "officer class" material, as he would admit with his tin-opener smile, transferring from a famous Scottish regiment to the Commandos. When he talked about the Highlander you listened. "Born to poverty, bred to it, nursed in it," this was McNab speaking, "he had to be tough. The bitter privations of battle were a bed of primroses compared with existence on the hills, in the glens." The hot clamour of war was all the Highlander had to cling to; it was the "mystic" union of blood that held the clan together. They peopled the land with mythical, fierce chiefs, snow-giants of prodigious valour, seers and prophets who foretold terror and destruction; it was to this spirit of tribal unity that the clansmen held, to this tribal society headed by bloodthirsty, fighting chiefs they owed total allegiance. The defeat of Prince Charles, the annihilation of the Jacobite Revolution announced the last half century of the clan system. Sometimes with speed, sometimes gradually, but remorselessly the clansmen's life-style changed.

Not only listening to McNab, but wherever else you listened, to the soft, regretful voices of shepherds and farmers, gamekeepers and pub-keepers, shop-keepers in the villages and small towns, you would hear of their lost heritage, a pride gone forever. Of how the *clanna* died, painfully and shamefully, betrayed by their leaders, thrown from the homes of their fathers, evicted from glen and hill, stripped of any cause to fight for or arms to fight with, the wild, heroic images of their savage past destroyed. Not only were they debased, but their chiefs and lairds debased themselves. Their eyes were intent only on their future self-aggrandisement, with little concern for their "children's" future and none for their past. The past was over; finished, done with, and everything and everyone with it. Chief and laird could see only the hills and glens filled with sheep, they watched the roads into the Highlands bear their new-arriving fortune, bleating along in the shape of mutton and wool.

"*Mo thruaighe ort a thir, tha'n caoraich mhor a' teachd!*" the prophets had wailed: "Woe to Thee, O, Land, the Great Sheep is coming!" They did not warn the fox.

The drove-roads from the Lowlands and the North of England, mostly trails already beaten out by thousand upon thousand head of cattle, led across moor, marsh and desolate hills, intersected by swift burns swollen often into raging torrents by pitiless rains; roads by Kinghouse and the Black Mount, through Strath Glass to Fort Augustus; over ancient tracks used once by her early kings and princes, monks and pilgrims, when Iona represented Scotland's spiritual heart and was the burial spot of these same kings; the stalwart drovers, wild bears of men, hirsute and shaggy, whose food was a few handfuls of oatmeal and two or three onions, or ewe-milk cheese and bannock, with the inevitable ram's horn filled with whisky. An addition to their diet was cattle-blood (cattle were bled in spring and autumn) mixed with the oatmeal and onions to make the popular "black pudding". Dressed in homespun tweeds reeking of heather and peat-smoke, armed against cattle thieves and gentlemen of the road with gun, sword and pistol, the drover himself may not have been credited with a high degree of honesty, except to his clan chieftain, but with tireless, determined devotion he brought the Great Sheep to the Highlands, huge flocks that did not drive so easily as cattle, but nevertheless made a dozen miles a day – night marches were ruinous to sheep. Resting at night, the exhausted drovers wrapped in their plaids, their crooks close to hand, lay until the morning frost showed white, or the morning dew shone on their sleeping forms, when they awoke, ate, and were off once more.

Every year after 1772, *Bliadhna nan Caorach*, the notorious Year of the Sheep, during the infamous Highland Clearances, between May or early June and russet October's end, for years to come, sheep swarmed up from the south into the Highlands, where sheep-farming on an unprecedented scale was to succeed in rooting out the impoverished crofters and smallholders far more effectively than had the Massacre of Glencoe and Culloden. The hills inadequately utilised by scattered small farms with mere handfuls of cattle and sheep of a thin, poor variety, now provided grazing stored with the accumulated rich fertility of centuries. Where once it was wolves who had been the detested murderous thieves preying on the livestock, for which crime they had suffered total extermination, now the villain of the piece was the red thief, the fox.

While a radical political, sociological and economic metamorphosis smashed the fetters which had gripped the Highland people in their old way of life, the fox became the accursed predator; during the years while the massive flocks of the Great Cheviot sheep – which for the quality of its meat and wool ousted the Blackface which had ousted the puny local sheep – grazed on the hills, with their "close, inquisitive bite", the fox was harassed as their baleful foe; with an obsessive hatred shepherds and farmers set about extinguishing the fox species as they had the wolf. While sheep-farming spread hugely and recklessly, for where the sheep had fed, the bracken was to spread to menace the Highlands' very existence, fox-hating ran amok, and even when cheaper foreign mutton came into the country and prices for Scottish mutton and wool inevitably declined, still the destruction of the fox proceeded with a zealous cruelty out of all proportion to his alleged crimes.

Is it against this backdrop of history that you should set the Highlanders' obsessive hatred of the fox and determination to wipe it from the face of their homeland, defamed and forever lost to them, in an attempt to expiate their guilt? They had exterminated the wolf, that handsome, gentle creature; and the bear that sought to harm no man. It wasn't for want of trying that they hadn't eliminated the harmless, beautiful wildcat, or the otter, or the eagle, or the osprey.

Until the arrival of the sheep, the fox hadn't attracted much attention from man. Virtually his only enemy at that time had been the golden eagle, which was known to carry off young fox-cubs, whenever it sighted one strayed from its den or parents. Although there has never been a fox photographed slaughtering a lamb, let alone a sheep, the crime of which it is most often accused, there are photographs of fox-cubs which have been borne off to a golden eagle's eyrie to provide food for young eaglets.

True, there were even in the early days of sheep-farming a few who foresaw the ruin to the farmer and the community's economy that the introduction of sheep would bring. *Donnachadh Buidhe*, Yellow-haired Duncan, a Gaelic poet of the time, wrote:

> *Destruction of the sheep from all corners of Europe!*
> *Scab, wasting, pining! Tumours on the stomach and skin!*
> *Foxes and eagles have their lambs; nothing more to be seen of them,*
>   *but fleshless skeletons!*
> *And the grey shepherds leave the place without laces to their shoes.*

Another Gaelic poet, even more famous, Donald Ban McIntyre – *Donnaichaid Bann*, born near the Bridge of Orchy, Glencoe; there is a monument to his memory at Taynuilt – early in 1800 wrote a poem denouncing sheep and praising foxes. As for James Hogg, the Ettrick Shepherd, poet and song-writer, he came to revile Jesus Christ's sacred animal in no uncertain terms, for he set up as a sheep-farmer himself, and went bankrupt as a result.

The fox's great asset in its continuing war with man, it's true, is its mobility. The badger, for example, could be wiped out by man tomorrow. Simply employ hunters to sit at the entrance of its sett and shoot it the moment it showed itself. A badger can always be found sooner or later in its sett, which is its permanent home. This applies to many wild animals and birds. But your fox, no. Your fox presents problems to would-be exterminators: it isn't a sitting target; unlike the badger it doesn't keep to one home. It moves around.

While it has adapted itself to man's continued attempts to destroy it merely by not remaining in the same place for any length of time, it has also learned to change its habits. It hasn't stopped learning; it's learned that food is becoming more plentiful and more accessible not in the dark, dangerous forest, or on the desolate moor or hillside, but, paradoxically, closer to human habitation. The fox is moving in on the outskirts of well-populated towns, the suburbs of cities, where there is an abundance of dust-bins and refuse-dumps offering food of all kinds thrown out by members of an affluent society.

At night the fox, like the Assyrian of old, descends on dust-bins and dumps, there to scavenge to its belly's delight; and when dawn's fingers lift the curtain of the night, silently as the Arab he folds his tent and steals away. Where food is the fox will be also. It is supply and availability of food which inexorably governs the number of foxes, not the number of foxes which governs the supply of food. Nature has got it the right way round. You would think that man would learn to do the same.

The cubs' dark chocolate fur was becoming increasingly sandy in tinge. Now their personalities began to alter. No longer was their entire life concentrated on pushing their heads into Frieda's belly; their attitude was more alert, more inquisitive. They were allowing their nose to lead them into every corner of the den. They were taking in the view of their immediate surroundings, limited as they were by the rocky wall of their shadowy home; they were pushing at each other in these efforts to reach the extremities of the den, soon they would be clambering over each other, or shoving under each other as they began more and more to explore their restricted living-space.

Frieda would call them out of their den with that strange, low-pitched "mewing", an enticing sound calculated to attract the cubs' natural curiosity. At first, the boldest, the biggest of the dog-foxes, put its tiny nose out of the den, sniffing the bright sunny air, its eyes, still of brightest blue, screwed up against the light, which made such sharp contrast with the darkness of its home. The cub withdrew its twitching nose, and disappeared from sight. Frieda, a few feet from the den, moving slowly up and down, her eyes fixed on the entrance, continued her calling. Now, another tiny, pointed nose showed itself, as one of the vixens followed its brother's bold example. It, too, took a brief sniff at the cool air beyond its home, nothing like so warm as it was within the darkness with which it had grown familiar. Then another cub's nose appeared, and Frieda kept up her calling. Very soon, all five cubs had put their noses for the first time outside their den, for the first time made a tentative exploration of the shining world that compelled them to screw up their eyes, used only to the darkness, against it, and withdraw. None of them, it seemed, would risk venturing any further that day.

Rufus drifted over from a slab of rock upon which he had been sunning himself and joined Frieda in calling his progeny. His call was similar to hers, a little louder, perhaps, with the resonance of paternal authority about it. And the cubs answered him – their curiosity at the sound of this other quite new voice overcoming their continued timorousness. The voice of the father they had barely met, though they would have scented him whenever he came to bring food to Frieda at the mouth of the den: the cubs, whose hearing was already fantastically sharp, heard this new voice and they could not resist it. One by one they again put their noses out to sniff the owner of this seductive tone – and Rufus could adopt a quite beguiling voice when he chose.

Still, they didn't show more than their tiny faces, faces that gave the appearance almost of pansies framed by the den's entrance. They were all beginning to take on a fox's characteristic colouring. The black nose, of course, the fawny facial markings. The three vixens were indistinguishable one from another. For a few moments, while Rufus and Frieda were calling them together, the trio appeared together, making an enchantingly appealing picture, impossible to tell which was which. Their faces seemed more delicate-looking, more flower-like in structure than those of their brothers. The colour of their bodies was growing even lighter, less chocolate-hued; each moult of fur brought a change to their colour. The fur was growing longer.

One after the other, both baby dog-foxes put out their quizzing noses, and then joined their sisters back in the darkness of their home. This was what was continuing to hold the cubs together at this stage: their home. They were suckling Frieda less each day, she was out of the den increasingly, obtaining food for them – placed by Don or me, or brought to her by Rufus. The cubs were experiencing less of Frieda's warmth, the comfort of her milk-filled teats, but they quickly learned to replace that desirable warmth by huddling tightly together in a corner of the den, moving away only on brief crawls of exploration towards other corners, or to take a piece of meat away from the others to nibble and suck alone.

They were weighed each week, Rufus and Frieda contributing as little help to the proceedings as ever – Rufus repeatedly removing the scales, just as Don was about to place one of the cubs in it, and Frieda predictably putting up her performance, adding to the confusion by picking up each cub as soon as we had got it into the scales and in place on the weighing-machine, and dashing off to hide it.

Rufus used to look forward to it all with gleeful anticipation. We only had to appear, Don with the scales, and I with notebook in which to note down the weights, and Rufus's eyes seemed to light up. He would at once adopt a strategic position, from which he could dash in and grab the scales, to dance away out of retaliatory danger. On top of their parents' contribution to the humour of the situation, the cubs themselves, now learning to crawl with increased speed and confidence, were no longer content as they had been before to lie, dark little bundles, blind and supine as their weight was registered. Not a bit of it; now they wanted to look over the side of the scales, and then scramble down and make off back to mother and warm, dark home.

The spring days melted away like snow before the soft rain that sweeps in from the sea beyond the loch. The cubs were maintaining their weight. At five weeks, the dog-fox, Robbie, weighed exactly three pounds, his brother three ounces less, and the vixens turned the scale at 2 lbs 12 ozs, 2 lbs 11 ozs, and 2 lbs 10 ozs each. They were beginning to look less like each other – as alike as three peas in a pod was no longer the right description of them. The sandy coloured mark on the cubs' fur just above their tails was now very distinctive, though it would soon match the rest of the fur. This was the mark of the special gland which the fox used to mark its territory; it excreted a definite odour when the fox sat and rubbed it against a tree-trunk. It was intended as a warning to other foxes that this territory was no one else's but his – or hers, in the case of a vixen. It was also the gland from which the fox exuded its characteristic scent when it was excited, or when under tension, such as when it was being hunted by hounds. Paradoxically, and where nature's special providence falls down, it is this scent which lures the hounds on and too often brings about the fox's death.

I would bring the cubs into the cottage. Frieda was even less troubled when I picked them up out of the den and took them away. She would drift off to join Rufus, and they would greet each other affectionately. You could almost hear her telling him that she was feeling quite glad to be rid of her cubs for an hour. Her teats were very raw and red, where the cubs were still suckling her: it had become almost a reflex action on their part, as if they suckled her whenever the thought occurred to them. Their needle-sharp teeth made it a painful business for her. So she was glad for them to leave her alone for a little while.

Don's work in the forest took up most of his time, and when he wasn't in the forest, there was paper-work in the office to keep him busy enough. When he had some time to spare, I would get him down to the glen to take photographs of the cubs. I spent a lot of time with Rufus in the glen, or he would come up to the cottage. He would explore every corner, every inch of this new territory. I would watch him, talking to him. Then, as if satisfied that he would know his way around next time (though, in fact, this was a routine he always went through every time he came to the cottage) he would come and sprawl on his back for me to scratch his stomach, while he chattered away. Presumably this was his instinctive way of "submitting" to me, showing that he was not prepared to attack me (though it was absurd to think of him attacking anyone), that he wanted to be friends. Or it may have been a game he was playing, shamming death, which foxes do in the wild, either to lure a victim into a sense of false security, or in an attempt to escape attack on themselves. His exploratory actions were almost certainly an instinctive search for potential danger, lurking under the sitting-room table, or behind a chair, or under my bed; and so he must have been experiencing a certain amount of fear. His rolling on his stomach must have meant that he

was relaxed, any thought of danger about the place having been
dismissed.

Sometimes he would stand up on his hind legs and place his
fore-paws against me, as if he were asking me to partner him in a
dance. Perhaps again he was playing a game, a hunting game – the
fox is noted for instinctively performing dances with the idea of
attracting a curious rabbit, who, mesmerised by the dance,
approaches closer and closer until it has drawn too near to escape
the fox's calculated, sudden pounce. Dancing with Rufus – we used
to take one or two steps together – you couldn't think he'd ever
entertained the slightest notion of mesmerising any rabbit; but the
instinct was there. Don used to recall his trying to return Rufus,
when fully grown, back to the wild. This was on Loch Aweside,
and Don knew the right thing was for him to go back where he
belonged. The wild, where all wild things belong. One night, Don
left him in the forest. But next morning, there he was on the door-
step with the milk. "Och, it'd taken him no time at all to realise he
couldn't hunt, he'd never learned how – so, like a sensible fox, back
he came to where he knew the food was. That's why he returned
home to me. He didn't know how to get food for himself."

Rufus's eyes were not only unusually round; they not only
seemed to slant less at the corners than those of other foxes I'd seen,
but they were large and very expressive. Sometimes, when you
sat with him, you would find him staring into space, and when you
tried to call his attention to something you wanted to speak to him
about, or show him, he would turn his head, but his eyes didn't
focus on you. He was still a million miles away, you felt. Perhaps
it was the daylight that affected his eyes, the same as it had affected
the cubs' eyes when they first opened. After all, he was really a
nocturnal creature: had he remained in the wild where Don tried
to return him, he would have spent most of his waking hours at
night, roaming the forest and hills, the glens and along the shores
of Loch Aweside.

Once, Rufus and I sat together in the old armchair, neither of us
saying anything, he'd gone off into one of his "trances", and I was
trying to remember when it was I'd had this feeling of sympathy
for the fox. It seemed that I had always been drawn to him, even
though I'd hardly ever seen a fox, let along met one; and despite
realising that he was rated such a despicable creature, robbing

Frieda with her newly-born family. The roof of her den has been removed to enable this unique photograph of a vixen and few hours' old cubs to be taken. Frieda looks as if she would have preferred to have been left with her young in the dark.

(*upper left*) Frieda cleans her last-born cub.

(*upper right* and *centre left*) Her family soon begin to show their curiosity for each other and their surroundings.

(*centre right*) Robbie characteristically has launched himself further (a few inches!) afield.

(*lower left*) Robbie on the scales, putting on weight every day.

(*lower right*) Eyes open, about a month later, anxious to learn about the outside world.

(*right*) Rufus, snoozing in the sun, relaxes from the strenuous efforts of fatherhood.

(*below*) He watches out for Frieda, keeping his distance from her and the youngsters.

(*above*) Rufus in spring moult, looking less than his best, and (slightly overweight!) Shuna.

(*below*) Shuna, taking a paddle in the loch, keeps a weather-eye open for Cronk, somewhere around.

(*above*) Cronk has appeared, and leads Shuna off on one of his games.

(*below*) Shuna, having given up the game with Cronk, returns for more gentle play with Rufus.

(*above*) Cronk pretending to be nest-building? Though she's lost her mate and anyway, it's rather late in the year.

(*below*) Cronk giving her ear-splitting imitation of a barking dog.

(*right*) Kee-wick . . . Keee-wiicck . . . shrieks the tawny owl, as phantom-like it sweeps through Ennochdhu Wood – The Dark Grove of the Birds.

(*upper left*) The wildcat, that strange "apparition" that appeared at Stalker's Cottage.

(*upper right*) Ernest Dudley finds the wildcat's lair – it was here under the cliffs near the Road to the Isles that he encountered the wildcat again.

(*centre left* and *centre right*) Frieda notes that Robbie is growing up.

(*bottom right*) Rufus takes a good look at Ernest Dudley – and he demonstrates his affection for his biographer.

(*above*) Roebuck, in velvet – the very one, perhaps, encountered by Rufus in Ennochdhu Wood.

(*above left*) His last bow. Rufus appears at the children's book-show; with Patrick Garland, the film-director, for whom he was going to "star".

(*above right*) Rufus with Don MacCaskill at Lloyds, where he was insured for his film-appearance.

(*below*) Rufus with some of his admirers at the book-show.

(*right*) The last time Rufus and Don were photographed together.

Shuna, alone – how long had she known Rufus was gone; that she would never see him again?

farmers of their sheep, and poultry-keepers of their chickens, a
thief and a murderer, skulking through life, persecuted and harassed
unto death, you begin to entertain a certain disbelief that he could
be all that evil; with this feeling for the fox had developed the same
sympathy you feel for the down-and-out, the human under-dog.
My father, who was often quoting at me, once said of a man he
knew who was having a rough time, being vilified from all sides:
"There, but for the grace of God, go I." And, because he was in
some respects prejudiced in his views, for my father to speak like
that about someone who he knew really was a no-good, carried
a lot of weight with me. This kind of fellow-feeling for the outcast,
the social pariah, sticks in your mind, and grows. And that's how
you come to think about the fox being less evil than he's
supposed to be.

The evening light was fading, and I realised Rufus should be
going back to Frieda and the cubs; and a shadow had fallen
across him as he sat there, and as I stirred he looked at me. His eyes
were bright in the shadow, they glowed just like a cat's eyes in the
dark, and I remembered a quotation from Michael Drayton's
poetic fairy-tale, *Nymphidia* (Drayton was a contemporary of
Shakespeare, and in fact was thought to be a part-author of *A
Midsummer Night's Dream*), in which he described Faerie King
Oberon's Palace being built of:

> *. . . spiders' legs, and*
> *For the roof instead of slats*
> *Is covered with the wings of bats,*
> *And its windows of the eyes of cats.*

As I picked up Rufus to carry him back to the glen, I wondered
who had been his ancestors? Half-dog, half-cat – where did you
come from? I asked him. He yawned.

Some days I would take the three vixens, leaving the two dog-
cubs to keep Frieda company, or for Rufus to play games with.
His idea of a game was almost invariably to hide the cubs somewhere away from the den, so that I would have to search for them
when I returned with the vixens. If I experienced any difficulty
about spotting the hidden couple, Rufus would condescend to
show me where they were, chattering and jumping up and
wagging his brush at the pleasure he was enjoying at my expense.

The cubs always remained exactly where he had hidden them. They never made any attempt to move away. I could have sworn that Rufus used to communicate with them in some way, warning them to lie low while I was looking for them. Both he and Frieda were able to signal to the cubs by some means when they were away from them, warning them to keep quiet, stay where they were, stay out of harm's way.

In the cottage the cubs would burrow into my jacket, hiding their heads, eyes tightly shut. Their tiny bodies were warm and trembling; their little tails resembled dark, small carrots ending in minute white tips. I would talk to them, crooning as if they were human babies, repetitive, rhythmic sounds, reassuring and comforting. At first I sounded so selfconscious that I felt pretty sure even the cubs weren't convinced – they seemed to wriggle about a bit more. But I began to get the hang of it, and could put on a tone of voice and murmur words of endearment that even convinced me. It had quite a good effect on the cubs. I'd never had any trouble with Rufus in this respect, he used to respond to my calling him "Darling", which I often did quite unselfconsciously, with apparent delight.

The days passed, the cubs began to look at you more squarely, their eyes becoming used to the light. The vertical "cat's eye" slit was more noticeable. These eyes that had been specially constructed for nocturnal vision; like a cat's eyes the amount of light that could hit the retina or light-sensitive layers back of the cub's eyes is controlled by the size of the pupils, the size of which in turn is controlled by the coloured circle surrounding the pupils, the iris. So as to protect the delicate retina from too much light, the iris by muscular contraction narrows the size of the pupil to a narrow vertical slit. At night, or in dimmer light, the iris widens the size of the vertical "cat's eye" aperture to allow it to use as much light as is available.

The cubs were beginning to display individual characteristics. One of the vixens would open her tiny, pink mouth with its baby milk-teeth bared to "cough" at me in anger if I startled her or made a sudden movement with my hand when I fed her a piece of meat. The others remained quiet, eyes tight shut, huddled up inside my sports-coat. The cubs were now learning to feed themselves on dead wild birds, rabbits, and pieces of venison. They were learning to chew the meat and extract the nourishment from it, spitting out the chewed-up stuff.

Sometimes I would take the cubs alone when Don was away in in the forest, and the cubs would sit and snuggle up to me, forever trying to get away from the light, to hide themselves in the darkness, the security they were accustomed to in the den. They would clamber under my jacket seeking the dark and the warmth of my body. They were warm and trembling as you held them. It was an extremely emotional experience, holding the cubs in your hands, feeling their trembling, the soft warmth of them; holding them against your cheek and smelling their warm, faintly musky scent.

Another mystery of the animal world which seems insoluble is the way that several animals born and brought up together in identical environmental circumstances should within a very short space of time exhibit widely varying personalities. It is true, of course, that you can only know this about animals with which human beings have been in contact, to a lesser or greater degree – only that way, after all, could you learn anything at all about animals. If they were left entirely on their own would they not exhibit individual characteristics among themselves? Does contact with man, however slight or remote, none the less trigger off something in the animal which it would not otherwise exhibit, so that it is impossible, really, for you to study animals without their being aware of it and therefore falsifying your picture of them?

Robbie would now open his tiny, pink mouth and give that "cough" at me, his flower-like face suddenly quite distorted in fury, at a sudden movement of my hand, even to give him some food. It was exactly the sort of angry, warning "cough", though in miniature, which Frieda would give Don or myself if we approached her in the den when she was with her cubs and she felt we were taking her a bit too much for granted, which she decided was likely to endanger her or her family. The dog-fox had picked up her warning "cough", and now he was warning Don and me not to venture too closely, not to try his patience or take him too lightly. And, while two of his sisters remained cuddled up under Don's coat, or mine, the other demonstrated from the word go that she was going to stand no nonsense from either of us.

This time, when we took the trio of vixens back to their den, we also took some raw venison which Don had obtained – a dead roe deer had been found in the forest the previous day – and fed it to Frieda and Rufus. Both of them took it into the den for the cubs to feed on. I watched while Robbie promptly showed who was the boss, by grabbing the largest piece of meat, and "coughing" his affronted anger at the presence of any of the other cubs who chanced to come near him. He bit and wrestled with his brother or his sisters if they didn't stay out of his way and leave him to enjoy his food. Behaving as if he were on the starvation mark, which his plump little body amply belied, he trampled all over his fellows in the cramped space of the den, while not one of them uttered a squeak of protest, and hardly bothered to shift their head as the "boss" cub poked his paw at their bright eyes.

"As good an example of the pecking order as you'll see," Don told me: the order of precedence in the animal world in which one animal dominates the other which in turn dominates the next, and so on, down to the smallest and weakest member of the group.

The last days of May and into June it rained sudden sharp showers mixed with long heavy downpours, when the raindrops smacked down on the earth like miniature bombs. And then the storm would pass, and the sky which had been swollen with grey and purple clouds would suddenly, miraculously brighten into an almost incandescent blue; the sun would blaze down, wonderfully warm so that the steam would start to crawl along the shining road-surface like gentle, helpless wraiths.

Friday afternoon, 2 June. The cubs were precisely six weeks old and due to be weighed. This time, we would rob Rufus and Frieda of their usual enjoyment of the proceedings by fetching the cubs indoors for their performance on the scales. A somewhat mean thing to do, you may think, but that was the way of it. Don opened the gate to the glen. We saw Rufus near the den. Normally he would have rushed to us, with his welcoming chatter, and rolled on his back to have his stomach scratched. But he remained still, staring at us as I shut the gate behind us. Don didn't say anything, didn't call out to Rufus. I was about to open my mouth to call to him, but I didn't. There was something in the air. I could sense it. At any rate, I thought I could. Something off-key. I hung back as Don went towards the den. Suddenly he gave a sudden exclamation. "Frieda —" I caught up with him.

Frieda was curled up in an old half-begun den she and Rufus had dug; it was several yards from the den where we expected to find her with the cubs. Don muttered something, which sounded like an imprecation in Gaelic and marched to the den, Frieda barely giving him a glance, and I went after him. He was quickly lifting up the den's cover, his expression faintly anxious. I joined him and we both looked in: the den was empty. The cubs had been in the den safe enough last night when Don had been to see that all was well; but they were gone, they might never have been.

"Frieda's hidden them." For a moment I thought Don's tone carried less conviction than usual, and the back of my neck went icy. Was he really thinking that someone had broken in and taken the cubs away and destroyed them? They were worth 50p each, at least, probably more: they were big cubs, and the children, too, of a famous father. And who knows what pleasure, what horrific pleasure it would give some fox-hater to be able to destroy them himself, personally? Like drowning them in a bucket as he would unwanted kittens – or he might devise some even more pleasurable way of killing the cubs.

I went rigid with apprehension, my mind full of horrible pictures. I could feel the perspiration trickling down my upper lip and under my arms. Don was already moving, his face calm. He reached the wooden shelter where Rufus often used to stretch himself out for a rest, and as he started to lift it, I gave him a hand and looked underneath. The cubs weren't there. We lowered the shelter, and began looking round, walking carefully for fear of treading on a cub hidden in the long, thick grass, Don all the time calling to Frieda and asking Rufus where they had hidden their young. But neither was telling.

Don noticed some freshly scraped earth under a raised hillock some twenty feet from the den; it was where Rufus and Frieda had some time earlier started to dig out a den. It had been filled in, wire-netting fixed over the place in an attempt to discourage any further efforts by Rufus or Frieda. Don was on his knees scrabbling away at the fresh earth so that it fell away to reveal a hole under the hillock about one and a half feet in diameter. He stopped, staring up at me. I thought I could hear a faint mewing down below. Don made as long an arm as he could, rolling back his coat-sleeve, but with a grunt of disgust withdrew his arm. "Too deep." He reached for a long, thin length of shrub and snapped it off at the root.

Carefully he pushed it down the hole. It vanished some four feet. He stopped and withdrew the length of shrub, and pointed out on the end some tiny hairs. The cubs were down there all right.

Frieda and Rufus after removing the pieces of rock and wire-netting must have put in some non-stop digging. What had been their purpose for all this? What motive had impelled them to go all out to hide the cubs? Don dragged them out, one after the other, kicking and struggling and squeaking their protests, and each returned home, Frieda now at the den-entrance watching them safely inside. The last one was the biggest, the "bossy" one, Robbie. The toughest, roughest of the cubs. Rufus all this time had continued to take no interest in what was going on. The feeling I'd had that there was something in the air hadn't left me. But Don seemed to take it all calmly, and so I didn't push any questions at him.

But even when Rufus came over to Don, and stood up on his hind legs to have his stomach scratched, as if the crisis was all over, I could still feel that chill at the nape of my neck. Don decided to leave it until next day to weigh the cubs. We filled in the hole, Rufus joining in as usual by getting in the way, and replaced the wire-netting and chunks of rock. He followed us to the gate. Frieda was still in the den with her family. Don locked the gate and we went up to the house. Suddenly, I had an idea that someone was watching us, and I looked back. But it was only Rufus, very still, staring after us.

2

Duncan McGregor came into the *Fisherman's Rest*, kilted and clutching his bagpipes and all. His father had been a piper with a Scottish regiment in the Second World War (and had died of wounds) in Normandy. Duncan spent the winter doing odd jobs, but blossomed forth as the Lone Piper of the Highlands in the summer, playing to tourists. He claimed descent from a Duncan MacGregor (he had spelt it M*a*c) who was born locally. *Donnacha Mor na Pioba*, as he was called, though considered to be daft in the head, had achieved renown as a bonny piper. According to Duncan, the Old One had been trained at the once-famous MacCrimmon College for pipers on the Isle of Skye, and could fetch a tune out of his *piob-mor* that fairly rattled the tiles off the roof, and the cows in the byre would run with perspiration. He travelled the Highlands, hoarding the money he earned for his performances by burying it in the ground. Once when he was asked if he knew where he'd hidden his money, the Old One replied: "Och, yes; I made a chalk-mark on a horse by Black Wood."

Over his drink Duncan McGregor gave me a nod, and winked at Rufus – we had gone on ahead of Don, who was working late. He put down his glass, and wiping his mouth with the back of his hand, "This one's top of the pops," he said. He began to play *Amazing Grace*. Rufus started to look uncomfortable.

I uttered a bit of a groan, and asked McNab to refill my glass. It wasn't so much that I didn't share McGregor's exuberant self-confidence in his ability as a performer on the bagpipes, it was just that you could hear the sound of *Amazing Grace* every time, it seemed, you switched on the radio. Everyone in Dunfuirich, you could easily believe, was walking about with a transistor which was incapable of playing any other tune; I was quite intrigued by the way it had become so popular: a two-hundred-years-old hymn tune, because that was what it really was, the words of which had been written by an eighteenth-century London clergyman.

McNab had become involved in a lively enough argument with the American wearing the cigar who had said that it was none other than David Rizzio, Mary Queen of Scot's dark-visaged court musician, later to become her trusted confidante, who had introduced the bagpipe from his native Italy into Scotland. The Reel of Tulloch, the Rothiemurchus Rant, and Jenny Dang the Weaver, from Italy? roared McNab. The Pibroch, Strathspey, the Lament, imported by an Italian? I had come across a reference to Rizzio and his connection with the bagpipes before, as a matter of fact, but I kept out of it as McNab's piratical moustache bristled with furious indignation. The American answered that bagpipes are common in both North and South Italy; he had heard them played there. In any case, McNab said, switching the line of the argument, playing the pipes indoors was all wrong in the Highlands. "No more intended for a house than an army band. The pipe's meant to call the clans to arms, to lead warriors into battle —" And he clapped his hands to his ears. While I was thinking what a strange twist in the skein of Fate, though not perhaps so strange when you're in the Highlands, as you soon come to realise, had brought me to Dunfuirich and this old pub?

By now Rufus had joined in, accompanying McGregor with spirited enthusiasm. The only thing was his howling didn't altogether harmonise so well with the bagpipes. *Amazing Grace* is one of those freaks whose success was inexplicable, even in the world of pop-music, that unpredictable business where the popularity of a song soars virtually overnight. The tune, of unknown origin, had emerged from Scotland's long ago Celtic mists, derived from two or three tunes played by the old bards. Then, two hundred years ago, London-born John Newton, famed hymn-writer, turned it into a hymn to which he wrote the words.

Newton, who had previously flourished as a rumbustious sailor, rising to the rank of captain of a slave-ship, had repented, turned strongly religious and was ordained in 1764. He became Rector of St Mary, Woolnoth, London, where his hymns numbered *How Sweet the Name of Jesus Sounds*, and *Glorious Things of Thee are Spoken*, and one which was to become *Amazing Grace*, this old Scottish tune he had heard and remembered during his adventurous voyages. "John Newton lived in wickedness a long time," his publisher explained, "but finally turned to the work of his Lord and Master, and entered the ministry, and was a power as a preacher, poet, and hymn writer. He expresses his feelings at the time he wrote the hymn, 'Amazing grace, how sweet the sound, That saved a wretch like me!'"

His hymn also travelled extensively on the Continent, and in Canada and the United States, where it was taken over by Negro singers, to become particularly popular in Texas. During the more recent popularisation of folk-music, several well-known singers had added the tune to their repertoire with varying success. In 1970 an American singer, Judy Collins, sang it to her own guitar arrangement. It became a hit in America and over here, and her recording was heard by bandmaster Stewart Wilson Fairbairn, of the Royal Scots Dragoon Guards, who enjoyed it so much that he arranged it for the Pipes and Drums and Military Band of the Royal Scots Dragoon Guards, the armoured infantry regiment stationed at the time in Herford, West Germany. The solo part played by Pipe Major Anthony Crease, 25 years old from Peebles, was so hauntingly moving it caught the public's ear when a recording made by the band was played over BBC radio, and they demanded more of it. It was this solo which McGregor was attempting to emulate.

As if the place wasn't in a big enough uproar, with Rufus's contribution growing louder than the laughter and *Amazing Grace* all put together, the barking started. The barking down the chimney. Cronk barking. What was a dog doing up the chimney, McNab wanted to know. I yelled at him that it was Cronk, he had already been told about Cronk's return several days before. The hideous noise was accompanied by soot and debris, it looked like the remnants of an old bird's nest. Cronk was making his presence known, and no mistake. Rufus seemed somewhat put out by this interruption – he knew who was causing it, all right – but McGregor soldiered on, though the cloud of soot from the fireplace made him cough a little. I was trying to explain to everyone that it wasn't a dog at all, but a raven, but what with the row continuing – Rufus, not to be overawed by Cronk, had resumed his accompaniment, and McGregor seemed to be getting off the note slightly – you could hardly blame me if I didn't entirely get the message through. Then Don came in, grabbed Rufus under his arm, we shouted our goodnights, and went out, Don calling up to Cronk that he was a black devil, and to come down from the chimney.

Cronk duly obliged. He landed on Don's shoulder, clawing on with grim determination, and rubbed that savage-looking beak of his against Don's cheek. It may have been the sentiment of the tune, or the words themselves of *Amazing Grace* . . . "how sweet the sound, That saved a wretch like me!" but, anyhow, the sight of that great black shape crooning like a baby and caressing Don, brought a catch in my throat.

With Rufus under his arm and Cronk on his shoulder, Don and I walked along the loch. He might have allowed Rufus to run on ahead, but he had become a little scared of doing this. Now, it was only in the immediate area of Ennochdhu Wood, where he knew where he was, near his home, that Rufus was allowed to run around on his own. Elsewhere, he might be panicked by a speeding car or noisy motor-bike, rush off to become lost, and meet a violent end at the hands of fox-haters. This was the ever-present fear, Rufus's safety. His life.

Tom Gordon smoked his pipe as he leaned against the gate of the corrugated-iron post-office at the side of the road. He was the sub-postmaster. He also supplied groceries, ice-creams, mineral waters, cigarettes and picture-postcards. With him, sitting on a broken chair with no back which he intended in due course to break up for firewood, was Hughie Drummond. He pointed a long finger at Cronk and, turning to Tom Gordon, said: "The Black Raven will come and eat ye!" At which Cronk gave one of her most grating barks, flapped her wings and flew off, still barking, to perch on the branch of a tree overhanging the road. "That's what my mother used to warn me, when I was a bairn," Hughie went on, "if I didna stay quiet and obedient." He stood up, but keeping one hand on his chair for support, he loudly vouchsafed the story of how the Vikings, in A.D. 845, or thereabouts, when they set out on their marauding voyages and warlike raids, took with them ravens as spies. Set free at the appropriate time, they would fly high and sight the distant landfall, to which they would head. Which was how, according to Hughie, they came upon the Scottish Highlands and mainland coasts. "Led by the ravens, the Vikings were, who came to pillage and destroy. That's why," pointing that long finger in Cronk's direction, "ma mother used to warn me of him" – at which Cronk gave a somewhat high-pitched bark, as if she had heard and resented Hughie's wrong description of her sex – "if I didna stay quiet and obedient. He would come and eat me."

"Didn't your mother also tell ye that Noah sent out both a raven and a dove from the Ark to sight the land," Tom Gordon said, "when the flood began to subside?"

Hughie let his pointing finger fall to grip the chair with both hands. "Aye, but that was when the raven was as white as Noah's dove. Then it was turned black as punishment for fouling a spring at which Jesus Christ had stopped to drink —" He broke off as if he had been reminded of something. He addressed me again. "I didna tell ye how I was also wounded here?" He had already started to let his trousers down, at which Cronk gave an affronted screech and took off homewards, with a great flap of wings. "That bluidy bird," Hughie said. "On the Somme, it was —"

I told him I'd heard his other dramatic account of how portions of his behind had been shot off by one of our own machine-guns, as he was returning from a sortie on the enemy lines. "Ye see, I was at that precise moment crawling backwards to give the Boche the impression that I was advancing – camouflage, ye understand — ?" But I put a stop to it, pointing out that the story had earned several drinks from me already. He pulled up his trousers reluctantly. "Anither thing," he went on, "ma mother used to warn me if I didn't behave, was that an *urusig* would carry me down into the depths of the loch."

Loch Fourich, like almost every Highland loch, yielded its full quota of ghosts and goblins, *urusigs* and *glaistigs*, from its depths. The most popular creatures to haunt the loch were sea-horses. Or to be precise, if you ever can be precise about occult manifestations or supernatural visitations, these phantoms turned into horses on gaining the land. The idea was, apparently, to lure human beings into catching the horse; it was always white, with beautiful mane and flowing tail. When it was caught and mounted, the rider would suddenly realise he was being carried at a terrible gallop into the loch; it was impossible for him to dismount, the horse quickly submerged, the rider drowned.

The object of this enterprise was never made clear, though Hughie Drummond, or it may have been Johnson, who was also steeped in these strange tales, had thought that what the sea-horses were really hoping for was that they would be caught and ridden by a beautiful maiden. This would ensure that the creature would remain a horse faithful to the girl, never returning to the loch. According to my informant, whoever he was, the beautiful girl and the sea-horse had to get together on the night of the yellow *gealach fhoghair*, or harvest moon, or the magic wouldn't work.

Hughie was quoting an old Gaelic notion at me, which he carefully translated, that up till the time you were adult, you belonged to the water, or sea, after that the earth claimed you, until old age, when your allegiance was to the air. "It's elementary," he said; it was one of his favourite pronouncements, uttered in his somewhat unctuous manner, "just like Sherlock Holmes."

We walked on, leaving Tom Gordon to refill his pipe, Hughie to rest a little on his chair, preparatory to heading for his tent. The sky was darkening, and Rufus comfortable in Don's arms, keeping one eye open and giving his tail an occasional wag as if to say he was glad to be on his way home. On into the misty, purplish distance stretched the slightly choppy waters, on the other side of which the forest-clad hills rose, dark greens and greys, broken by glens and ravines, with a glimpse of a white waterfall perpetually cascading down to a burn, hidden by rocks and foliage, on its way to the loch. Beyond, a great gash in the forest, where a storm had struck and uprooted the trees, throwing their huge trunks and branches aside like matchsticks, to fall into grotesque, sinister shapes down the hillside. The white, round lighthouse lay low-built on its spur of shore ahead. Beyond it the bend in the road hiding Captain Bailey's house. But I wasn't giving him a thought, as we turned off up a narrow track, a short cut to the top of the road wriggling up to Don's house.

I was looking down on the loch, its surface ruffled by evening gusts, which seemed to me to carry a taste of sea on the air. Seagulls dipped low, every now and then leaving ripples where they had scratched the loch's grey, glinting surface. The wind rustled in the larch plantation further along the road and then a sparrow-hawk cock called his mate: *Kek-kek-kek . . . Kek-kek-kek*. There was a lot of low cloud, trailing black ribbons of it. Only a few early stars – one was the North Star, I thought – flickered in the sky. Don paused, and while Rufus licked his nose, listened. He had watched and photographed a pair of sparrow-hawks in this same larch wood for nine years. Each year they had nested higher in the trees until the last time he had observed them they were forty-five feet high in the branches. We watched the hen appear for a moment, swift, yellow-eyed and manoeuvring its short, powerful wings through the close-growing larches, now darkening in the fading light, in answer to its mate's cry. *Kek-kek-kek . . . Kek-kek-kek*.

Hughie Drummond's tales at the post-office had set me off on a story about my grandfather who, when he was a medical student, had stayed the night at an Edinburgh hotel and had heard a strange noise in the street below. Looking out he saw a crowd, very quiet and subdued, black in their cloaks, hurrying as if to witness some sight. The noise was the crowd's murmuring. There was a drizzle of rain, the street gleamed with black mud. My grandfather found himself outside the inn, then being caught up with the crowd, carried along with them. He was outside the Tolbooth prison, where above the heads of the milling throng packed like sardines, he saw a man swinging from the gibbet. The man wore a white cap over his face, but now the whispers of the crowd rose in a shout: "Deacon Brodie . . . Deacon Brodie . . ." Grandfather knew he was seeing the hanging of the great thief, upon whom Robert Louis Stevenson was to base his Dr Jekyll and Mr Hyde story, Deacon Brodie. The date was 1 October 1788 – my grandfather hadn't yet been born. He woke next morning, convinced that it had been no nightmare, that he had gone out to join that dreadful mob. And his boots which were clean when he had gone to bed, were bespattered with mud, and his trousers damp with rain.

Don was asking me if I'd seen the plaque on the garden wall of the house at Kinnaird, which was out on the Kirkmichael Road, which said that Robert Louis Stevenson had stayed there in 1881, when he wrote some short stories, before he turned to *Treasure Island*, and I was saying I hadn't been to Kinnaird, yet, as we reached the screen of trees. Beyond them lights glimmered from Don's house. He muttered to Rufus, anxious now to get back to Frieda, to be quiet.

He began recollecting the flitting from Loch Aweside. Neither he nor Catherine had quite settled down in the house, they still thought of their old home, where they had lived ever since they were first married. They had both "belonged" to that part. Don gave a sigh. Seventy miles, that's all the distance they'd flitted. They liked the house, it had an odd shape, but it was warm and had plenty of light. They had slept on the bare boards the first night of their arrival, with Rufus and Shuna, Cassius and Frieda lying on some old newspapers in the kitchen. They'd been late arriving. The removal-men hadn't shown up – a breakdown on the way, and in fact they didn't show up until next afternoon – but they had some blankets with them, and some food, and they had made coffee. It was October, the house had been left unheated for several weeks while it was being redecorated.

Don had woken in the early hours, stiff and chilled. He had got up and dressed in his anorak and woollen tammy. He heard Rufus chattering in the kitchen, and he opened the door and told him to lie quiet. He didn't want to take him, in case he ran off – it was all strange to Rufus, and he might have been confused and become lost. It was moonlight, with a good spatter of stars in a light-coloured, wintry sky. The first frost-brittle leaves of winter crackled underfoot as Don made his way up to a hill looking over

Loch Fourich. He heard the bark of a roe-buck in the forest. It was a harsher "wouff" than that uttered by the doe.

His new job meant advancement; he was really very glad about it, but at this hour he felt as if it was starting all over again. He looked back at the house. It appeared strange and unreal there in the moonlight, its windows dark blanks, without curtains. He wondered what the future held. New friends to make, strange faces with which to become familiar. Och, well, he had Rufus. That was something to be glad about. And there was Shuna and Cassius, and Frieda; all old, true friends. He looked down over the loch, its surface dark and smooth, almost as if it was frozen over. He turned and glanced back, where he could make out the icy peaks of Glencoe far away, but clear in the frosty night. He began walking back to the house.

Don broke off his abstracted gaze and turned to me. We started down to the glen to return Rufus to Frieda, and to listen to the cubs squeaking. He warned me not to step too near the entrance to the den, just in case Frieda dashed out to give me a nip round the ankle – she might think I was getting a bit too near her family. A friendly warning, that's all she'd mean.

We watched Rufus hurry off to the den, outside which he paused, and we heard the cubs squeaking. He turned and looked back at us. You could almost swear that he gave Don a nod as much as to say everything was all right. The cubs were safe with Frieda and he was there, so there was nothing to worry about. "I suppose," I said, "he loves you about as much as he can love anyone."

Don thought for a moment. "If I was to drop dead tomorrow," he said, "I don't believe he'd feel a thing. Why should he, what does he know about death? Who's told him about it, communicated to him the inevitability of his own mortality? He can't foresee it, he has no idea that it must come. So why should he mourn me?" He shook his head slowly, as we moved back up to the house. "We mustn't humanise him. He goes through life totally ignorant of what lies round the corner for him. It might be a nice, juicy rabbit, it might be a blast from a shotgun."

My mind flashed back to when I was working on the Rangi book. Rangi's mate, Tiki, had just recovered from an operation on her ear for the removal of a cancerous growth – and I had the chance of observing a similar operation, also on an Alsatian. I recalled the two nurses bringing the dog into the operating-theatre and placing him on the table, all bright-eyed and friendly, his tongue slobbering affectionately over the nurse's hands as she prepared him, shaving the fur off his ear. The veterinary surgeon produced the hypodermic syringe. It could have been a lethal shot for all the dog knew; it occurred to me, then, that a dog, or any other animal, possessed no means of knowing what the future, immediate or distant, held in store for him. The hypodermic could be bringing him total extinction, instead of merely putting him to sleep so that his illness could be cured.

If, then, Rufus knew nothing about death, what could he know of mourning, of sorrow? Of love? Could he weep for a lost love, could his heart ache for an absent loved one? It seemed unlikely. Could you attribute to him the love of a husband for his wife? You can't compare Frieda's love for her cubs with that of a mother and her children. Frieda could hide one, or two, or three of her cubs and forget where she'd hidden them, or that she'd even given birth to them in the first place. In a few weeks she would forget them as if they had never been hers; she wouldn't acknowledge them as her children if she met them face to face. All that she experienced towards her cubs was instinctive reflexes which she had inherited, which were genetic. It was her maternal instinct. It wasn't mother-love, as human beings understand it.

The sound of Cronk barking reached us. It was less harsh now, more of a grumbling to herself, as if she was trying to settle down for the night, and wanted everyone to know it. Don gave a wry smile, and I could read his thoughts. What went for Rufus and Frieda applied just as much to Cronk and her love for Don, even for him. When the time came she would leave him. Fly away on her black wings.

We went back to the house.

7 Watchers of the Night

Rufus greeted Frieda with a wag of his tail, and they touched noses; she had just come out of the den, leaving the cubs to search for food. The evening sky was light, with no stars. Frieda went off to dig up some rabbit that Rufus had brought her, provided by Don the previous night, and which she had buried. Rufus stood for a few moments staring into the mouth of the den, where the dark, furry shapes of the cubs huddled together for warmth which they had lost when their mother left them. Rufus's scent reached them, and they whimpered for him. He had begun to take his paternal rôle with them and they were blossoming out under his tuition. He was teaching them to hunt; performing his dancing pounce for them to imitate. He hadn't hunted himself, but instinctively he knew that it was his job to teach his offspring, and instinctively he knew what it was necessary for them to know. They were responding to his presence, now, outside the den. He was their friend, their father. They wanted him to warm them in place of their mother. But he knew a thing or two better than that. He knew that to venture any nearer to the cubs than he was now would earn him Frieda's maternally roused, biting fury. He was remembering how the first time she had given birth to cubs, and he had allowed his natural curiosity to get the better of him, she had chased him out of the den, snarling and snapping her teeth at him. He never allowed his paternal feelings to run him into this sort of trouble again.

Curiosity was, you might say, the breath of life to him, the same as with all foxes as with most wild creatures; those that have survived. Curiosity must have saved a fox's life time and time again;

hardly ever could it be said to have caused its death. Rufus always wanted to know what was going on, and was always ready to explore the unknown. Come to think of it, curiosity has been a forceful compulsion with human beings. You might think it's been more compelling for us than any other urge, even the biological urge. It's what has driven man to explore the earth and beyond it; the drive of curiosity is what has brought about the miracles of science, from the time of the discovery of the wheel or the use of fire. A power greater than love? With only love to power us would the human species have survived? If the force of curiosity hadn't driven us to discover the use of axe-flints, arrow-heads, the weaponry which has made us master of the animal-world, wouldn't we too have become extinct? Where did love get the brontosaurus or the iguanodon, the miacid – you might say it wasn't curiosity that killed the cat, but not enough of it – or our nearest relative, the anthropoid?

If it's curiosity more than love which has saved our species, it's certainly not love but curiosity which has saved the fox; driven from the forests eroded by civilisation, hunted down from the hill by sheep-farmers, Rufus's kind moved into suburban areas, where those refuse-bins brim over, and where the city-dweller's reflex-action is not to reach for a gun so much as to view the invader with a kind of amused tolerance.

Rufus had turned away from the den and loped down to the gate, where a hole in the wire-netting had earlier aroused his curiosity and which he considered might be rewarding to exploit. The tear in the wire-netting was hidden by tall weeds, which was why neither Don nor I had noticed it. Rufus worked away with the particular kind of diligence he always exercised in matters of such importance, and in twelve minutes had extended the hole sufficiently to enable him to wriggle through. The diameter of the gap was less than six inches, but he contrived to make his body extraordinarily thin, and he was free.

He glanced back in the direction of the den. He glimpsed Frieda briefly as she paused at the den-mouth. She was carrying some food, and she uttered a gurgling note to her cubs inside, then she vanished. Rufus knew she would not leave the cubs to accompany him on his exploratory trip; she was still tied to them maternally. They were not yet weaned. Rufus gained the top of an incline some fifty yards from the gate. From this vantage-point he was able to stare at the loch, scintillating in the moonlight, which was mistily pale. A hare appeared, eyes bulging, tall ears twitching. It didn't wind Rufus, nor did it observe him, as it paused to nibble at its hind leg, teeth glistening. Rufus gave a little grunt, and the hare's ears were suddenly erect, its bulging eyes white round the edges as it sighted him. With a flash of its scut it was gone.

In the shadows the velvety blackness behind Rufus's ears threw their whiteness in front into startling relief; the white jawline contrasted equally with his black, shiny nose, which was even more emphasised by the whiteness of his throat extending down his chest. It appeared almost luminous – to friend it may have conveyed some particular information, to foe it must present a terrifying sight, as frightening as the macabre, painted faces of those warriors – Zulus, Red Indians, whose war-paint resembles the fox's mask – must have appeared to their foes.

He was free, yes; but what would he do with his freedom, now that it was his? His thoughts went back to Frieda and the cubs, and for a moment he almost decided to turn back – the security of the glen suddenly seemed more important to him than the adventure of searching out strange places. A whiff of breeze off the loch with a faint touch of the sea in it caught his nose and he turned away and made off down the other side of the low hill. He came to some pines on the edge of the forest and stared into the darkness beyond.

He could hear the branches of the tree above him squeak as they rubbed against each other in a hatful of wind which blew up from the loch, and he felt a sudden itching along the side of his jaw. He rubbed his jaw against a short length of branch jutting out from the lower part of the trunk. But the branch felt too smooth and he moved round to the other side of it. It was rough, and he enjoyed its roughness as he moved his itching jaw against it. A feather detached itself from the rough side of the branch where it had fallen from a bird perching above and become caught. The feather fluttered like a delicate grey snow-flake towards the ground. It was a ring-dove's feather. Rufus watched it, his eyes crossing grotesquely, as it slowly settled on the tip of his quivering nose. It teetered there precariously, until Rufus gave it a puff and it sailed up a few inches in the air, while he observed it, his eyes now properly focused, speculatively. Then, as it fell again very slowly to the ground, he turned away and he moved towards the water's edge.

Down past the blue-grey outcrop of rock he padded. He stared out across the silent water, paws sinking into the soft, silvery sand. The loch was shadowed and misted with grey wraiths in the moonlight; and looking down he saw three silver birches uprooted by last winter's slide of snow and thrown headlong into the shallows, where they lay half-submerged like the whitened bones of three enormously tall skeletons.

Rufus began paddling towards the topmost skeletal branches; soon he found himself up to his shoulders. The branches were still too far for him to reach. He began swimming. It was at best a kind of "dog's paddle". But he was soon swimming over the tops of the trees. He swam around for a few moments, then he was past the three trees, heading out towards the centre of the loch, and he turned back hurriedly. He seemed to be anxious to regain the shore. His paws reached the sand once more. Shaking himself vigorously, he blinked as if in surprise as the water sprayed all about him. His mouth wide, his tongue lolling out – he had enjoyed his dip – he began moving up the bank, back towards the forest. A piece of weed hung grotesquely from his right eyebrow, and he stuck his tongue out further and licked it away. He paused to sniff at the primroses and some daisies, but their faces were too tightly closed against the night. He heard an otter bark somewhere along the loch. Then he watched a young salmon float slowly past, moving slowly because it was dying. It gave an occasional shiver, so that it sent ripples from its body; there was a long jagged scar in the uppermost side of it. Caused not by the otter, but by the spear-like beak of some bird, perhaps a heron. The fish had somehow escaped from the bird's attack, and had eluded the otter, but it would not live long. Rufus watched it out of sight. He heard the otter give a long-drawn-out groan culminating in a whistle, fading into the distance. He began moving up the bank, back towards the forest.

Now, his nose quivered. This was not the scent of primroses, now, or daisies. It was the scent of a badger which it had left on the ground from the glands beneath its tail. It was a warning; the badger had left its scent as a warning to its own kind, and other animals could interpret it as a warning that there was danger about. And despite the fact that Rufus lived as well protected as possible from the dangers that beset every creature of the wild, he recognised the warning. He raised his head, his ears pricked. It was the threat of human danger; the menace he knew, instinctively, information which all his senses, eyes, nose, ears and his whiskers presented to him, was that of man. And of man that killed foxes; it was not that kind of human being who was friendly towards him. It was not Don's scent, or mine. The badger had known, and had left his warning.

He went into the trees, to encounter a roe buck, who was gently rubbing his antlers against a tree-trunk. They had grown from knobs extending from the frontal bones of his skull and were still covered by the nutrient skin which was known as velvet, and it was this putrefying skin which the buck was now rubbing off. The buck turned on Rufus and tossed his head at him. Rufus was invading his territory, which was something Rufus shouldn't have done.

But the buck was scared of injuring his precious antlers by attacking Rufus with them. Instead, and Rufus sat back with a surprised expression, he rose up on his hind legs and thrust at the air with his fore feet. It was as if he was inviting Rufus to spar with him. Rufus felt relaxed, he wanted to flex his muscles; but he had no intention of lending himself to such an exhibition. He refused to stand on his own hind legs and box the buck, who thereupon changed his tactics. He arched his neck to prod Rufus with his antlers. Rufus at once realised you needed to be pretty smart at dodging the probing antlers, and after a couple of minutes backing and weaving he retreated. His tongue was lolling out; he wasn't used to exercise as strenuous as this (after all, he was over five years old) and he was quite happy to let the buck toss his antlers in triumph as much as he liked. But not at him.

He moved off. Unhurriedly, jauntily, not the least bit discomfited by having been forced to retreat; let the buck have his territory all to himself, and good luck to him.

Rufus paused and listened intently. His black, white-edged ears were cupped forwards as he bent his head to the ground. The grass was thick, providing good cover and tunnels for voles. Rufus could hear them squeaking as they hurried along, about their particular business. He moved to a weed-covered clump and poised there, ears still bent to the squeaks of the voles. Suddenly, he leapt up and dived down in one flash of movement, and in his fore-paws he held a struggling, squeaking vole in his mouth. He crossed his eyes at it – and released it. The vole squeaked even more loudly as it dived into a grass tunnel and shot away. Rufus had acted instinctively, he had gone through all the motions of hunting, but he hadn't known what to do with his prey when he'd caught it. Still, it had provided him with some sharp exercise, and he derived a certain satisfaction from holding that tiny little creature, struggling helplessly in his jaws; that had provided him with sufficient reward for his activity.

He proceeded on his way, on his toes – like the cat-family, except that he had only four toes to each foot, against the cat's five, and his claws weren't retractile – his paws were digigrade, he moved on tiptoe. His distant ancestors must have walked flat-footed, using the entire forepart of the leg (in human terms, the "wrist" and "ankle") as the foot. The process of evolution required the fox, like the cat, if he was to survive, to be able to run fast, spring and climb; accordingly he lengthened his legs by getting up on his toes.

The waters of a burn, glinting and shot through with moonlight filtering through the trees, raced past Rufus on his right and he halted, listening to the noise of the water. He moved cautiously down to the burn's edge, his paws skidding a little on wet moss-covered rock-slabs, and drank. His eyes were close to the surface of the burn and he stared at the dark long weeds which swayed in the current. He dipped a paw in and patted a length of weed; tiny bubbles rose from it, and it tangled round his foot. The weed clung to his foot when he withdrew it, and still hung on when he tried to shake it off. It straggled behind him as he padded off. It didn't seem to bother him. Anyway, it became caught on some undergrowth and he lost it.

Reaching a rowan tree which had been half-uprooted by a storm that early spring, so that a branch stretched out horizontally about five feet from the ground, his attention was diverted by some pellets, comprising mice's fur and bones, scattered about on the ground, which an owl had regurgitated and ejected. He considered a pellet for a few moments, turning it over speculatively with his nose. Would it be good to eat? He sniffed at it once more and decided he wasn't that hungry, after all. He had enjoyed a good meal, provided for him by Don, before he had left the glen. He turned to the rowan tree again and sprang up the trunk like a cat.

As he proceeded along the branch, it bent and swayed a little beneath his weight, but his claws bit into the bark, and he reached the fork of three branches, into which he fitted himself comfortably. Curled up, he enjoyed the gentle movement of the branches. He shifted his weight and settled himself.

Swaying there at the end of the branch like a great cat, his brush round his face, he did not, however, relax; an urge began to niggle at him, the inevitable pull reaching out to him from Frieda and the cubs. There came a sudden swish and flap of wings above him and a tawny owl was setting about him – he had invaded its territory, this was its perching site, and there was nothing for it but to move. While the bird, with its white moon-like face implacable, continued to harass him, Rufus slowly made his way, head hunched between his shoulders, along the swaying branch. He gained the trunk and leaped to the ground.

Irresolutely, he stood, tail wagging slowly to and fro. His nose, a phenomenally powerful in-built scenting apparatus, was still picking up Frieda's scent and that of the cubs. He was still keeping within a relatively short distance of them. Frieda, too, could scent him. He could get back to her in a matter of minutes. As well as scenting each other, they would be conveying information between them. Was Rufus picking up some signal from her which was causing him to feel uneasy, so that he couldn't make up his mind whether to go back now or adventure a little further first?

As well as whatever information he might be receiving from Frieda, the very atmosphere everywhere around him quivered with intelligence. His whiskers, thick, long black hairs on either side of his face – *vibrissae*, bristles – running up from the corners of his mouth, together with those sticking out from where his eyebrows would be if he had any, possessed extraordinary sensitivity. If you ran your fingers along them, they would seem almost charged with electricity. They were Rufus's extra sense-organs, augmenting his powerful scenting ability and his acute sense of hearing, a powerful aid to his sensory perception, enabling him to pick out of the air wonderful and vital pieces of information. Pieces which he could fit together, like working out a jigsaw-puzzle, to give him a complete picture of what was going on all about him. In the darkness of the night, this was tremendously useful. It was of life and death importance to him.

Put to its most elementary use, he was able to gauge, in the same way that a cat can, the size of any aperture he contemplated entering, but he could also sense the vibrations of any man-made element about it, so that he could be sure he wasn't putting his head into a trap, for example. These powerful, uncanny antennae he possessed could pick up vibrations in the atmosphere due to the movement of animals, or birds, or human beings about him. The rustle of a bird's wing, the stirring of a hare, these he was made aware of at once.

He was moving deeper into the forest, and he turned back. He found another rowan tree in some rocks. Now the scent from the glen came more strongly again on the breeze from the loch. He was still moulting his winter coat, a few tufts of fur still decorated his frame, which appeared thinner, and he felt a little chilled. He would have been warmer in the shelter Don had provided for him. He curled himself in a small hollow among the roots of the rowan, where some primroses straggled, their flowers closed against the night.

It is totally impossible to imagine Rufus's life-style: you could only hope to understand by comparison the difference between his world and Don's or mine. For instance, his world was made up of scents to a degree beyond our comprehension. He could eat and enjoy, so far as is known about what he enjoys or doesn't, rotted food the smell of which could make you vomit. He could live near the putrefying carcasses of birds, rabbits, hares, voles – Frieda and the cubs, of course, lived for weeks on end in a den with rotting food, excreta, all about them, although she carefully washed the cubs continually – Rufus could give off smells from his scent glands, the sub-caudal glands beneath his tail, and glands in his feet (these helped him when retracing his steps), which are pretty pungent to human nostrils. He could scent all the smells, of varying intensity and types, given off by animals, birds and insects in the forest.

These scents produced by his own and other creatures' normal bodily functions made up his world; he pondered them, reached conclusions concerning their meaning, to him and perhaps to others, tucked them away in the appropriate compartments of his memory. And acted on the information they supplied him. The scent of primroses now under his nose may have given him little or no enjoyment, but you shouldn't rate him the less because he derived something of more particular interest to him from the smell of some putrid meat than from the scent of flowers. After all, perhaps he obtained important information from the primroses' scent which humans simply possess no capacity to estimate. Our own powers of scent have been so diminished by the pressures of civilisation, the ever-increasing pollution of the atmosphere, that perhaps we aren't able to appreciate what we're missing. The ability to scent danger is not so essential to man's survival; in any case you can use animals to do the job for you, guard-dogs to scent thieves, police-dogs to smell out cannabis. Rufus had no nose to rely on but his own. His marvellous nose which could sniff hatred, violence, death in the air.

Add to his antennae-like receiving apparatus and his phenomenal scenting powers, an acute sense of hearing – alerted, his large ears pushed forwards, wonderful "ear-trumpets" capable of picking up the cracking of a twig a hundred yards distant, or the rustle of a gamekeeper's breeches – and you have a creature who could truly express his central life-values. Inarticulate by human standards he may be, but he communicates with his world with unerring precision, stating exactly his attitudes, his emotions. Can we with all our sophisticated means of communication, say as much? It is our world's loss that we cannot pick up his signals. Transmitted through a flick of his brush, by his fur's guard-hairs, by his howls and barks, his facial expression, his grimaces, he expresses, spontaneously, without any artifice, his feelings, his nature. Human beings, because they can't tune-in on his peculiarly subtle wavelength, reject Rufus's kind. Vilify, hunt, and exterminate them.

He caught the badger's scent once more. It stirred a warning note at the back of his brain, set off that bell ringing again. He stirred uneasily. He went forward again, but there was less uncertainty about the direction he was taking. He was heading towards the glen where Frieda and the cubs were. Now it was her scent that he picked up again as he neared the glen, and now the other scent, the scent the badger had dropped was replaced by that friendly, familiar scent.

Suddenly there was a swish and flutter of wings, as a tawny owl – it may have been the one he had seen earlier – descended and went for him in another effort to drive him away. He was too near her nest, now, which was in some rocks nearby. He moved off again, ducking low to avoid the owl's attack and found himself among some spruce trees. He paused for a moment, realised he was moving further into the forest, away from the enclosure, and Frieda and his cubs. He turned and made his way back some twenty yards. He found another rowan tree in some rocks and now he shivered; his coat was thin, and the breeze from the loch was chilly; he thought of the warm and comfortable shelter which Don had provided for him; but he decided to curl himself at the foot of the tree where some primroses straggled, their petals closed against the night, his brush shielding his nose. The silver birches' leaves rustled soothingly in the breeze from the loch, and Frieda's scent was brought to him reassuringly. He would be on his way soon. He dozed. Perhaps he felt safe under the rowan. The rowan that used to be planted at the gate of most Highland dwellings, or at the doorway, for it was supposed to possess magical properties; it was supposed to keep the Devil out of the house.

At dawn, with its sky flowing like running water-colour all pink and pale blue, mingled with gold and orange and reflected in the waters of the loch, Rufus's dreams, if indeed he was dreaming, were interrupted roughly. He gave a sharp bark, awaking with a start. The roe-buck was back, nudging him cautiously with a shove of his antlers. Rufus barked again at the buck, this time less sleepily; he was feeling quite irritated by the roe-buck's attentions – especially being woken at this hour. The breeze whipped up from the loch coldly. He stood up, shivering and yawned, while the roe-buck backed off a little. Frieda's scent reached him, and Rufus stretched himself. As the roe-buck advanced towards him aggressively, he turned his back on him and loped off towards Frieda and the cubs. He reached the slope on the edge of the forest leading down to the enclosure and loped off down it, home.

2

I had been over at the Fasganeoin Hotel that evening. I had been on the 'phone to Bernard Smith, arranging to meet him in London next week. Don had fallen in with the idea of Rufus appearing in the *Lady Into Fox* film. It now remained for me to reach agreement with Smith on the final details. One problem that was going to take some settling was that of insuring against Rufus being lost, or meeting with an accident, sickness or death between now and the date when production of the film was due to begin. Performing animals are, as a matter of course, insured, but Rufus was a wild animal, virtually living in wild conditions; moreover he was by law rated as vermin, a pest, so that anyone who succeeded in causing his destruction couldn't be held liable, sued, for maiming or killing him. On the contrary, they would be congratulated, even suitably rewarded. Who would agree to insure him, taking into account the hazards under which he normally lived?

These hazards had been taken into account by Don from the first day he had owned Rufus as a young cub; after all, it was only by sheer luck, a thousand to one chance, that he'd survived being wiped out with his parents and the rest of the family just after he'd been born. When he came into Don's hands it was impossible to guarantee that he would be secure without his being confined – penned up, caged. From the start, when he wasn't close to Don, in the house, or out with him for walks, or travelling, he had been allowed to run free in a big enclosure, wide open to the skies, to the forest around him, simulating as realistically as possible his wild home. Had his surroundings been anything less than this, he might as well have been in a zoo. You had to accept that his comparative freedom increased his vulnerability. It was a risk you had to take. It was a high risk, because you knew there were people about who were always on the look-out for the chance to destroy him. But it was better that way than that Rufus should be made a prisoner. You had to rationalise it, realise that if he had been totally wild he would by now almost certainly have been dead.

Don couldn't change this pattern, now, simply because of Rufus's prospects of becoming a film-"actor". He couldn't start curbing him, ensuring his greater safety by allowing him less freedom than he had enjoyed. This was the way of the game, and you had to make up your mind to play the game, or get into some other game, less dangerous. So this was the risk that he had to be insured against, that he would end up by losing the game. That he would be stopped from appearing in the film.

Mrs Turk also had a message for me to telephone Iris; she was still in Edinburgh. When I spoke to her she said she was on her way back to London. She would be going back to New York in about a week's time. I told her I would be in London myself by then and looked forward to seeing her before she left.

I stayed to have dinner with Mrs Turk and the family. The hotel was full, except for one room which had been taken yesterday afternoon but vacated that same evening. Mrs Turk was about to elucidate the mystery of the young man who (didn't I remember?) had kept a candle burning in his wash-basin all night – he and his mother had returned home, though they had remained a further two days, they had enjoyed their stay so much – when she was interrupted by Mr Klein. He came into the sitting-room, and launched into his dramatic account of yesterday's young woman who had booked and then so soon vacated this room.

It was late afternoon when she had arrived. She had explained to Mr Klein that her car had broken down and she had left it at the garage nearby. It wouldn't be ready until next morning. She was very tired, she would rest until dinner-time. She was very thankful that she had got the last available room. She would fill in the visitor's book later. Dinner-time, but no young woman answered the dinner-gong. Eventually, Mrs Turk had gone up to the bedroom. Empty; the young woman had gone. Taken a bath-towel with her. It had Fasganeoin Hotel in the corner. She must have slipped out without anyone seeing her go. Later, a call from the local police. Inquiries about a young woman who answered to the description of the guest who had stayed so briefly. They had a name for her different from the one she had given Mr Klein. The police were anxious to ask her about the car she had left at the garage. No, there was nothing wrong with it that some petrol wouldn't put right. Except that it didn't belong to her. It answered the description of a car stolen in Inverness. Mr Klein couldn't offer the police much help, and after commiserating with him about the lost bath-towel and promising to do their utmost to recover it, they went away.

Sabrina and Norbert had now come in to have their dinner; the guests had all been served with coffee, and both of them had theories they wanted to expound concerning the young woman, but Mr Klein was more concerned with the vanished bath-towel. He felt convinced, somehow, that it would never be recovered. "Never mind," Mrs Turk said, "it has got the name of the hotel

on it, so that's something—" Mr Klein failed to see how that
helped. "Well," Mrs Turk pointed out to him, "it is a good
advertisement for the hotel." Mr Klein didn't see how advertising
the hotel to friends of a young woman who was wanted by the
police was likely to be of much advantage. Mrs Turk urged him
not to judge her too hastily. After all, there might be a perfectly
reasonable explanation for her behaviour. While Mr Klein was
grumbling that he couldn't see what explanation she could offer for
stealing a very nice bath-towel, and Sabrina and Norbert had
their theories to explain the young woman's behaviour, Mrs Turk
took up her account of the young man and his mother, and the
lighted candle in the wash-basin. "It was his mother who put it
there, you remember? It was to protect him from evil powers.
According to her, there are two different kinds of spirits, those at
night – which are evil; and those in the day-time which are good.
Light, you see, wards off evil powers. So, according to his mother,
if you make the darkness light – even by a single candle-light, you
keep evil powers at bay. What do you think of it?"

It seemed to me that her expression was quite serious, but whatever I thought Mr Klein and Sabrina and Norbert didn't think
much of it. To them the young woman who had taken the bath-
towel was a much more intriguing case. I left them, Sabrina and
Norbert, listening to Mr Klein practising Rachmaninoff's Second
Symphony. Mrs Turk came with me to the front door. She was
asking me about Rufus – how was he? And Frieda, and the cubs –
how were they? And she hoped she could come up and see them
again, very soon.

I stood in the hotel-drive for a few moments. It was a pale, moon-
lit sky. Rachmaninoff in my ears – Mr Klein's touch was light and
expressive – and from the distillery on the other side of the road, I
could sniff the sweet, balmy scent of whisky on the air. It made an
agreeable combination, the night-sky, the music, and the scent of
whisky. I drove slowly down the drive; as you turn into the road
you can glimpse the distillery windows brightly lit, and the figures
of the night-shift moving about their task.

I reached Stalker's Cottage, parked the car, and walked back to
the *Fisherman's Rest*. It looked blackened and begrimed against the
sky, the wooden sign with the indecipherable name was rotting
away as it creaked in the gentle wind off the loch. The tiles were

thick with lichen, paint flaked off the wooden shutters. Wally Ness came out, shouting a good-night to Johnson and clutching his fishing-gear. He was on his way to the caravan in which he lived several months every year. It was near Hughie Drummond's old tent; and was in about the same kind of shape. But then Wally hadn't got much money either. Which was one reason why he had set up as a window-cleaner in Glasgow.

You don't need much capital to set up business as a window-cleaner, and since capital was what he had least of all, he found the career most suitable. Lack of capital wasn't the only reason why he'd become a window-cleaner; he was a fisherman. And there was another reason, too, which he would expound to you, with Johnson to support his every word. You see, Glasgow, according to Wally, supported by Johnson, owns up to a greater number of poor than any other city in Britain, and it has 11% male unemployment. It looks like a blitzed city, torn apart for redevelopment plans. "A ring road," says Wally, "so that the rich living in the suburbs can drive to their work in the city, polluting the atmosphere and congesting the streets"; and tower-blocks to replace the tenement slums. "Though no one wants to live in them high-rise monstrosities," Johnson would chime in; he knew Glasgow all right. "All they want is for their slums to be cleaned up and made decently habitable – indoor sanitation, ye ken?"

And so, according to Wally – and he's not only supported by Johnson, he's read the latest City Father's report – 25,000 quit Glasgow every year, fleeing the place as if it lies under the spell of doom. Some go South, some to the Midlands, some North, Bradford, Leeds and so forth. Others get out of the country altogether. A few, a very few, head for the Highlands. Like Wally.

"It's not only escape from Glasgow," he says, "it's escape from the industrial rat-race. Industry, what good's it brought? Pollution of the air, the rivers, the sea. What's the working class become? Walking zombies. No thought for their craft, because they haven't got a craft; no thought for doing a good day's work, because the work is inhumanly monotonous. They've only got thought for screwing as much as they can out of the employers they hate, despise, and envy, for as little work as possible. Thought for booze and betting, and watching TV."

No, he wouldn't lend himself to servitude like that. Besides, all he wanted out of life was to fish. Ever since he'd been a kid, it had been his dream to get to the Highlands and fish. He couldn't explain. He'd just happened to read about it as a school-boy. It had caught his imagination, he had window-shopped outside fishing-gear shops, he had gone fishing on nearby rivers and lochs, either legally or illegally. But his job – he went from one to another when he wasn't out of work – had to take first place. Until the day several years ago, when he decided he wouldn't stand the servitude any longer. He would be his own boss. He would take the whole summer out, and fish. He became a window-cleaner, working throughout autumn to spring only; that way he earned enough to spend the summer fishing. And so every summer he headed for the Highlands.

He was wearing an anorak which I hadn't noticed before. "Got it from the Pakistanis in Moulin," he said; Moulin was a nearby village. "Sell everything, they do. Stock up a van in Glasgow, work their way up to Stornoway. Och, taken over Stornoway, they have. Ye ken? Shops, the caffs." He smoothed his anorak. "Pakistanis are clearing out of the Twilight City, too – can you blame 'em? I tell ye, no human being can take it any more. Used to be the pilgrimage to Mecca you had to make, if you were a good Muslim. At least once in your life-time, wasn't that it?" I shook my head. I didn't know. "Now, it's the pilgrimage to the Highlands."

I was thinking of the Asian girl as I went back to Stalker's Cottage. I opened the door and thumbed the light-switch, but nothing happened. Must have been a fuse, I decided, and I found the candlestick kept against such an emergency in the kitchen. I didn't bother to do anything about the fuse then; I thought I'd leave it till next day. It would be easier in daylight. There was plenty of illumination from the moonlight, aided by the candle-light, enough for me to see to get to bed.

I was lying there, feeling sleepy and was just about to put out the candle, when it went out by itself. It was a bit uncanny; you could have thought that someone had blown it out. I struck a match. The flame burned steadily; there didn't seem to be any draught. I re-lit the candle. The flame was steady enough. I watched it for a few minutes, I suppose, and then I must have fallen asleep.

I woke up suddenly. The light was out, but that wasn't what had woken me. It was the sound I'd heard in my sleep. It had invaded my dream – had I been dreaming of Rufus? Dreams are strange like that, sometimes you can't remember anything at all about them a couple of seconds after you have woken up; and then the dream will come back to you, much later on, sometimes a day or two later even, quite clearly. Suddenly, for no reason at all. This time, the moment I was awake, with that echo of sound still in my head, I knew it was the bark of a fox that had woken me. At once I wondered if it was Rufus. Fear gripped me as I pulled on some clothes and went outside.

It was dawn, the forest was alive with movement; it seemed to pulsate with life. As I hurried towards Ennochdhu Wood, there was a sudden clatter of birds in the trees, shrill cries of warning of an owl on its last swoop for prey before it headed homewards to sleep the day through. I glimpsed its wraith-like shape for a moment, silently speeding through the forest, and the crescendo of the birds' cries rose and fell, to rattle away in the distance. There came that familiar: *Ke-wack . . . Keeee-waackkk . . .* faint, and I thought it sounded frustrated, and finally fading into the rustle of the tree-tops in the dawn wind off the loch. Mist curled across the water; the sandy shore just below looked silvery in the pale light, washed by an ever-changing edge of wave that glimmered like antique lace. I caught sight of a dark blob, suddenly glistening above the surface where the mist had cleared, then it was gone; only the faint splash and the ripples to betray an otter, out hunting at first light. As always, whenever I found myself facing an early hour in this part of the world, I experienced that eerie tingling at my nerve-ends as if I was trespassing on a territory of darkness's ending, unfamiliar and forbidding; when spirits and phantoms had barely taken their leave and resented my appearance so soon. I might have been an actor over-anxious for my cue and stepping on to the scene too early, where the ghostly shadows still lingered behind.

The girl stood quite still against the blues and pinks of the dawn sky, her black hair caught in the breeze. She must have heard my approach, but she didn't turn her head. Her attention seemed to be concentrated on listening for something in the direction of the glen. She wore the old sweater and jeans, the canvas shoes. She made such a strange, confused impact, that for a moment time and distance stood still for me. Again she recalled to me those Graeco-Buddhist friezes sculpted thousands of years ago – the trees behind her might have been temple columns – but this time, too, Wally Ness's words rang in my head, and I saw her against Glasgow's dark, gap-filled streets, drizzle-damped pavements, the stench of abysmal poverty, of the rotten dust of bull-dozed houses. Her skin seemed especially pale, with a kind of glow reflecting the sky. When she did turn towards me her eyes seemed enormous, shining and dark. There was a glint of her white teeth as she smiled.

"It is Rufus," she said. "Och, but he is okay, all right," she added quickly.

She had sensed my sudden tautness of apprehension. I looked towards the glen in the direction she had been staring. How long had she been here? How did she know about Rufus, that he had escaped? And, anyway, I thought she had gone away. Funnily enough, I realised that I hadn't been at all surprised to see her again, here, near the same place where I'd seen her the first time. I suppose I'd been too worried about Rufus to give much thought to her still being around.

"I came to see that he is okay, all right," she said.

I started to put into words the questions that were in my mind, but she made a sudden movement. She gave a sharp intake of breath. I heard the unmistakable bark of Shuna up at the house. Out of the corner of my eye I saw a glimmer of light and knew that Don was awake. He would have heard Rufus bark. I turned my head as Shuna's "woof" sounded again, and as I did so the girl seemed to disintegrate. When I turned back to her she had gone. I caught a brief glimpse of her black hair flowing over her sweater, then she disappeared from sight, running down the road towards Dunfuirich. Shuna was hurrying towards me, her tail wagging, her eyes as ever soft and maternal of expression. Don followed her.

He had awoken at dawn and thought he had heard the bark of a fox. He had wondered drowsily if it was Rufus – the sound had carried unexpectedly clearly on a wind-gust from the loch. He'd thought he must have dreamt it, and fell asleep again. But only briefly: a few minutes later he woke again with a start, got dressed quickly. He knew he had heard Rufus.

I was only half hearing what he was saying; I was too busy trying to make sure that the girl had been there, that she wasn't some phantasmagoria of a Highland dawn. She had vanished so totally. But I knew I couldn't have imagined it; she couldn't be part of my dream continuing into my wakefulness – my confusion was clarified by something Don was saying. Something about Shuna barking. "What made her bark like that?" he said. "As if there were some stranger about? She doesn't bark at you."

I didn't answer. Instead I expressed my anxiety for Rufus. Where would he have got to? We were hurrying down to the glen, Shuna running ahead. How the devil had he got out? He answered that he didn't know for certain that he had escaped. But as he opened the gate there was no sign of Rufus. And when he called out his name, no reply. Don had told Shuna to wait behind, and I stayed with her while he went to the den. Still no sign of Rufus. My hands were clammy with fear. Shuna gave a little whimper and stared up at me, her expression miserable.

I heard a grumble from Frieda in the den, and a faint mewling from the cubs. They were safe enough, at any rate.

Don calculated intuitively that Rufus would return, that he would not desert Frieda and his family: and he decided, as he searched for the means by which Rufus had made his exit, that he would not be long away. The pull of mate and family would be too much for him. Don let himself into the enclosure, to search for Rufus's exit. He swept his torch-beam along the length of wire-netting which extended from the gate. He came upon the high grass and clump of weeds, noting at once that they had been trodden down. There was the hole torn in the wire. He bent down and pulled off tell-tale strands of fur which were caught on the wire-ends. This was the way Rufus had got out, all right.

It was growing lighter. Don glanced about to see if there had been any cause for the wire being broken at this particular point. He could see nothing; a piece of branch nearby might have become caught in the netting, perhaps. But he knew that there need be only the merest weakness in a strand of wire and Rufus, or Frieda – she was just as eager as he was to make something of it – would spot it and begin to test it, then if it proved encouraging, exploit it. To try to escape, to seek new territories, to satisfy their eternal curiosity, was as instinctive in both of them as breathing.

Frieda appeared at the entrance to the den. She raised her nose in the direction of the forest, towards where the slope climbed upwards. Don and I glanced in that direction; we couldn't make out any sign of Rufus, but none the less Don interpreted Frieda's appearance at the den-mouth as an indication that he might be returning. We waited. The minutes passed. Frieda turned back into the den as if in answer to whimperings and grumblings from the cubs. Still no sign of her mate. Don was used to waiting and watching for a wild creature to show itself. He scanned the edge of the forest. The sun was just about to begin to show, throwing its light on to the loch, the tiny waves ruffled by the early morning breeze glinted and flickered with gold. Then suddenly, silently Rufus appeared out of the forest, trotting casually down towards the enclosure.

He hadn't caught sight of Don or myself, or winded us. He might have been out for an early-morning stroll by his manner: not a suggestion of guilt about his beautiful head as he vanished once more in some undergrowth.

Suddenly Shuna gave a "wuff" and, her tail wagging excitedly, headed out of the wire-netting gate. "That's him," Don said. We went after Shuna, who was wuffing loudly, more excitedly. We could see her tail and head above the undergrowth. Then she stopped. She sprang forward. As she did so Rufus jumped up, and the two of them pawed at each other in a kind of dance, Shuna barking and Rufus chattering. When we reached them Rufus was lying flat on his back, with Shuna standing over him, one fat paw on his stomach. His mouth was wide open, tongue lolling out, while Shuna blinked up at us as proudly as if to say, there you are, I've caught him for you, single-handed: alone I did it. As for Rufus, you could have sworn he was laughing at us.

8 Children from the Twilight City

Before setting off for a few days in London I made up my mind to meet Captain E. A. S. Bailey, C.B.E., D.S.C., R.N.

A couple of weeks earlier, late one night, one of his shepherds had found two dead lambs, which he felt sure had been the victims of a fox. The shepherd was an ex-schoolteacher who had sickened of his occupation, forever indoors, the scholastic rat-race, the pressures and tensions of urban life, and had opted out. Off to the wild, free Highlands, and a job on the hills. His enthusiasm for fox-hunting was no less than his employer's, he kept a sharp lookout for signs of foxes, and together, aided by the recently acquired pack of fox-hounds, they had lately accounted for a vixen (she was in cub which slowed her up – this after a mile sprint along the loch-shore), then another vixen with her cubs. Tony Bailey shot the vixen, and his two terriers, Lulu and Jim, soon sorted out the cubs in the earth. Where was the vixen's mate? They longed to add him to their bag, and for three nights they had both waited with their guns for the dog-fox to show up. He failed to oblige.

The ex-schoolteacher turned shepherd had kept watch on his own for the next few nights; Tony Bailey was busy with the hounds answering calls from neighbouring farmers complaining that their sheep were being killed by some murdering fox. The hounds enjoyed no success. Then, his shepherd came to Bailey's door two weeks ago, despair on his face, haggard from nights without sleep, throwing down the two lambs, and the seemingly conclusive evidence that they were freshly killed. Tony Bailey had placed a sympathetic hand on his shepherd's shoulder. "You get some shut-eye," he said: "The Navy's going in."

He had to act quickly if he was going to have any hope of success. He fetched his other shepherd. His wife, Sukhi – "Bless you, darling" – was quick to offer to help. By 05.00 hours, the three of them, Tony Bailey sporting his "pink", a red anorak, and the six hounds from his own kennels, were off. The two fastest hounds, Gallant and Charity, led, with Mustang and Loyal followed by the pair of "pensioners", Ragman and Clancie, all going like the clappers. The full pack included hounds named Rascal, Waspish, Cragsman, Waifer, Steadfast, Dowager, Lively and Trinket, Loyal and Dragon; the whole business smacked of John Masefield's poem, *Reynard The Fox*, based not on the old fables, but on a real-life fox-hunt – "Oh God, let them get him: let them eat him," a huntsman, named Bill Ridden, urges on the hounds as the fox looks like escaping. The schoolteacher-turned-shepherd had found the dead lambs the far side of Glen Gour; Bailey's other shepherd had a hunch that the killer-fox would be 2,500 feet high up on the far side of the glen. A fox in his attempt to escape always heads up into the hills, up to the highest summit, but when – thank God! – he begins to tire and there is nowhere further he can go, he tends to circle back to his own territory. The hunch proved right. The three of them heard the hounds' sudden exultant baying. Then a defiant screech of a bark that was nothing like a dog's bark. Racing on, they were in time to see Gallant and Charity to the fore, with the others close after them, form a terrible star dark against the rocks in the pale dawning light around the crouching, teeth-bared creature. Then, in for the kill. The horrific screech, the agonised scream. Tony Bailey turning to his wife with a triumphant grin. "Got him." Her answering smile.

Silence. Then came the hounds' growling worrying, and soon there was little left of the dead fox except for the nose sticking out of old Loyal's muzzle, and the tip of the brush, which Tony Bailey pocketed, lying among the rocks. The six-mile hike back home in the wonderful, pink dawn with "that varmint's bit of tail in my pocket, was," as he was later to describe it, "an agreeable swan-song to a memorable undertaking". The death he logged at precisely 07.14 hours.

Three days afterwards, late afternoon, he sighted a fox up on a ridge, silhouetted against the skyline. By the time he had scrambled up there, it was nowhere in sight, but on his way down again he came across a den.

That night he waited by the den. He had lashed a flashlight to the barrel of his shotgun; an idea which he had come up with to help him find his target in the darkness. He sat there for three hours. He had dozed, his mind had filled with the pictures of the time when, on escort-duty accompanying a troop-ship to Burma he had helped destroy a Japanese U-boat with torpedoes, after riddling her with gun-fire – though not before she'd torpedoed one of the troop-carriers, with only a few survivors, and hadn't there been Wrens on board? He awoke with a jump. He shook his head to clear his thoughts. A movement near the den. By his flashlight he saw a vixen dart off. He was too late for her, but not too late for the cub with her. Mesmerised by the sudden light, it died, its head blasted off.

It was a big cub; he could see by the flashlight that its colour was changing towards that of a full-grown fox. He bent over it triumphantly. If only he could nab the vixen as well. He waited until just after 24.00 hours, and was about to return home with his trophy, when he heard a dreadful scream. He paused. It was the vixen, screaming for her lost cub. The sound seemed to come from above him. He could make out a ledge of rock, black, jagged-edged against the starry sky. The ledge hid him from the vixen's view. He had snapped off the flashlight. Hoping that she might show herself against the starlight long enough for him to take a crack at her, he held the shotgun in readiness. Her screaming continued, a dreadful cry, almost a human cry, high-pitched, like a woman more terror-stricken than in pain. He waited two hours, the night turning to the pearl-grey dawn. All that he saw of her was when she drew closer to the edge of the ledge above him, screaming, so close that he distinctly saw her breath. Then she must have scented him, and was gone.

He trudged back to the farm, the dead cub dangling from his hand. It had stopped bleeding, what remained of its shattered head was a congealed mess. He was trudging up over a ridge when he heard a sudden movement which halted him. Was it the vixen, or perhaps her mate, the dog-fox? He snapped on his flashlight and aimed. Two eyes glared back at him balefully. He was about to pull the trigger, when he heard another movement and he swung his gun in its direction. Another pair of eyes shone back at him. He hesitated, his trigger-finger itching. Came an affronted bleat from the darkness and he lowered his gun. He had nearly shot one of his own bloody sheep.

He was back next night, determined to get the vixen. He waited beside the den from 23.00 hours to 05.00 hours; he could hear her, continually screaming for her lost cub, that dreadful, blood-curdling cry. He found himself counting the screams. He made it nine hundred and forty. He never caught a glimpse of her, though once he heard the scrabble of loose scree as he passed within ten yards of him in the dark; before he knew what had happened she was in the den. He waited for her to come out, but there was no sign of her. There must have been another exit. He heard more screams, and he tried to stalk her, but without success. He gave up to return home as the dawn light flooded the sky from the east, the pinkish tinge changing from orange to palest blue.

Tony Bailey heard my car, and came out to greet me. His grey-stoned house, two hundred years old and shielded by tall trees, stands back from the road some fifty yards. Over the front door hangs a ship's bell from HMS *Paladin*, his first command in 1943. He had put in a claim for it, when the ship was broken up. The Admiralty allowed him to buy it over other officers' heads – perhaps because he had fought in her against Germans, Italians and Japs. Round the walls of his office were citations in black *passe-partout* frames – Captain E. A. S. Bailey, C.B.E., D.S.C., R.N., was a brave fighting officer; he also possessed considerable charm, belying his shrewd toughness. There was a Peter Scott picture over the mantelpiece of Male Swan "Brimstone", which Tony Bailey "owned" under the scheme by which the famous naturalist's swans could be subscribed for by wild swan-lovers and reared at their expense. On the mantelpiece two World Wild-Life Fund collecting boxes were included in the clutter of pipes and odds and ends. A large glazed case of sporting-guns and a fox-hunting water-colour adorned another wall; and a fox-hunting tapestry hung above a bookcase stuffed with volumes: *South China Birds*, *Birds of East & Central Africa*, pocket-guides to British birds, wild-flowers, the seashore, *Debrett* 1964, and *The War At Sea*, together with *Hunting & Stalking the Deer, Deer-Stalking Grounds of Great Britain*, and volume after volume of natural history.

Trapping foxes by use of the horrific gin-trap in England Wales was made illegal. It was unnecessarily cruel; it was also unselective. İt caught, maimed and inflicted days of agonising suffering or killed not only foxes, but badgers, otters, wild birds and even dogs. Scotland, however, would retain its use until 1973. But my information was that Highland sheep-farmers, poultry-keepers, gamekeepers generally were, through their lobby in Parliament, intent on retaining the gin-trap indefinitely. The RSPCA and others anxious for wild life preservation and protection of animals against cruelty, had their own Parliamentary lobby working for them. But it was Tony Bailey who very soon after his arrival on the scene took on, with typical ardour, the leadership of the local "vigilantes", sworn to exterminate foxes wherever they were found, and helped obtain a £3,000 Government grant enabling them to buy a Lake District fox-hound pack and pay a professional huntsman from Yorkshire to help them do the job. Because he and his followers had feared the use of the gin being denied them, he sounded off unequivocally, he had turned – in desperation – to foxhounds. "They have solved the problem in the Lake District for two centuries, why shouldn't they solve ours?" It never occurred to him that if Lake District farmers had been using fox-hounds for a couple of hundred years – and still continued to do so – to deal with the fox "problem", it could hardly be said to have been solved.

But this is the brick wall against which you can bash your head forever if you try to reason with the fox-haters. They swear to the efficacy of the gin, yet despite its use ever since sheep came to the Highlands, the foxes are still here. The fact is that the gin is a convenient method of trapping. You set it and leave it; you aren't required to visit it regularly, any time to suit you will do. Once its terrible steel jaws have clamped on its victim there's no escape. It'll be there waiting for you to bash its head in, or shoot it mercifully – if you want to waste shot – any time you choose to come along. (Rarely has a fox or badger or other wild thing been known to bite off its trapped foot, to free itself.) Some farmers, some shepherds, don't always care for their sheep as well as they may; trudging the hills can be wearisome, especially in the sort of

weather you get in the Highlands; sheep and lambs can be neglected. If you're not too bothered about them, then you're not
likely to bother about some "bluidy fox" caught in a gin. "Let the
bastard suffer, that'll teach it."

Tony Bailey opened a drawer of his antique kneehole writing-
desk and produced the brush-tip from the fox his hounds had
slaughtered high on the hill. "I regard foxes as I did U-Boats in the
last spot of bother, my dear fellow; I respect 'em, but by God, I'm
out to destroy 'em." He returned the souvenir to the drawer, and
indicated the wall over the desk which, apart from a long-tailed
hunting-whip hanging together with a pair of Japanese binoculars
which were in a German U-Boat's binocular-case, was given over
to maps of the surrounding area, and charts studded with multi-col-
oured pins, indicating known or suspected fox-dens in that area.
His desk was a mass of papers, documentary evidence, he claimed, of
foxes' depredations. Facts and figures categorically supporting the
farmers' claims for Government help against the fox. He handed
me a large scrap-book filled with press-clippings from the *Scottish
Daily Express*, *The Scotsman*, the *Oban Times* and other newspapers
– including an amusing *Observer* interview, it seemed to me, rather
ridiculing him and his "vigilantes". There was also a stack of
"letters to the editor", almost all of them full of praise and
encouragement for the worthy efforts being made to protect sheep
from their hated, traditional foe. One or two correspondents
thought it all a waste of effort and ratepayers' money, merely an
excuse for the farmers to indulge their sporting instincts; some
even suggested that farmers and shepherds might spend more time
and trouble in their flocks' interests – for a start, if they saw that all
sheeps' and lambs' carcasses which scattered the hills were buried
(which is a legal obligation), the foxes would take themselves off
to seek other, easier, sources of food.

Tony Bailey took it all with characteristic good-humour. "I
don't mind what they say about us, the more controversy we stir
up, the more publicity we get, the more the Government will hear
about how we're trying to save our sheep. That's what we want.
It's good propaganda; what you need to help you win a war." He
went on to discuss the campaign he was waging in terms of
intelligence and deployment of his forces. A local Army major, an
M.C., "very enthusiastic, very knowledgeable", had aided and

abetted. "Been a sort of combined naval and military op, you might say." He jabbed a finger at the wall-maps. "You see, my dear chap, ours is not only the northernmost pack in the world, it must surely cover the biggest area, 2,500 square miles, and the most rugged – up to 4,400 feet – the furthest meet from my lash-up kennels here is 65 miles away." He extolled his Yorkshire huntsman's expertise. "Despite hellish weather to start with, aided by his splendid hounds, he's accounting for half a dozen foxes a month. Earning the respect of us all for the way he's tackled his challenging task."

Sheep lamb mostly on the hill, which he explained was why losses didn't come to light at once. This was an important factor when dealing with the fox – no, he couldn't agree that this very factor was consistent with the probability that the fox took only lambs which were already dead from natural causes such as malnutrition and exposure. There were always plenty of carcasses lying about to provide enough food without having to kill for it. He was preoccupied with the problems of terrain. "The country's very 'blind'; there's a scarcity of roads; there are fifty deer for every fox – we have to watch out that they're not harassed by the hounds; folk are very thinly spread out."

He took from a drawer a device which provided his "spotters", usually shepherds, with a means of signalling the rest of the hunt when they were in action. The "spotters", stationed on strategic hill-tops, ignited the device, virtually a domestic fire-starter, when they observed the hounds working a fox to ground, using it as a smoke-signal to alert the hunt – "all hands on deck, so to speak" – to make for the quarry full speed ahead. As he enthused away before his pin-pointed charts, you found it difficult to believe that destroying foxes was really what it was all about; you could imagine that he was Naval Intelligence, that it was a cover for his presence here on much more sinister business. Wasn't there a hush-hush installation in the hills? Top-secret submarine anchorage in the loch? You could be in the dream world of Ian Fleming and John Buchan, with a touch of P. G. Wodehouse. And then – what had brought him here, you couldn't help wondering, in the first place? You couldn't imagine that come peace-time, after the war he'd enjoyed, he would find himself farming sheep in the wild, desolate Highlands.

It had been his wife's idea – "Sukhi is Hindustani for 'Happiness'"

– she had joined him on his leaves when his ship was in Rosyth; they had come up to the Highlands, which both had loved from the start. When peace-time came and he was "the sailor home from sea", there had been no job he had particularly liked: city-life, business, that kind of thing wasn't for him. Then his wife had heard of this house by the loch, and become interested in farming in the hills. They had viewed the place together; within a few hours, backed up by his wife, he had made up his mind.

"Yes," he was saying, "the hunting-season for us is from Trafalgar Day, 21 October, you know, after the deer-stalking's over, through April into June, when we're on call for lamb-worrying." He had been working on the first annual report of the Fox Destruction Society, as the hunt was known officially, complete with its Board of Directors, Chairman, Hon. Secretary and Hon. Treasurer, Hon. Auditor, and Hon. Veterinary Adviser. "We've pitched into a difficult enterprise as absolute greenhorns, don't y'know." Then: "Of course, the chaps enjoy it. Get their bit of fun out of it – keeps up their enthusiasm for the job in hand."

There was his own first annual report, as the huntsman, to make. It would deal with the mechanics of the hunt, costs, upkeep of hounds, the difficulties of terrain. It would pay due tribute to the Fox Destruction Society's sponsors, "90 to 95% of farmers and landowners around"; who were backed by an "army of well-wishers and active supporters", which included the Masters, Chairmen and officials of various Scottish and North Country hunts who had provided hounds, and instruction on how to use them; and there were the Scottish National Farmers Union – actively seeking to legalise the use of the gin – and the Highlands & Islands Development Board, one of whose objectives in the worthy cause of developing the Highlands was the extermination of the fox; together with the Ministry of Agriculture, who made direct allocations of money for fox-trappers' wages and to meet the cost of gin-traps, poisons and gases. Also included in his report would be Appendix (B), the Tally. It was appreciated that in that extensive and "blind" terrain, it would not invariably be easy to prove a kill – the fox's carcass might not be produced. It seemed the best way to reach a satisfactory assessment of the hunt's successes would be as follows: a "possible" kill, when nature and duration of the hunt coupled with subsequent behaviour of hounds suggested that a kill was likely; a "probable" kill, either (1) smell of fox about hounds; or (2) a "possible" kill corroborated by fresh blood (not their own) on one or more of the hounds, coupled with an empty belly. The empty belly is significant, as a hound finding a sheep or deer carcass will gorge itself, whereas Bailey's hounds would only break up their fox if they arrived on the scene in force as a pack, in which case they got precious little meat each. A "kill" would be claimed when the carcass was recovered. And there would be notes on "probables" and "possibles". Then: Cost of killing an adult fox. Taking every expense into account – wages, and provision of house for huntsman and his family, transport, feeding hounds, man-hours spent – estimated minimum cost, £30, "which will be adopted by the hunt as a yard-stick". It was a lot of paper-work; and he had enough of that already, farming sheep. But you had to be business-like. Your lobby liked to be provided with plenty of ammunition. The Government department concerned liked you to have everything on paper, in triplicate. "The more they realise we're serious about this, the more they'll recognise our efforts need rewarding. They'll either continue the grant – or agree that we should keep our gin-traps. Which are cheaper than fox-hounds, anyway." Good thinking. You had to admit it, Tony Bailey had the right strategy.

Then there was another report he was making to the local Farmers' Union on the Drowning Set type of gin, complete with two diagrams. You provided an artificial boulder in a convenient pool, baited enticingly. You set the trap on a "pier" 18 inches away from the side of the pool on which the fox would step in order to reach the bait. Tony Bailey's Note: "On stepping into the trap fox instinctively bounds forward into the pool and is drowned. Trap does not require regular inspection to dispose of the trapped fox. This answers any objections on humanitarian grounds against the use of the gin-trap for dealing with the problem." You knew now what, in the event of the grant to maintain the hunt being discontinued, would inevitably result. He had an iron-clad case for the gin-trap's retention.

Both he and his wife wanted to hear about Rufus, of course – "Sounds a fascinating beggar" – "Never fear, we already have a high regard for the fox – it's just that there's not room for both of us on this farm, unfortunately" – yes, they'd heard about the book; no, they hadn't read it. I would send them a copy. "Autographed by Rufus?" Autographed by Rufus, I promised. It isn't easy to explain Tony Bailey's disarming charm. Even though you couldn't see eye to eye with him, to say the least, about foxes, you would find it difficult to show any anger or bitterness towards him. He didn't go berserk at the mention of the word, as his neighbours seemed to do. To him it was almost an absorbing hobby, a form of relaxation like fishing or model trains. And after all he was a professional hunter; Germans, Italians, Japs, foxes, were all quarry to him – *Father, forgive them; for they know not what they do.* But for all that, I felt increasingly disloyal to Rufus. I found myself hoping that he wouldn't sense that I had shaken a hand that was stained with the blood of foxes. I hoped next time we met, he wouldn't turn his back on me.

It was a black night as I stood at the door beneath HMS *Paladin*'s ship's bell, saying good-bye to Sukhi and her husband. As he accompanied me to the car he started telling me about the otters, who were attacking his lambs. They rose up out of the waters of the loch like phantom monsters, came ashore and killed his sheep or lambs that had strayed near the shore. His ex-schoolteacher shepherd had recently come across a beheaded lamb. He then saw an otter swimming in the loch. He began patrolling that part of the loch for the next several nights, armed with a rifle. He saw the otter again and shot it. It was an old dog-otter, $4\frac{1}{2}$ feet long. "No more lambs were lost in that part," Tony Bailey said, "so we concluded that this beast was the villain. It seems that when an easterly wind made the loch difficult for the old gentleman to go fishing, he turned to lamb-killing." He had noted that lambs killed near burns, which an otter would use to cover his approach, or near the loch-shore, were beheaded and only the head eaten. "A lamb's nasal bone is not unlike a fish-bone, you see."

He was making out a report. He suspected that more lambs were being attacked by otters than was supposed. Perhaps the killings were the work of only one or two otters, rogue otters. I watched him in the reflection of my mirror stride back to the house, as if eager to scan the wall-charts and maps, to plan the strategy for dealing with this latest menace. You could imagine him back on the bridge, seeking out this new, appropriately submarine, foe. Seek and destroy. Driving back, my headlamps slicing the blackness, a starless night, no moon, I slowed as I saw a dark, sinuous shape run across the road. It was an otter: keep out of sight of Tony Bailey, I prayed. I drove on, full of foreboding. I felt that I had been putting up a case for an accused who was already condemned, always had been from long ago. Against the fox the dice were so heavily loaded, the cards so implacably stacked, that his cause must be irretrievably lost.

2

The cubs were nine weeks old; they were weaned, they no longer tried to worry Frieda to suckle them. They were learning to feed themselves – Frieda was giving them regurgitated half-digested food, and she and Rufus were both bringing them food left by Don. They had given up the den which for so long had been their warm, dark home where they were safe, and they wouldn't return. Already it was forgotten; their brains were full of fresh sights, sounds and scents of this new world into which they had ventured. It was a world full of play and games in which their father joined; he helped them learn the games, kept a watchful eye on them all the time. Sometimes, especially in the evenings, Frieda would join in. There would be chases round the trees and rocks, with a lot of yelps and yapping. Their legs and paws weren't yet always co-ordinated, so they moved about in jumps. Hind legs and fore-feet together – more like a tiny kangaroo, you could say – they weren't running like an adult fox. Sometimes, though, there would be a stiff-legged "fox-trotting" by a pair of the cubs, or games of hide-and-seek behind tree-trunks. Once, Rufus picked up one of the vixen-cubs by its tail and swung it round and round, to the delighted amazement of the others. At once they chased after Rufus, wanting in turn to be given a swing round by their tails. You could see Robbie trying his best to be given the next turn. But Rufus refused to be bullied or persuaded to favour the toughest and strongest of his children; he dropped the first vixen and picked up the next one and gave it a swing. Then the next one, then the dog-cub – Robbie didn't get his turn until last, after all.

It was all very exciting; and the cubs were quickly getting the hang of feeding off insects. There were lots of rough-and-tumbles over the food that was brought to them – which made it all the more appetising. Robbie nearly always won these squabbles, but sometimes one of the vixens would out-manoeuvre him, and he would "cough" with fury. One of the vixens, weakest of the bustling, yelping quintet, always the last to get some food, hardly ever yelped, and I never saw her give an angry "cough".

It was my idea that the cubs were now old enough to be separated from their parents. A small enclosure was built for them just out of sight of their old home. They had a shelter provided, and there was plenty of room for them to play. We would keep them there for a few days, to see how they would react to Don and I handling them; this was all to do with the film in which they might be used in one or two scenes.

The cubs reacted perfectly happily to Don, but the first time I went to them in their new enclosure, they retired to the shelter, from which they all, except the third vixen, "coughed" at me. She stayed still and quiet in the corner. Both Robbie and the other dog-fox cub dodged out of my way whenever I went to the new enclosure. I tried to make friends with the vixens. The two "coughed" at me from their shelter as soon as I approached, pushing the third vixen, still very quiet and shy in contrast with her sisters, into the corner. Eventually I got out first one angry cub, then the other. I was nervous handling them, I was afraid of hurting them, and that made me slow in getting them out. Eventually I shifted them; they glared angrily at me, and though their eyes still seemed to me to be unfocused, I knew they could see me distinctly enough; they had seen me as I came in the enclosure-gate. Now, outside their shelter, they crouched, "coughing" at me, and they would blink in such a way that their inside eyelids would descend over their eyes, making them look as if they were rolling their eyes – this inside lid was a white film which I hadn't noticed before.

Then, with them out of the way, I took out the quiet vixen without any trouble; she remained quiet and nervous as ever. I cuddled her in my hands, spoke to her softly. I could hear her, as I pressed her against my face, whimpering very softly to herself. Then I let her burrow her face into the inside of my jacket, and I cradled her like that, while I sat chatting to her very softly, smoothing her soft, velvet ears and lulling her into a sense of security. Both her sisters had hurried back into the shelter and crouched in their corner, staring out at me and opening their pink mouths every time our glances met in their angry "cough". How to explain that while the others showed by reflex action their fear and dislike of human beings, the third vixen hadn't followed their example? Sometimes Shuna would join me, and then all the cubs would relax, the tension would slacken, they were all friendly towards me.

Then, when I was making a determined effort to handle Robbie, he bit me; a second time he bit me, drawing blood. Each time he had been quicker than I, twisting round and snapping at me with his sharp teeth – they really were needle sharp – and getting my fingers, so that I let out a yelp of pain. The most cursory glance at his teeth, and I was having many opportunities of seeing them at close quarters, showed me that they were very similar to those of a puppy, which is one reason why the fox is rated as a carnivore, and also why he is classed with the dog family, *Canidae*, which includes wolves and jackals. The cub had a total of 42 teeth – upper jaw: incisors 6, canines 2, premolars 8, molars 4; lower jaw: incisors 6, canines 2, premolars 8, molars 6. These were his first set of teeth, and would be lost to be replaced by a similar number of adult teeth. His long upper canines projected below the lower part of his bottom jaw – these were the ones that did the damage!

It wasn't that being bitten by him was so very painful – no, it was more the shock of it that caused me to feel a flash of irritability. I mean, you would think by now, wouldn't you, you would think that he would know I was his friend? You would think that it would have dawned on him that I meant him no harm – that I was the last person in the world who would intentionally hurt him. I was his friend (at a time to be in the future the only friend he ever had). And with this feeling of annoyance, rather than pain, was my disappointment that he wasn't gentle and loving the way Rufus, his father, had been.

And this was where I was so wrong, badly wrong. This was something in yourself that you had to cure. If you are to become his friend, really his friend – to love an animal without any thoughts about whether he loves you in return – then you need to concentrate your feelings upon what he was, a wild creature. I had to make myself remember that Robbie was a wild thing, without any power of knowing how I felt, or wanted to feel, towards him. All he knew with his as yet underdeveloped senses, aided by his whiskers, his power of scent and acuteness of hearing, was that I felt as unsure of him as he did of me. This was all the information I was conveying to him, this was how he was reading me. He didn't possess the cerebral processes to work out what I really meant to him. He didn't have the intelligence to reason that I wanted him to enjoy life *his* way, to feel relaxed and secure.

Don decided the cubs should be returned to their parents. He took Robbie, who made no attempt to bite him, and the other dog-fox; I took the three vixens. When we put them back in their old home, the five of them at first moved slowly towards Rufus and Frieda, who made no move; just waited tentatively. You could see the cubs' little noses lifted. Then they got their parents' scent and off they shot to them. Their personalities changed dramatically. No longer tense, no longer fearful and insecure, they were relaxed and confident; they were affectionate and playful. Rufus and Frieda greeted them – Frieda reacted a little more slowly to her offspring, as if she was experiencing a certain amount of difficulty recalling them, who exactly they were – "mewing" and chattering as their children yapped and danced around them. It was welcome home.

I felt a catch in my throat as I watched Robbie, now proud and head-high, dance a little jig of love for his mother. And then, suddenly, he sighted, or scented me. He paused – you could see his brain ticking over, as he danced over to me, full of friendship. The others all chased after him and played round me. You could see that their movements had, all of a sudden, it seemed, become much more co-ordinated. Their legs were more controlled, not so floppy. I knelt and held Robbie in my hands. He "laughed" at me, opening his mouth, his tiny tongue sticking out, his nose wrinkled, his expression exuberant. You couldn't help feeling a bit shaky at the knees, you felt yourself trembling with emotion.

Don thought we should wait until the cubs' bonds with their parents were completely broken before we tried again to separate them. Come August and they would be totally independent of Frieda or Rufus. They would be on their own; they would be thinking of going their own individual ways. Then would be the time to work with them, handle them, get them used to us, to become familiar with human beings, unafraid of them.

It was later in the week that a farmer who owned a camping-site the other side of Ennochdhu Wood came to the house and warned Don that he would shoot Cronk. She was pecking holes in the tents of his early holiday-makers. Don did his best to mollify the man; he would think of some way of keeping Cronk from the camping-site. When the farmer had gone, Don shook his head hopelessly. There was going to be trouble with Cronk. Several caravan-tenants on another nearby site had complained to Don that she was becoming a nuisance. At first her antics had amused them. The way she barked at every dog she encountered – terrier, Peke or Alsatian, all were fair game – who of course, barked back and gave chase. Cronk would tease the dog, lure him on to race after her, and then just when it seemed she must be caught, she would take off, barking derisively down at the frustrated animal beneath. Cronk could play this sort of game with half a dozen dogs at once. Their combined yapping and barking became pandemonium. It also became less and less entertaining to the caravanners.

Cronk arguably possessed several failings, not least being her failure to suspect her growing unpopularity; she continued to attach herself to one occupant of a caravan or tent after another. She would appear at the caravan-window and bark and peck at it to be allowed in to enjoy a tasty tit-bit which she had become used to receiving. She would bash her beak against the window so hard that you would fear she must break the glass. Against less resistant canvas, that beak of hers could gash and rip great holes. She wasn't so popular any more with the children on the sites or out on the forest nature-trails. She thought it great fun to pounce on an ice-cream just as it was on its way to a child's mouth, or, appearing out of nowhere, to snatch the coin a child or parent was proffering to purchase an ice.

Families picnicking found her a less than welcome guest; she would insist on snatching the most delectable cake right out of your hand. It wasn't so much that she was greedy for something good to eat, it was more that she was greedy for your attention. She wanted to be invited to the party; once you had shown you thought she was fun, a great "character", then you had continually to demonstrate your need for her company. Perhaps it was really just love she needed, now that she'd lost her mate, and in the natural order of things would not mate again. Something human about her, you might think; all that so many human beings want is just love. And she had no compunction about borrowing a shiny tea-spoon that took her eye, and never thought of returning it. She had also developed a technique of making off with any woman's handbag left lying about; or, if it was too large and heavy for her to lift, she would contrive to open it and remove the shiny compact, or mirror; whatever appealed to her. She would cache these treasures away, up in the roof of Don's house, or in tree-holes in the forest, or under rocks. On her walks with Rufus and Shuna she would fly on ahead to look up her caches, and satisfied that her treasures were still safe, return them to their hiding-place.

It was a worry. The farmer would without a doubt carry out his threat the next time he saw her. And if he didn't, someone else upon whose nerves Cronk grated wouldn't hesitate to get a gun and do the job. Of all birds, ravens are rated by farmers, shepherds and gamekeepers in the Highlands as the most deadly predators, attack-ing sheep and lambs, pecking out their eyes, or pecking them to death, or taking game-birds' eggs or chicks – all of which activities are largely mythical and legendary. In fact, whatever damage ravens may do is far outweighed by their enthusiastic scavenging efforts, feeding off carrion, insects and rodents, entitling them to an important place benefiting our environmental plan.

We could hear Cronk barking now. We went to the glen, where she was playing her old "stealing" game with Shuna's bone. Rufus had joined in as he often did, acting as Cronk's accomplice – she would stalk Shuna, who would guard the bone recently given her as if it was the last she would ever enjoy. Rufus would divert Shuna's attention for that split second when Cronk would be in and away with the bone. She would proceed a few yards and drop it for Shuna to retrieve. Once more Shuna would go through the performance of guarding her precious gift, again Cronk would stalk her, and Rufus would play his part. It had long dawned on Shuna, of course, what it was all about, but she was so kind-hearted and helpful that she was prepared to pretend with quite remarkable realism to Cronk that she was in danger of being robbed.

While we watched the performance, there came the sound of a

dog barking nearby. At once Cronk paused in the game, she switched from stalking Shuna and, uttering her own hideous bark, flew off to tease and harass the dog; no doubt she recognised the bark as that of an old adversary, whom once again she meant to do her utmost to drive berserk. Don and I turned away, we preferred not to stay and hear the pandemonium that would result from yet another confrontation between the two.

It wasn't only the danger to Cronk. Through her, jeopardy could threaten Rufus. This was the biggest worry. Cronk attracted irate callers, which brought them near to where Rufus and Frieda and the cubs lived. This was what Don feared could only too easily happen. Unwelcome strangers, trigger-happy farmers or game-keepers were the very last humans we wanted around. I got that horrible chill in my gut at the thought of it.

Something would have to be done about Cronk. For Rufus's sake as well as hers.

You have to rely on the facts of the case, even if sometimes you must wonder where realism gives way to fantasy; you can't pin-point where the borderline between the two lies, life day-by-day isn't comprised of facts alone. Chance, which you can't foresee, has nothing to do with facts, yet can in a moment totally alter them. So that only by looking back can you disentangle realism from that which is unreal. The pattern of life for human beings can be changed out of all recognition, simply by chance. An unforeseen encounter in the street with someone may result in your making a life-long friendship, or, as you move on about your business, slipping on a banana-skin which hadn't been there a few seconds before.

Which is why, looking back, I can't always recall my motives for a particular course of action. Why, for instance, did I, two days later, make up my mind to go to Moulin? Was it on account of Wally Ness? It must have occurred to me that there was a link between the Pakistanis from whom he had bought his anorak and the Asian girl, but I couldn't have imagined that she might have any connection with Rufus's destiny. Yet this was a time when he and what could happen to him filled my thoughts. Certainly, at any rate, Moulin always seems to me to be a place with a full quota of ancient eeriness; its atmosphere fairly hummed with vibrations.

In A.D. 145, or thereabouts, Ptolemy, the Egyptian geographer, published a map of the world which included the British Isles depicted as they then appeared to the eyes of the ancient world. Ptolemy had obtained his knowledge from Greek traders who claimed that they knew Scotland well, although according to their reckoning the Scottish coast-line showed the upper part beyond the River Tay running almost due east instead of north. But they did mark large rivers and certain towns which are still identifiable with those on today's maps. There was "Orrea", today's Abernethy, "Victoria", which is now Perth; and "Lindum", known nowadays as Moulin. Then it was an important Pictish town, a great marketing centre, where deals were concluded with a solemn handshake, "clasping hands". All that remains is this small village of Moulin, a short distance from Dunfuirich. The surrounding neighbourhood is dotted with tombstones of the earliest Pictish age, long before St Columba and Christianity. Some commemorated the grave of a great hero of the time; a Pictish poet wrote:

> The Stranger will not know of my grave,
> He will see a grey stone with ragweed o'ergrown,
> And he will ask whose grave is this?
> We know not, the children of the glen will say,
> The song of his fame has not lived to our day.

East of Moulin lies a low hill, "Cnoc dubh", or Black Hill, reputed to be an ancient place of Pagan worship. Here was once a circle of stones, not tombstones, these, but marking the site of strange rituals. Until they were removed, the place had a reputation for occult occurrences, the uncanny. It wasn't until I had lived at Stalker's Cottage for some time that I learned that stones from Black Hill had been used in its construction.

I saw the girl at the door of the village hall. She caught sight of me as I approached, and though I smiled at her, she gave a frightened gasp and, her black hair flashing in the morning sunlight, disappeared into the hall. I paused for a few moments, noting two posters on either side of the door, hand-coloured, announcing a sale of goods within. Ahmad showed himself, a short, thin man, looking hardly any older than his 21-year-old son, who also watched me, before darting back into the hall behind his father. Ahmad gave me a grin. He wore a neat, light-grey suit, with a white, stiff turn-down collar and brightly coloured tie. Wally Ness had pointed him out to me one day when we had been passing the village while taking a short cut to a stretch of Loch Fourich; Wally had seen an otter when he'd been fishing the evening before. He thought it appeared so large it might have been a sea-otter, and would I like to take a look at it? (It didn't show up at all, as a matter of fact.)

The girl wasn't in the hall when I went in, and Ahmad began showing me round the various goods he had displayed. There were several prospective customers. It cost him £4 a day to hire the hall, and business was quite good. I asked him who the girl was that I'd seen as I arrived. His daughter? She looked pretty, I said. He smiled at the compliment, but shook his head. I didn't refer to her again for several minutes. I bought some tea-towels. I looked around. Where was the girl, then? He looked uncomfortable, though his long, white teeth glistened in smiles. His voice was low. I pretended that I wasn't very interested in what he was telling me, I was looking round at what he had for sale.

"She a wild thing," he said. "She been in trouble. Absconding. I not know this, for sure. Maybe they will come for her, and I will get into trouble also." He spread his hands. He did not want to say any more, and I did not want to know any more. Was the girl related to him? Perhaps she was, perhaps she was his niece, but he preferred not to admit it. His son stood by, glancing in our direction every now and then, and you had the feeling that he had sharp ears, he was listening to every word his father was saying. Ahmad muttered something about a band of thieves in Glasgow. "Not Pakistani, you understand," he said. The girl had been associated with them, he thought. He only thought it, he did not know for sure. There was plenty of thieving in Glasgow, wasn't it so? There were many poor people in Glasgow. He spread his hands once more, as if it was a condition of life, a state of things which you had to understand, to accept.

He himself had worked so that he would not be poor, so that he would not be tempted to become a thief. For several years he had driven a 'bus in Glasgow. He had put in as many shifts as he could, so that he could earn money to keep his family, not only his wife and son (a previous son had died aged only a few months), and he sent some money home to his parents in Pakistan; and he saved. Every week he saved money. This was why he had come to Glasgow, this was what he had left his home for. Glasgow transport authorities failed to recruit 'bus-conductors or 'bus-drivers locally, wages and shift-work system were unacceptable. So they sent to India and Pakistan and recruited labour there. It was the same as with London Transport having to recruit in the West Indies, because white labour refused to work for basic low pay and the shift-hours. "We come, because we are wanted," as Ahmad put it: "The transport cannot go without us. We are offered the job. We come and we do the job."

The Asians, Indians, Pakistanis, had first made their mark on Glasgow in the 1930s, some of them crew-members of ships from Chittagong, docking at Greenock; others had followed, somehow scraping together money to pay for the trip, or working their passage. They had taken various jobs, waiters and kitchen-staff, door-to-door salesmen with silks and exotic materials to offer, cheap, easily transported from India. It was in the 1950s and on, that they became British Rail stewards, or worked on the 'buses. Now, after the hard work and saving the money, Ahmad had quit his job. He had earned enough to set up on his own. Now he could achieve the dream of every Pakistani who comes to this country: to own his own business, his own restaurant, his own shop, be his own boss; not have to drive 'buses or work as a 'bus-conductor. That was the means to the desired end, the heartfelt desire: your own business, you are your own boss, God has been good to you. You have been a good Muslim. A good Muslim works, he mixes with others and shares their burdens. Muhammad the Prophet has said better this than to live a life of seclusion and contemplation. The Muslims had built their own mosque in Oxford Street, in the Gorbals, converting it from a run-down billiards hall. They had spread all round Glasgow; in 1958 a score of Asian drapery warehouses flourished in the city – the owners of these businesses lent their fellow-countrymen capital to set up businesses of their own (no trying to borrow money from the bank as a local man would have to do, and invariably fail to obtain credit).

With the money he had saved, Ahmad bought this huge motor-van. I had glimpsed it at the side of the hall. He had obtained credit from his friends, and stocked up his van with anoraks and men's shirts, football-boots and watches, kitchen-towels and women's knitted dresses. There they were spread out in Moulin's village hall, cheap and attractive.

Ahmad had little to add about the girl. Quarrels with her parents and leaving home; Asian families had their problems, no less than white families, with the young who wanted no part of the old ways, who wanted freedom to live their life their own way. A Muslim girl was not allowed to mix with white girls on the one hand, while on the other she would be attending a Protestant school, learning to speak English (with that strong Glasgow accent); she was not allowed to wear latest English-style clothes, and must not uncover her legs. She wasn't allowed to go to dances with girls or boys, nor to go swimming. Against the background of the so-called permissiveness, such parental restriction could be regarded as totally outdated, the teachings of Islam seem unrealistic, contradictory. At any rate, the girl was safe now, for the time being. This was all that Ahmad could say. She had attached herself to his family. She was coming with them to Stornoway. That was the idea; whether it would work out, who could say?

Stornoway, main town on the Isle of Lewis, and biggest town in the Hebrides, is a busy port. Its harbour, overlooked by heather-covered hills and the woods around its castle, is jammed with fishing-boats, ferries, mail-ships and cargo-vessels from the mainland and European ports. Prince Charlie reached here in 1746 during his wanderings in the Hebrides. Today, Pakistani families fleeing from the City of the Twilight (Wally Ness's description of Glasgow) had opened up cafés and restaurants, general stores, drapery shops. They were integrating with the islanders, you could say that they had found a new Mecca. (As Wally Ness had pointed out to me, this was nothing new, in the 1930s Italian hokey-pokey merchants had moved in all over the Highlands, opening up ice-cream parlours – and fish-and-chip shops.)

There was no sign of the girl when, with my tea-cloths neatly wrapped, I left the hall. Ahmad expected to be remaining in Moulin for another two or three days before moving on. I hadn't learned very much about the girl. I hadn't even learned her name.

Next afternoon found me trudging a path that led to the Road to The Isles, except that I struck off towards where the bluish-greenish-grey rock-face jutted out in huge buttresses, with edges that appeared as sharp as razors against the intense blue sky; faint tendrils of cloud like wisps of cotton-wool moved lazily across the blue. And all the time there were the calls of birds alarmed by my approach, circling above before settling for a few moments to cry their alarm once more and circle the air again. The short light *chirck* of the greater spotted woodpecker. The harsh grating of the jack-daw. The clear, melodious call of the mavis.

I had come up through a mile of scrub and rock foothills to reach the densely wooded lower slopes of the crags. The aromatic tang of young Douglas Firs and Scots Pines, resinous and sharp, filled the warm air. I began slogging up through the brown fern and bracken with only a glimpse now and then of moss on the path I trod. I looked up at the rock-face, towering even more menacingly, again. Limestone rock, a rich site due to seepage from the crags. Could the birds so high make me out so clearly? I noticed three peregrines flying above the cliff-face, disturbed by my approach, waiting for me to quit the scene. All the falcon family possess phenomenal sight, all predatory birds possess an acuteness of vision difficult for man to comprehend. I saw two of the peregrines mate. I observed the winnowing of their wings. They were a pale fawn colour, with bright yellow eyes and black moustaches. The pair were near the nest on a piece of rock jutting out from the face. The third peregrine was a loner, it had failed to find a mate; it remained as close as it dared to the other two, like some unrequited lover, you might think, hoping for its love to be returned. Brown grass clung to the rock-face, moss covered the ledges above the foothills, and all about me were dozens of tiny Scots Pines; huge boulders lay where they had split away from the ancient rock, the oldest rock in the Highlands – perhaps the oldest on the planet.

Looking back the way I had come I could see the vast panorama of hills, pine tree and heather patched, the hills' humps edged sharply against the sky, with beyond them low slow-moving cloud. There were moments of stupendous silence; as you stood there it seemed to brush against you. Then that silence was broken by the cooing of rock-doves. Some of the pine trees had been uprooted and pushed down by a rush of melting snow that winter. As I shifted my eyes to take in the vista of hills, I noted several tall black skeletons of trees. My gaze moved on; further to the right, high up, the hills were chocolate-coloured with here and there driblets of snow still remaining in the crevasses, like a rich cake with its icing mostly picked off by children's fingers. I moved on, tough green grass and grey-green moss underfoot. I halted as an extraordinary sound soughed along the cliff-face, the wind, echoing among the crags and boulders. Now I came to within a dozen yards of the lair of the wildcat.

I had learned that there was a wildcat here, almost certainly the one I had seen near Ennochdhu Wood. And if there was one wildcat, it was almost certain that it had a mate. The previous day, Don had shown me the den. I had reported to Don that the wildcat had black striped fur, and that its tail was black-tipped and rounded, not pointed as it would have been with a feral cat. The black stripes, as against the blotchy markings of a domestic cat, were conclusive. Wildcats have larger, flatter heads than the other variety; their teeth are larger, too, though both animals are about the same size.

Cats have always attracted me, though I've never kept one myself, living as I do mostly in London, without a garden or the open space which I believe a cat requires to keep happy. This was one reason for my love for Rufus; it seemed to me he was much more cat in him than dog. But my father had owned a wonderful cat, named Black Sambo – Sam, for short – a starving stray which had turned up almost dying from starvation and exposure. My father's prescribed medicine, whisky and hot-water bottles throughout the night and day for a week, saved Sam's life. He grew into a handsome black Persian of a marvellously loving nature, devoted to my father, whom he used to follow regularly to the village pub every evening. At closing-time, however, it was my father who preferred to follow Sam back home.

Like the fox, the wildcat has been harassed and hounded to death by man; only a few survive in the Highlands. Here they are likely to become extinct, the few that are left being shot on sight or trapped by gamekeepers and farmers; if their den is discovered, the entire family, parents and kits, are mercilessly exterminated. Fearing man as they do, they are difficult to observe – I had spent hours at dawn and dusk, when they are most active, watching them. Mice and voles are their usual food, but centuries-old myths and stories have been handed down depicting them as cruel

predators, forever attacking lambs, game and chickens; and consequently Man – apart from whom they have no enemies – has
virtually wiped the wildcat out.

I had noted several trees near the den, marked by scratches deep
in the bark, where the wildcat had been sharpening its claws. I
thought I could make out some fresh scratches – and then I heard
the rasp of claws on rock. I looked up and the wildcat was staring
down at me from the rock-slab over its den. For a few breathless
moments it poised there. Its eyes glowed at me, just as they had at
our first encounter (I was convinced it was the same wildcat I had
seen before), except now we were only a few feet from each other.
No mistaking that wild, savage face beneath the flattened skull. Its
long, white whiskers stuck out several inches from the sides of its
mouth and above its eyes, *vibrissae* – antennae, which just like
Rufus's could pick vibrations and signals out of the air. Dead these
whiskers may have been, as is all hair, but at the roots of each are a
bunch of nerves very much alive. What signals was the cat receiving
from me? You could almost feel the electricity that charged each
separate whisker. I whispered to it – I don't know what I said – and
it tensed. Was there a flicker in those eyes, a slight loosening of
tension in that taut body? Involuntarily, I must have made a slight
move towards it, and it was gone. Soundlessly, it seemed to disintegrate. The wildcat might never have been there.

I reached the road again leading to Stalker's Cottage, and saw
the girl waiting for me. My mind was full of the wildcat; I was
deeply thrilled by this second encounter, and longed to see it again
– I must come here one evening, or at dawn when I got back from
London, where I was going on the sleeper that night; I would
learn how to keep watch on the den without betraying my
presence.

When I spoke to her, the girl said nothing about our seeing each
other at Moulin. I asked after Ahmad. When was he leaving for
Stornoway? "We go this evening," she answered. I said something
about it being a coincidence my also going away that night.
London. For a little while. She said: "But you go long way. We
go short distance only. We stop at other places on the way. We
take two, three weeks reaching Stornoway. You return here before
then." Ahmad hoped to pay his way from sales of his stock; what
remained would help him set up business at his journey's end. I

hoped all would go well for him. And for her. I sounded serious, I suppose. She didn't turn her face to me. She gave a little shrug.

"I not hope very much – I not believe in Kalimah Shahadah," she said. "Och, I not have the faith, okay, all right? I not bear witness there is no god but God, same my family believe. They see God in their minds as a man. Why not see God as an eagle? An eagle more beautiful. Or," and she glanced at me, her eyes narrowed, sharpened at the inside corners, "an animal? Rufus more beautiful than a man. He live a more Godly life than any man. Muhammad said all animals must be treated with kindness, okay, all right?" I supposed so, I answered; I was reminded of a letter in my pocket which I'd shown Don that morning. "But Muslims sacrifice animals in memory of Abraham who was ready to sacrifice his son, Ishmael, in obedience to God." She shook her head.

She was saying all this for effect, with the idea of shocking me, as she must have shocked her parents. That was what I thought as I took the letter out of my pocket. Rufus was asked many times to appear at religious functions, Catholic or Protestant, the denomination didn't seem to matter. It was usually some scheme aimed at raising money for an animal charity or a trust or society for animal welfare, especially an event which it was hoped children would attend. Then Rufus would be the big attraction. I read out to the girl that Rufus was invited to the forthcoming Blessing of the Animals service at Worcester Cathedral, where, as usual, it was the children especially who would come to see Rufus. "Unfortunately, Worcestershire has a number of hunts," the letter said, "and there are several pony-clubs attached to them. It may be that some children who go hunting will bring their ponies." But if Rufus was there to be blessed, in the name of all foxes, the children would think twice before going hunting again. Don hadn't sounded over-enthusiastic. Security for Rufus wasn't likely to be easy. There would be the risk, also, of him encountering too many with the blood of foxes on their hands. It could be too much for him to take.

The girl thought that for Rufus to be blessed by a priest at a cathedral was a wonderful idea. It entirely supported her rejection of her family's religion. I realised that she was deadly serious. I had nothing to say. I had never thought about God and animals in that way. "Rufus," she said, "he blessed by God – och, that is okay, all right." To her, it made marvellous sense. I had nothing to say. I was still experiencing surprise at the depth of feeling she showed. There was something wild about her – off-key; I recalled our first meeting, the night of my return to Ennochdhu Wood. The dark forest about us. This phantom figure reminding me of Rima – who had met that dreadful death at the end of the book. And I remembered again how she had spoken about danger. Danger? Danger for her? She was saying something in a whisper that sounded like a benediction; I didn't understand the words, I only caught the tone of her voice. She turned away. I watched her until the bend in the road hid her from sight. She hadn't looked back.

That night, as I lay in my swaying bed on the *Royal Highlander*, my thoughts went out to Ahmad and his son in the van, stuffy with goods and materials from Glasgow, on the road. And the girl. On their way, along their Road to the Isles.

9 The Tumult and the Shouting

My father spent some time as a doctor on the West Coast of Africa among the gold miners, and one of his stories was about how, when black labour was short, Chinese coolies were imported to work in the mines. Their main fear was not that they had left their homeland for hell-hot, disease-ridden darkest Africa, but that if they died so far away from their native land their bodies might not be returned home for burial. A simple, if sentimental, request, and the mine-owners were prepared to guarantee to meet it; they could take out insurance to cover the cost of transport in cheap coffins back to China. They ran into a small snag, however. They could insure their employees against death by accident, but what about death from disease? Disease was rife enough – and, they were suddenly made to realise, could at any moment hit epidemic proportions; what did you do with thousands of dead Chinese to be shipped back to their own country? You couldn't insure against that. No personal accident or life company would look at it; nor would marine insurance cover it.

The coolies were insistent that they be guaranteed this last request, and the mine-owners had to come up with the answer. The answer was to insure them as livestock. They had been transported from China in cattle-boats, why shouldn't they be returned, dead, the same way? After all, no live coolie had complained, or if he had no one had taken much notice, on the trip over; he would have less cause to complain on the way back. All he wanted to know was that he would be buried at home. And so, according to my father, that was how the matter was solved. The insurance was duly effected, and as it happened there weren't any serious epidemics during his time: those Chinese who did die on the job were sent back for burial to the land of their ancestors.

This was not the sort of business that Lloyd's would underwrite, though they are famous for never refusing to insure any risk, from a herd of elephants to a performing flea. It isn't quite the case: in fact, they are remarkably flexible, but, for instance, they won't write long-term life assurance or financial guarantees.

Terry Hall, a leading Lloyd's underwriter, was recently asked to quote a rate for All Risks of Mortality on non-pathogenic ectoparasites in transit by air from New York to Atlantic. These were, as you will have guessed, performing fleas, 20 of them, *en route* from one exhibition to another, whose naturally anxious and responsible owner-trainer was determined that they should arrive safe, ready, willing and able to perform – they were, after all, his living. Now, Mr Hall is a leading underwriter in the sense that where he leads others follow (a risk is not normally covered by one man, several – sometimes, a large number of underwriters – chip in; this is the practice at Lloyd's) and although, like most of his fellow-members, he possesses a strong sense of humour, and some risks may seem to be of a frivolous nature – like insuring an actress's legs or the Loch Ness Monster – it's doubtful if money is lost on them.

On the face of it, this little matter of the performing fleas seemed an amusing risk, but, as in the case of the Chinese coolies, a snag became apparent. It was to do with the business of identification of each flea. It became even more complicated when it was learned that six Rhesus monkeys were travelling on the same flight. There followed not a little to-ing and fro-ing between the broker and Mr Hall, who finally, with his charming if somewhat enigmatic expression, neatly sidestepped the proposition by intimating in his quiet-spoken tones that he would underwrite the risk – on the strict understanding that the broker would earmark each individual flea.

Terry Hall is not unused to the oddities of the kind of business in which he specialises, livestock insurance. It ranges over a wide field, from horses – thoroughbreds, performing horses, or show-jumpers – and cattle, sheep, pigs and poultry to rare animals, *en route* to and from the world's zoos, and a creature whose existence has so far not been established, the Loch Ness Monster. A famous Scottish whisky firm decided to cash in on the news stories and sensational reports broadcast annually claiming a sighting of the monster. One million pounds was offered to the first person able to prove conclusively that the living, breathing creature existed (there was no requirement that the claimant must drink a bottle of whisky beforehand). It was a good publicity idea but, as the rush of competitors swelled, the whisky firm prudently decided to insure against having to pay up. Their insurance broker accordingly found himself in Lloyd's famous Underwriting Room – buzzing with business, its elaborate system of telephones and indicators going flat out, enabling brokers and underwriters to keep in instant touch with one another – in close discussion at the pew-like desk of Mr Hall, who duly underwrote the risk.

It was he who also underwrote Rufus. Without Rufus being insured against full Mortality Risks including theft, mysterious disappearance or escape during the anticipated several months before the film of *Lady Into Fox* went into production, I couldn't complete the deal with Bernard Smith. It was the essence of our contract (Frieda and the cubs were also part of it), and without this stipulation the project couldn't get off the ground. This entailed the inevitable health and fitness check-ups, veterinary certification, all the rest of it. John Morton, an insurance broker who also special-ises in livestock (both he and Terry Hall are concerned with wild life preservation, as it happens) whom I consulted about obtaining the cover, invited Rufus and Mr Hall to lunch; afterwards we planned to take Rufus to visit Lloyd's.

Rufus was due to appear at a children's book-show in London during the week. I had come on ahead to straighten out with Pan, the publishers whose book-display it was, the publicity people and everyone else, a time-table for Rufus's appearances; and to arrange for him to be put up at the RSPCA's accommodation in Jermyn Street, where he had previously stayed when in London. He was also to meet Bernard Smith and Patrick Garland, neither of whom had yet made his acquaintance and both of whom very much wanted to get to know him. There were also meet-ings between Bernard Smith, his lawyers and my lawyers, for the final drafting of the contracts; and then the inevitable script-conferences with he, Patrick Garland and myself, and work to put in on the sequences of the script in which Rufus would appear.

Soon after I arrived in London I telephoned Iris. She was staying with friends in Knightsbridge, and she asked me along for a drink that evening. I had expected that she would want to come and meet Rufus, at the book-show, perhaps, or somewhere else we could fix up. But she made an excuse. She was off back to New York sooner than she had expected, and there was so much at the last minute to deal with. I thought she sounded a little brisk over the 'phone, and it occurred to me that returning to London had made a difference – something had happened, something was going on. I had gone along to Lloyd's after seeing John Morton, which was when I took the opportunity to check out McNab's yacht, *Penelope* (I suppose it wasn't just curiosity – I probably intended to mention it to Iris when I saw her later). There it was, of course, recorded, and it gave me a strange feeling seeing it written down. I was also given a sight of a copy of the broker's slip showing the cover for Francis Chichester's *Gipsy Moth IV* when he miraculously circumnavigated the world; reading the note concerning the details of the policy, the rates and the time covered, I found among the facts and figures a phrase which gripped my imagination: "Periods to be agreed by Ldr. only after the tumult and the shouting has died down and Assured knows his commitments."

Next morning I was with John Morton again at his office in the City; the papers, veterinary certificates, the film-contract, had all been given the green light – Terry Hall was underwriting the risk. Don would travel down with Rufus overnight; he, Don and I would spend tomorrow morning at the book-show, before going to the lunch that John Morton was giving for Rufus, at which he would meet the directors of John's firm, and Mr Hall and some of his associates (in fact, Rufus was introduced to the entire office-staff, revelling in the affectionate admiration of all with his usual bright-eyed chattering). Of course, champagne would be laid on for him. Not that this was any light-hearted jaunt – I knew only too well it wasn't going to be anything of the kind. All the time I knew I was going to be on edge in case trouble, disaster or death hit Rufus. Anything could happen to him. Some little thing could cause him to panic and make a sudden dive for it, into the street and under a bus; indoors, someone just for the hell of it might bash him with anything lethal that happened to be at hand, a walking-stick or an umbrella. In a way, though there were enemies all around him at Dunfuirich, danger could threaten him more in London – at least, on his home territory we were as prepared as was reasonably possible for any premeditated strike against him – but in London there was the risk of some totally unforeseen accident.

The policy was carefully prepared so that Bernard Smith was effectively covered against any eventuality which might prevent Rufus, Frieda and the cubs starting work on the projected film under the terms of the film-deal. It was in the works, now, and that afternoon Bernard Smith and I met to talk about the film-script. He gave me a graphic run-down on the trials, tribulations, the hang-ups and headaches of an animal-film producer. His experience was long-standing and included such sagas as MGM Cinerama's *How The West Was Won*, with John Wayne, James Stewart, Gregory Peck, and hundreds of horses and not a few dogs – it was the dogs gave you the most trouble. The horses came with their own stunt-riders, who very often owned the animal, and they were taught to perform precisely what was asked of them: basically, to fall at exactly the right moment in the action and with breathtaking realism. These horses were so remarkably well-trained and their riders so expert on the job there never needed to be any retakes, there were never any accidents, and no one was ever killed.

With dogs it was different. True, what they were asked to do was usually more complicated than with the horses, and what was required of them usually took up more time. The trouble is that an animal has a limited attention span, especially when it has to apply its attention to some action which normally it wouldn't perform. Your dog, for example, will take many minutes stalking a wild bird; you can see him concentrating every sense and muscle on his objective. That's because he's normally always deeply engrossed in matters of the stomach. When he's hunting for food, which is naturally his favourite occupation, he'll give the task unlimited attention span. Not so if you ask him to perform some action out of character, such as to express an emotion of which he isn't capable, a human emotion. You have to teach him to do that – to be more precise, to give the impression that he is doing it – and loses interest – and bring in a "stand-in" dog to continue the scene.

Sometimes you come up with an individual animal who possesses a special talent, though usually you can't rely on it being able to perform more than one "speciality". In the film *Elmer Gantry*, which Bernard Smith produced, Burt Lancaster, as the character who is denouncing Darwin and his ideas on evolution, is addressing a meeting, holding a chimpanzee in his arms. Do you think, the actor harangues his audience, you and this chimp are brothers? The chimp raises a great laugh by the contemptuous manner in which he regards the crowd. It was a highly risible piece of animal "acting"; but of course the chimpanzee, even though it was very intelligent, wasn't really contemptuous of human beings: he was simply looking at them with characteristic curiosity. It was the dialogue and the angle from which the chimp was filmed that achieved the required effect. There was a scene in another of Bernard Smith's films in which the hero, off to fight in the American Civil War, is followed by his faithful dog and is eventually compelled to send him back home. The dog cast for the rôle was given intensive training by its owner, taught to follow the film-actor, then reluctantly, dejectedly turn back according to the scene as written. Its talent, and the expertise of its trainer, was evident in the dog's dejected walk – when the scene was shot you saw only its back, by which it managed to convey with marvellous conviction its utter misery at being sent packing by its dearly loved owner. But . . . that individual dog happened to have that sort of back, that was all there was to it; it wasn't feeling miserable at all – almost certainly it was wondering when it would get its next meal. Bernard Smith was able to make use of the dog's special talent for that one particular scene.

He envisaged Rufus looking fine for the close-ups, and that Frieda, or the cubs, who would be fully-grown when the film was set to go into production, would be suitable for scenes photographed in medium or long shots. All the time, you would need to script the sequences in which Rufus, Frieda or the cubs appeared in a simple and straightforward way so that too much wasn't asked of them. It would be up to Rufus to contribute most of the "acting" for the rôle of Sylvie (as the husband, Richard, continues to call his wife after she's turned into a vixen); this was because he would figure in the close-ups. The wife's metamorphosis into a vixen forms the basis of the plot and occurs a third of the way through the film, so that Rufus's performance would take up a considerable amount of screen-time. The "vixen's" scenes were almost entirely with Richard, and were close-ups or scenes just between the two of them. "She" had virtually no action on her own, except in the middle and far distance, where Frieda or one of the cubs would play the rôle.

This meant the actor playing Richard would in fact have to do most of the work during his scenes with the "vixen", although it would appear as if "she" (that is, Rufus) was having as much to do. This is the secret of making a film which features animals – you write the script and you direct it so that the audience are persuaded they're watching the animal when in reality they're often doing nothing of the kind. It's the actor they're seeing. He would be playing the scenes between himself and Rufus, speaking to him, touching him even, when it would only be Rufus's shadow, the movement of his fore-paws, the flick of his brush, that would actually be shown. Only when it was absolutely necessary would Rufus be completely in the camera's lens – because it was these shots which could be so time-consuming and expensive: at the crucial moment – the take – you just can't rely on any animal not to falter, break down or act in a totally different way from that rehearsed. The tension that builds up normally when the actors are ready, lighting and camera-angles exactly right, can be tremendous. This tension inevitably communicates itself to the animal, it loses its concentration, it forgets what it's been taught, and it's – "Cut" – and you have to start all over again.

It was fascinating, going through the script, page by page with Bernard Smith. He showed me how the very utmost could be made of Rufus's "acting" potential, while at the same time taking care not to over-tax his limited attention span. Here and there, because I'd been handling him increasingly and observing him with Don, and had been able to form a reasonably clear idea of his capacity for concentration, I could give Bernard Smith some guidance on how Rufus could be expected to perform. I felt hopeful he would come up with a "bonus" or two as an actor. Observing him again and again when we were together, talking to him (and he'd be chattering back), you could hold his attention; he could be looking at you, meeting your eye for all the world as if he was understanding every word you uttered, then – that strange, faraway look; he had shifted his eyes from yours, and you knew he had left you, he had gone. Both Don and I would be with him during the time he would be performing for the film, and between us we reckoned we could keep his mind on the job he had to do, bring him back from those dreams he was dreaming, the visions that took him so far, far away.

Patrick Garland joined Bernard Smith and myself; he had made the script from the novel and now had some revisions to discuss. As I was concerned only with the vixen sequences, I could sit back and listen while they plotted away together, re-shaping this or that piece of the action. The script had reached the first draft stage and there was still plenty of work to be done on it before filming began. Garland had suffered his quota of headaches over filming *The Snow Goose*; he gave all the credit for the marvellous performance of The Princess, as the snow-goose in the story is named, to Ray Berwick, a quietly drawling Californian who had attained marvellous results training the birds in Alfred Hitchcock's horror-film, *The Birds*. There is a sensational scene in that film where black, evil-looking birds attack the house in which the human beings tried to hide from them – this was all achieved by several weeks of patient work from Berwick; first the house's windows were replaced by screens smeared with food. The birds went for this, naturally. Then when they were fully trained to go without fail for the food, and everything was ready for the attack, at the crucial moment the screens were replaced by the windows; the birds flew at them pecking violently, mistaking them for the screens they had been used to feeding off. Of course, the basis for training birds or animals is always the same – rewarding them with food.

In *The Snow Goose*, Berwick even persuaded the bird, in the scene in which it is wounded, to lie quiet and totally relaxed while the actress playing Frith bandaged it. (Geese especially are supersensitive to human beings touching their wings.) Garland employed half a dozen of them in the film, and I had no doubt that if such marvellous results could be obtained with geese then Rufus wouldn't present any problem.

"Absurd though it is to equate animals with children," Patrick Garland was saying, "nevertheless there are points of contact, and it's easy to equate dumb animals with more eloquent ones." I was nodding my head, realising that he was serious-minded, he wasn't mouthing cliches; that he'd learned something from Ray Berwick and the geese which went deeper than his concern for the film; and he added something which stunned me with its simplicity. Had I, he asked me reflectively, watched the big cats in their cages at the London Zoo? How they paced up and down, up and down, up and down? And had it occurred to me how horribly similar this behaviour was to that of human beings in the process of a nervous breakdown? What he said struck a chill chord in my heart; I'm always uneasy at the sight of caged animals or birds. I'm used to the argument that a caged lion, for all his lost liberty, is well-fed, well-cared for, secure, but it has never blotted out for me the fact that, despite all the blessings he can count, he isn't free. He is a wild thing constrained, captive, and therefore really suffering as much as any human being would suffer under similar circumstances (I know something about the effects of long-term imprisonment upon men, and have always felt that the sudden loss of freedom is much more destructive of life than has ever been generally understood). I warmed towards Don more than ever before – for the first time I grasped the unsentimental truth that lay behind his unswerving determination that any wild animal that came into his care should be free. It was better for Rufus to run the risk of death living a free life in the glen by Ennochdhu Wood than for him to be caged and confined for his protection and better security.

2

Late that afternoon I was at the Tower of London. Nothing to do with Rufus, this was to do with Cronk.

Don had been compelled to reach the decision that she must be sent away. Either that or she would be killed. And so she was to come down to London with him and Rufus on the *Royal Highlander*. No use waiting around, hoping Cronk would oblige with a change of nature overnight. Don knew too much about her, too much about the behaviour of the corvine or crow family, of which ravens are the largest member, to hope for any improvement in Cronk's attitude towards human beings. Ravens are the most "human" of birds. Unquestionably, it seems that they play games like those Cronk and her mate had played, and the "stealing" game with Shuna – as human beings play, for sheer enjoyment, and not as an exercise in hunting techniques or predatory activity, which is the object of games and exercises in the case of most young birds and animals. Watch Cronk flying on the winds of a storm and you are watching her enjoying a game with the elements; she twists and turns, using the thermals to throw her high into the sky; she pirouettes with the skill and humour of a ballet-dancer giving a comic turn; she spins in an air-pocket with nonchalant dexterity, and then, timing it to the split-second, she will fold her wings about her, and barking with pleasure, throw herself headlong down the sky; then suddenly – and chuckling to herself for the fun of it – spread her wings to hang on the air like a parachute jerking open.

And so her thieving exploits, robbing children of ice-creams and sweets or bright coins, were all meant to be in fun; women's handbag-snatching, gashing holes in tents, bashing windows with her beak, were all part of Cronk's repertoire by which she tried to gain your attention. She wanted you to join in the game, either as an accomplice or a "victim", just as Rufus joined in "stealing" Shuna's bone. Perhaps, too, if she hadn't lost her mate, she would have felt less deprived of love, she would have felt more secure, not so desperately anxious to attract everyone's attention and affection. Perhaps it wasn't so much an emotional disturbance, if you like, with her; nor that she was suffering from a lonely heart – perhaps it was simply a reflex, an instinctive reaction. Anyhow, there wasn't any way you would get her to change; you would never teach her, she would never learn to mend her ways.

Don had been in touch with the London Zoo, and then the Tower of London, but both were already full up with ravens. Then he had found a home for Cronk – or thought he had – with a family near London, whose pet raven had just died. When I arrived in London I had telephoned to make arrangements for them to come up to collect Cronk – only to be told there had been a last-minute change of plan. That day a friend had brought them a young raven which they couldn't very well refuse. So Cronk was without a home. However, Don decided to stick to his plan to bring her down with him, so would I do my best to find someone to take her? If I hadn't done so in time then the RSPCA would look after her until a home for her had been found.

Yeoman-Quartermaster John Wilmington, Keeper of the Ravens at the Tower, introduced me to three of his own magnificent ravens, Brunai, Kala 2, and Hectora.

"Some folk refer to them as an 'unkindness', of ravens instead of a flock – maybe because of the stories of bad luck and death they're supposed to bring." He had a version which I didn't know of how the raven, originally supposed to be white in colour, was turned black. According to this story, Noah, when the Flood was subsiding, sent a pair of (white) ravens to sight the land; instead they turned their attention to feeding off the corpses of the drowned, for which sin God changed their colour to black. Yeoman–Quartermaster Wilmington now thought that perhaps room could be made for Cronk, after all, in a few weeks' time. This was good news. Straightaway I was put in touch with an Essex family who kept ravens and who would look after Cronk until she could join Brunai, Kala 2, Hectora and the others on the Tower "establishment".

Next morning, 7.30, Euston, and Don, with Rufus under one arm, and Cronk in a large container under the other, stepping off the *Royal Highlander* – Rufus chattering his happy greeting to me and Cronk giving her barking performance, which, as it happened, other travellers attributed to Rufus, inevitably mistaking him for a dog. Fortunately Cronk's temporary owner had offered to drive up and collect her at Euston. He was there as prearranged to greet us as we came off the platform, Cronk still barking, and he took her over. It would have been difficult to bring her with us to my flat – animals weren't allowed there normally, although this rule can be dodged if discretion is used: discretion is impossible with Cronk. She would have advertised her presence to everyone in the building at an unpopular hour of the day (or night), almost certainly harvesting a huge crop of complaints. There was a slightly emotional scene as Don said good-bye to her through the side of the container, during which Cronk subsided into prolonged incoherent muttering. Then she let loose with more barking, rising to an ear-shattering crescendo as she disappeared in the direction of the car waiting to convey her to her new home. Rufus had been too interested in his surroundings to take in the farewell scene, though he contrived to have the air of a seasoned visitor to the Big Smoke as the three of us got into the waiting car laid on for us by Pan's publicity department.

Wherever he went, whoever he met, on his tours of children's hospital-wards, book-shops, television stations – wherever it was –

after the initial astonishment at the sight of a wild fox who could behave like Rufus, not only did he receive the V.I.P. treatment, he was always accepted as a friend. A sort of friend of the family, you could say, whom you could trust – you knew he would never let you down, he would be at the book-shop, paw ready to sign his "autograph", on time; at the television studio on time. Everyone, from shop-assistants to tea-girls, make-up girls (not that he ever needed make-up, but everyone of the studio staff crowded round to watch him when the show went out), to the interviewer, took him to their hearts at once. When he left there remained an unforgettable memory of a wonderfully loving creature. It was the same at every pub to which we would adjourn with the media men and women, every hotel or restaurant – he would sit down quietly beside Don, roll on his back for a good scratch, or give an occasional yawn if he felt that perhaps it was time we should be moving on.

It wasn't as if you were with a fox or any other animal, it was more like being with another human being, a warm, loving human being who was there alongside, happy to do all he could to co-operate, however best he could. It was only in the studio, when there was the inevitable wait while everything was being set up for his interview, that he became a little bad-mannered. The lights would become unbearably hot and he used to start to stick out his tongue and pant a bit, and then there would be a rush to find him a bowl of water – champagne or the hard stuff was not allowed so soon before transmission, as the possibility of his uttering a hiccup wasn't thought to be good for his image – and in his haste to get at the water he might upset the bowl, which gave him the idea of racing round the studio with it in his teeth. Apart from an occasional lapse of this sort, there was never any fit of temperament, he chattered and showed his teeth in his happy "grin" on cue; he was the perfect television interviewee.

It was the same today. After breakfast, in which he didn't join – his one-meal-only-at-night routine never varied – we were whisked off to the book-show, where publishers, media people, photographers, and children, some with their parents, some in parties with their teachers, took him, literally, to their bosoms. He disappeared from sight to the accompaniment of the usual oohing and aahing, squeals of disbelieving enchantment and then the roar

of joyful admiration. At last, Don and I between us, aided by the
publishers, who were alarmed in case something awful happened
to him, managed to "rescue" Rufus and get him going on the
serious business of gracefully yielding to autograph-hunters'
requests, hundreds of them waving their *Rufus* books – some bought
on the spot, others which had been brought along. Untiringly
Rufus stuck his paw on the ink-pad, then placed it on the page.
Ink-pad . . . book. Ink-pad . . . book. Ink-pad . . . book. And the
cameras popped. And the small boy, school-cap knocked awry
over one ear by Rufus, to whom he held on as if he would never
let him go, begging: "Can I keep him? Please let me – he doesn't
bark all the time, like my dog. You can have my dog in
exchange —"

Bernard Smith duly arrived and was duly beguiled and
impressed. Other film-people, friends of his, who would be concerned with the business aspects of *Lady Into Fox*, showed up and
managed to get near enough to express their admiration of this
new-style "star". Patrick Garland was there, and was photographed
with Rufus; he stayed the longest, talking to him, and to Don and
me, astonished and totally enchanted by this handsome creature
(Rufus was now in his best coat, rich and glowing red, the silvery-
white of his throat and chest dazzlingly bright), and most of all,
as he held him in his arms and they chatted away together as if they
had known each other for years, marvelling at his loving friendliness. In a way, it was one of his most triumphant hours. Of course,
it's stupid to "humanise" an animal, even Rufus, but in the excitement generated by the children, the obvious admiration Bernard
Smith and Patrick Garland held for him, and the exuberant delight
of everyone around, the thrill of meeting this marvellous creature,
the wonder and the enchantment of it all, you could perhaps be
forgiven if you felt that he knew what it was all about. That he
played to the gallery, showed off, and obviously revelled in being
the centre of attention, the focus of so much love and affection
from everyone around him, seemed understandable, added to his
appeal.

Now we were at John Morton's office, meeting his fellow-
directors, Rufus being embraced by the secretaries and the
switchboard-operators – flashbulbs popping; then into the ele-
gantly mirrored dining-room, Terry Hall joining us for lunch in

Rufus's honour – he was a heavily insured "hot" film-property – his health duly drunk, while he stared at himself in the huge mirrors (he had partaken of the tiniest nip just beforehand, in reply to the toasts in his honour). Then he had his stomach scratched and, after surveying the territory from corner to corner, sprawled himself out, curled his splendid brush round his face and regarded us over it with his bright eyes.

And arriving at Lloyd's, to pose for the photographers with John Morton, Terry Hall – and the famous link-man resplendent in his traditional magnificent uniform, with the crowd on the pavement, craning their necks to see what the excitement was all about, and tourists viewing the sights of Old London and their inevitable cameras clicking – and more flashbulbs pop.

Now, it was late afternoon, Rufus was at the RSPCA's Jermyn Street offices, where emergency accommodation was provided for birds and animals, and he had settled himself down for a good rest. Don put his feet up at my flat, and we talked and planned; then returned to Jermyn Street to give Rufus his meal. The car took us off to Euston, Rufus as usual full of interest for the passing traffic, the busy brightly illuminated streets, in good time for the *Royal Highlander*'s return trip. I held Rufus in my arms for a few moments, then he was with Don, staring back at me from the compartment window as the train pulled out.

Two nights later, I was back at Dunfuirich. Don met me off the train and drove me to Stalker's Cottage. We chatted over a drink – Rufus was fine; he's been none the worse for the 30-hour trip to London and back, and Frieda and the cubs – Robbie was bossier than ever – were all in good shape. I brought fondest thoughts for Rufus from his friends in London, Bernard Smith, Patrick Garland, John Morton, his fellow-directors – everyone in the office – Terry Hall and others, not forgetting the link-man at Lloyd's. I'd had further meetings with Bernard Smith, his solicitors and my solicitors; the deal was sealed, signed and settled.

I stood looking at the sky after Don had gone; the horizon was veiled by the mist from the loch, overhead the distant stars glittered in a black dome. My ears were quickly accustomed to the gentle roar of the burns, so that it formed a background to the rustle of wind in the trees. I wondered if Rufus knew I was back.

Yet at that moment I could not repress a shiver – was it warm enough, even though it was early summer? Must it be some weeks before the night-air, at any rate, was really warm? The portents for a summer of truly hot, sunny days hadn't been too promising. Or was there some other reason for the chill in the atmosphere? I tried to will Rufus to catch my scent, so that he would know I had returned, that I was near, a friend who was close at hand.

My eyes were used to the darkness. I could make out the hills across the loch and the white burns spilling down them. Beyond, the mountains massed against the sky-line. This was the terrain that man had done so little to save; the Highlands knew no human beings until thousands of years after they had arrived in the southern part of what were to become the British Isles. Ice still covered the Highlands long after the rest of the land was free of it, yet man had done more wantonly to destroy its forests and hillsides in the relatively short time he had known them than anywhere else in the country, even perhaps in the world. This was the miracle of the place, that despite the ruthlessness of man's onslaught on its wonder and natural beauty, so much of it remained.

There came that *Ke-wack . . . Ke-wack . . .* the long hoot of an owl from the forest, and then after the barest pause, the reply from its mate, so that it might have been an echo, far off. *Ke-wack . . . Ke-wack . . .* Listening carefully, you could hear the whirr of wings disappearing into the darkness of the trees. Then from down by the loch-shore, over someone's radio, hauntingly on the misty air, comes the sound of *Amazing Grace*. I went in, the old, old words running round my head. "Amazing grace, how sweet the sound, That saved a wretch like me! . . ."

I was in my pyjamas when I heard a noise at the front door. Scrape-scrape. Two images flashed through my mind as I pulled on my dressing-gown and went to the door. Rufus? The Pakistani girl? I thought, perhaps, Rufus might have escaped and decided to drop in to see me. Or that the girl had come back; she had wanted to see Rufus again, before she went on to Stornoway.

But it wasn't either of them, as I found when I opened the door. It was the wildcat. It crouched, its teeth glistening, its long whiskers bristling, those marvellous eyes blazing. It was as if it had come to the cottage, and then as we faced each other, had decided that it had been a mistake. I stood perfectly still. I made some welcoming, muttering sounds at it. The wildcat's ringed tail swished very slightly; it was held stiffly, but it kept moving slowly from side to side. It uttered a kind of snarling hiss. Then it stopped any movement, it stood there quite silent. Once again, just as I thought it was going to relax, a tremor passed through its tense shape. I felt certain that this time it would make a move towards me (I was positive it was the same wildcat I'd encountered before). You could sense its longing to make some contact, you could see its brain clicking into place, to activate its limbs – then its eyes no longer focused on me. Abruptly, and yet with a sidelong movement of its body as if it was still reluctant to do so, it swung away. It was gone.

Gone into the darkness of the forest.

10 Watch and Pray

The days rushed past; daily the cubs grew more independent, Robbie bossier than ever, though he was always less bullying with the vixens than with his brother. You could watch them growing more independent of one another. They would play their games, yapping and squealing and giving each other playful bites – though sometimes Robbie's bites seemed less in play than for real. His jaws would close round his brother's neck as if he would bite the head right off – and there was plenty of stiff-legged pouncing, in imitation of Rufus's mouse-hunting practice. Often nowadays each cub would venture off on its own, though they always grouped together when they rested.

Frieda had made a shallow den for herself far away from the old home (which was now abandoned), usually ignoring and ignored by her children. She seemed to be anxious to be left to herself while she recovered fully from the arduous months of motherhood. Rufus, too, had little to do with his offspring. He spent his time basking in the sunlight or snoozing in his shelter. Occasionally he would drift over to Frieda to chatter to her, and she would "mew" or grumble away to him. A lot of the time he would spend with Don, or with me, or with Shuna. At first he and Shuna would stare at each other, then look around, as if puzzled by Cronk's absence. Shuna would go through the motions of the "stealing" game, leaving the bone she had recently been given, to wait for that barking black apparition to flap out of the sky to tease her. But she soon gave it up – Rufus showed no interest whatsoever in her antics; it was no fun without Cronk – and the game was forgotten.

From the news Don received about Cronk, she was settling down in her new home; no definite date, yet, when she would join the ravens at the Tower of London.

These were often harassing days for Don and his forestry-staff, dealing with forest-fires started sometimes by vandals, or by fools who threw lighted cigarette-stubs from passing trains. Not only did Rufus spend hours with me at Stalker's Cottage, but I was down in the glen with the cubs, handling them as much as possible – Don would join me whenever he could, and we soon decided that of the cubs Robbie showed the most potential as an "actor". Already, he was in appearance the dead spit of his father, although his eyes weren't so innocently round, and temperamentally he was very different. Aggressive and pugnacious, and still inclined to give you a nip; though now he didn't draw blood. His teeth would close over your finger, and then his jaw would "freeze" while he stared at you with a look which was a palpable warning that he could bite, and would if you didn't watch out. His brother and the three vixens were much more gentle, and responded to being handled – the vixens were becoming prettier, more and more like their mother; Don and I knew that we had a useful team of "actors" to back up Rufus.

We hit a week of overcast skies and storms – the day would start off all right up till about midday, then the sun would give place to heavy cloud and rain-squalls. The last Tuesday of August didn't even get off to a decent start. Storm-clouds and rain throughout the day, which consequently I spent with files of notes, reading, listening to the radio and trying to write several letters urgently in need of writing, none of which I finally got round to finishing. In the evening the rain slackened, though I could see the loch where it wasn't obscured by rain-mist chopped up by rain-squalls. The hills and mountains beyond were black, mingling into the livid darkness of the sky.

I forgot to take the key to the wire-netting gate from its secret place back of the house, only realising this when I reached the glen. For the life of me, I can't think why I forgot this; it had been an almost reflex action with me, collecting and returning the key. At the time I didn't give it too much thought. I know I thought about going back for it, then decided that Rufus, like Frieda and the cubs would be sheltering, and he wouldn't want to talk to me, anyway. I was about to return home.

Then I heard a movement in the glen, and turned back and called Rufus's name. At once he appeared from the direction of his shelter and raced towards the gate. He paused a few feet away, chattering and looking at me, head on one side. He was obviously expecting me to open the gate and hold him in my arms.

The shadows seemed to darken very suddenly. Ennochdhu Wood, the Dark Grove of the Birds, I thought to myself, with the trees marching up to you, black and thick, the ends of their leafy branches drooping like dreadful hands. This was what gave you the creeps, the sense that the trees were animated with some kind of life. The rain splashed my face and Rufus blinked at me. I knelt down by the gate and called him. He dashed forward and stood on his hind legs. It was wet and muddy. I managed to push my fingers through so that I could scratch his stomach; then he rolled in the muddy grass, his mouth wide open, "laughing" in submission and chattering away. He sprang up again, fore-paws pressed against the wire-netting and I stood up and touched his wet, black nose. A flicker of lightning flashed across the sky, thunder rumbled in the distance as he and I stood there. I was becoming soaked by the rain, it was running down my neck, my trouser-legs were sticking round my ankles. "Good-night, Rufus," I said, and turned away.

Trying to recall what my thoughts were, I can't honestly say I experienced any premonition. I was frustrated and I was annoyed with myself at having forgotten the key; I was sick of the squalls which howled round the glen and the rain that ran off my face and shoulders. I did look back – something made me do that, but it was something I would have done, anyhow – and perhaps that is how I will always remember him. As he stood there, head on one side, jaws open, staring after me. Blurred by the rain, but his chest and throat silvery in the fading light. And after we had looked at each other for a few moments, there was the flicker of the white tip of his brush as he turned away and was gone. I don't really think of him as a fox. Looking at him I saw him as a wonderful, loving friend, a human being, who in some strange way was capable of helping me with my human problems. This is the best way to describe the emotional impact he had upon you, the emotional involvement you shared with him. In that weird light, the light that must have illuminated the primeval world, the shadows of the trees, the chill of the storm, that inevitable idea of savageness that filled the fast-descending night, Rufus glowed. There was a luminosity about his being that radiated love.

The storm blew, the strong winds increased to gale force, with hail and sleet conditions on higher ground, and a crash woke me – at least that's what I thought it was – at a few minutes after eleven o'clock. I had dropped off to sleep half-an-hour earlier. The radio was still playing dance-music. I switched it off as I looked at my watch. It wasn't the crash which had awoken me, I decided, as I heard footsteps hurrying past my door. It was the voices and laughter caught on the wind. Men's voices, young men's voices, and their laughs sent prickles down my spine. I was out of bed and staring at the window against which hail rattled. Such panic and fear gripped me that I pulled some clothes over my pyjamas, pulled on rubber boots and, belting up my raincoat, still wet from the rain earlier in the evening, I grabbed a flashlight. The door slammed after me as I dashed towards the glen.

The rain came down like stair-rods. Don was already there; it was the crash of the large birch which had stood near the gate which had woken him. The tree had fallen across the wire-netting gate and smashed it down. Shuna stood close against Don's legs. She raised her head at me and gave a low whine; her tail drooped. There was no sign of Rufus. No sign of Frieda or the cubs. Don had heard the voices and the laughter. He made no comment about it. In the reflected light of his flashlight his face was grey and taut. I think he knew then what had happened; after all, you didn't have to be all that psychic, you didn't need so much Highland clairvoyance to really know. We barely spoke to each other as we searched the glen, shouting for Rufus, Frieda and the cubs. Our voices were caught by the wind, the blackness was broken every now and again by a flash of lightning, and thunder rumbled above the thrashing squalls and the hiss of rain and hail.

We searched until the dawn. Don found a length of stick, its end bloodstained, and a thick blob of fur on it. There was no doubt about what it had been used for. We carried on our search past Stalker's Cottage, past the *Fisherman's Rest*; along the road to Dunfuirich, retracing our steps, up the road past Don's house which ascended to the view over Loch Fourich. The hail and the rain

slanted into our faces; we didn't bend our heads to it, we must
search straight ahead, from side to side. We screwed our eyes up
against the rain and the hail. Still barely speaking to each other, our
minds concentrated on our searching, we scoured the terrain,
shoutirtg for Rufus or Frieda. There was never any response. If it
hadn't been for those voices, the laughter, and finding the bloodstained stick, Don and I wouldn't have been so worried. It wasn't
the first time Rufus had escaped and stayed away several days.
Like Frieda, he had turned up again as if it had been nothing out of
the ordinary. He was a wild thing, you had to remember it, and
when the opportunity presented itself, he took it, and ran wild. But
what had happened tonight made it different, we knew he was in
desperate danger. It might be too late.

Don and I were utterly exhausted. We were acting like zombies.
We must reach some plan for continuing the search. First, we had
to take into account the facts, so far as we knew them. It seemed
certain that vandals had been in the vicinity at the time when the
tree had broken down the gate to the glen and released Rufus,
Frieda and the cubs; or alternatively, the broken gate might have
admitted the vandals. Don carefully examined the ground by the
gate – by now it was almost daylight, and he could make out only
our own footprints in the mud; no sign of anyone else having been
there. It seemed then that the vandals could not have come upon
their victims until they had actually escaped from the glen. It was
then that they must have attacked them, by which time Rufus and
Frieda might have eluded the vandals, as might some of the cubs.
Could we feel entitled to hope that Rufus, Frieda and some of the
luckier cubs were alive, hiding in the forest? We must redouble
our searching. But first we must get some sleep.

Don put food in the glen, in the hope that it might attract Rufus
and Frieda or any of the others, then he went to his house, Shuna
accompanying him, to sleep, and I to Stalker's Cottage. He had an
alarm-clock – I hadn't – which would wake him at 8.00. He would
come and wake me, then, while he went to his office, I could start
searching again. That was how we worked it out, in watches of
half a dozen hours – there was Don's work in the office and in the
forest which, of course, he had to carry on with, so that he was
unable to get as much sleep as I was. Catherine MacCaskill was
away; there was no one else Don could enroll to help search – no

one knew Rufus or Frieda well enough, so that they would come
when called. This was even more so in the case of the cubs. In fact,
Don was well aware that if Rufus or Frieda had been severely
shocked by the events of the night, the storm, the vandals' attack,
they might never trust human beings – not even Don – again. Even
Shuna might be suspect; Rufus or Frieda might associate her with
human beings who had attacked them. This was assuming that any
of them were alive, that they hadn't been killed by the vandals and
their bodies disposed of, thrown into the undergrowth never to be
seen again.

The storm was much less violent during the Wednesday, though
the sky was still mostly overcast, and rain-squalls still kicked up the
waters of the loch and rattled the branches of the trees. Between us
during our watches Don and I covered the roads, paths, and forest
between the loch-shore and High View, the topmost hill above
Ennochdhu Wood, overlooking Dunfuirich. The caravan-sites,
the camping-sites – we tried to act as discreetly as we could,
attracted as little attention to ourselves as possible. Everywhere,
Shuna stayed close to Don or to me, except when she would rush
ahead, as if she had picked up a scent. Don and I several times
thought she had caught a scent, but it came to nothing. Only
Shuna's frustrated whimpering.

She accompanied each of us everywhere, with the idea that she
would attract Rufus to her. At first she was very enthusiastic;
obviously she was anxious at Rufus's absence and realised that
something must be wrong, but as she spent hour after fruitless hour
with either Don or me, she became increasingly dejected and less
anxious to come out with either one of us. She was rested, of
course, but every time she was asked to help once more to search,
she got out of her basket with increasing reluctance. I didn't say
anything to Don, but it seemed to me that she knew that Rufus
was dead, that it was pointless to continue to look for him.

Don and I agreed that nothing would be served by informing
anyone other than the forest-workers and the gamekeepers – who
were on the spot and would keep their eyes peeled on Don's behalf
– of what had happened. We believed publicity was more likely to
encourage the vandals, if they knew that Rufus, or Frieda or any
of the cubs were in fact lost, but unharmed, to return to the glen
with the object of finishing off the job. There were, of course, no

gin-traps in the forest where Don worked, but the gamekeepers normally laid snares, and he and those responsible checked the area against Rufus, or Frieda or any of the cubs having been trapped; there was no sign of this having happened, but the horror remained that any of them could have been trapped in one of the gin-traps we knew were set further afield, but whose whereabouts we did not know. As Charlotte Elliott the eighteenth-century hymn-writer put it:

> *Christian, seek not yet repose;*
> *Hear thy guardian angel say,*
> *"Thou art in the midst of foes:*
> *Watch and pray."*

The night proved stormy once more, torrential rain sometimes turning to hail, but Don and I – and Shuna – kept to our watches as we had done the previous night. Once, in a lull in the storm during my watch, I thought I heard a scream and my mind flooded with images of the vixen whose cub Tony Bailey had killed. With Shuna dragging wearily at my heels I made for High View, where I thought the scream had come from. But there was nothing to be found there.

Every road and path Don and I covered, from the loch-shore to Ennochdhu Wood and up to High View; across the caravan- and camping-sites, where caravans and tents stood tightly, depressingly closed against the rain and howl of wind, with not a soul in sight; every time returning to the glen, calling for Rufus, sometimes Shuna joining in with a bark. The desperate hope was that if they were alive Rufus, Frieda or the cubs would return for the food put out for them – Don felt certain that they would have not been able to find food for themselves. They must return to the glen.

That Thursday afternoon, one of the forest-workers reported to Don he had seen an old lady outside her cottage near the loch-shore, beyond Hughie Drummond's tent, with a bowl of bread-crusts. She asked the forest-worker if he had seen "her tame fox", which she had been feeding since Wednesday morning. Don hurriedly went to see the woman. She was aged about 70, and was quite certain that this fox had shown up in her front garden Wednesday morning; she had seen him while she was having breakfast and had come out with pieces of bread, which she had thrown to him. He had eaten the bread hungrily and then run away. From her description, it could have been Rufus. Don's hopes rose. He begged the old lady, who lived alone – she was visited daily by the District Nurse – to put out food for the fox – and if he showed up again, to act without any fear towards him and with friendliness. Don would visit her again that evening, in case she had any more news about the fox.

Don gave me the news, and my heart, too, lightened. He wanted to talk to the District Nurse who visited the old lady, and while I kept my watch, accompanied by Shuna, he went off to see her. I covered the area which extended towards the old lady's house by the loch-shore. There seemed a good chance that Rufus might pick up Shuna's scent, or she his; or he might scent me, and come to us. From what the old lady had said he was hungry enough: he might come to me for food. But still no sign of him, nor of Frieda or any of the cubs.

It was Shuna who was conveying to me the bitter truth which I would not admit. It was not only in the droop of her tail, the slowness of her movements; every time she looked up at you her eyes told you what she knew. Quickly, she would turn away to glance over her shoulder with a low whimper, as if to say why not go back home, where it was safe. No good could come of this continual searching. If she had found words to speak, or spelled it out with a paw in the mud, she couldn't have made it any plainer. She knew. Was she now remembering those pangs of jealousy she had shown towards Frieda when she had arrived on the scene to become Rufus's mate? Jealousy, short-lived, though sometimes revealed in brief flashes, quickly forgotten – and she had always exhibited nothing less than deep maternal love for the cubs (Shuna had not had pups of her own). Did she remember Rufus's first bow before the public a couple of summers ago at Edinburgh's great Highland Show? She had appeared with him, and the effect upon thousands of visitors was sensational. A dog and a fox playing games together, and obviously the best of friends: the children especially, dragging their parents with them, had been entranced, newsmen and BBC Television were on the spot fast, and the resultant news-stories, photos and television coverage boosted attendance so that the Highland Show figures were the highest ever. And the games Rufus had got up to, whipping off pieces of camera equipment (camera lenses glinting in the sunlight were his favourite toy) at the crucial moment; and Shuna somehow contriving to get in the way of those chasing him, to add to the confusion and hilarity. Was she remembering the games with Rufus and Cronk? Was she remembering the deep, tranquil bonds of affection forged between Rufus and herself? Perhaps her head was too full of what she now knew to remember anything.

It was dusk when I returned with Shuna to find that Don was back from seeing the District Nurse. His face was drawn and he shook his head. According to her, the old lady could not be relied upon. Putting it as tactfully as she could, she explained to Don how she herself had heard from a forest-worker's children about foxes belonging to Don MacCaskill having been stolen or let loose. She felt sure, she said, that she had mentioned it in conversation with the old lady, who had made up her own story about seeing Rufus and feeding him. It came as a dreadful let-down to Don; he was now convinced that Rufus and Frieda, together with the cubs, had been killed. I couldn't find it in me to feel anything but agreement. The game was over. It was all over.

I went back to Stalker's Cottage, however, thinking I would continue the search on my own, though Don was convinced that it was hopeless. He had his work to deal with, in any case; he would be away from the forest for several days on that account. He thought that all I could do was check with the forest-workers and people round about in case they did have any news. It was dark, the air heavy and oppressive, rain spattered down in large blobs. I swung my flashlight from side to side as I went along the road. Just in case Rufus might appear.

As I went into the cottage a sudden gust of wind slammed the door behind me. At the same moment I heard a loud crack. It was a curious, almost metallic rather horrible sound. I switched on the light. I looked round the sitting-room, I didn't know what I expected to find – a window-pane broken, a picture fallen from the wall; but there was nothing amiss. I felt all in and low. Perhaps I wouldn't go out again, yet, after all. Perhaps I'd get some sleep first – an hour or two – and go out later. I moved to the bedroom and happened to glance at the big marble mantelpiece. Its greenish colour seemed brighter than I'd ever noticed it, it almost pulsed. It seemed very alive. And then I saw the crack almost in its centre.

The marble was split right across. I felt the split with my fingers. Perhaps it was the slamming of the door which had caused it? And yet, I recalled that the crack I'd heard as I came in had occurred at the precise moment the door had slammed – *or might it, even, have been a fraction of a second before?* It seemed to me that the door-slam, loud and jolting though it was, hadn't been responsible for the cracked mantelpiece.

I went into my bedroom. I couldn't resist the feeling that it was an omen. The ancient marble mantelpiece cracking like that, it wasn't normal.

I thought I caught the sound of some animal. Perhaps it was the yelp of a badger. Or it might have been a wail from Shuna to the moon masked by the heavy clouds, borne on a capful of wind from the loch.

2

I began the book with the end.

Now, you are back with me where I began; the second bad storm in two weeks which shifted the tiles off Stalker's Cottage, and finding Robbie underneath the chair, his fore-paws crushed. I had taken him to Mrs Turk at the Fasganeoin Hotel. It is two weeks since Rufus had gone, with Frieda and Robbie and the four other cubs. After the false hopes raised by the old lady by the loch, there had been nothing else to encourage Don or myself that we would ever see Rufus again. Don had gone away on forestry business, Shuna with him; and Catherine was still away.

I have described how after I had got Robbie to Mrs Turk's, and she could do nothing to mend his crushed bones, I had realised that the only thing that could be done for him was to get him to an expert veterinary surgeon. And I had set off for London. I wasn't acting rationally – the proper thing to do was to put Robbie out of his misery; he must be in pain, he must be suffering. But I was in no state of mind to act rationally, I was in an emotional mix-up; there was no one to help me, and I had this sense of guilt, the inner conviction that I had betrayed Rufus, that if it hadn't been for me, my idea for the film, he would still be alive. I was "humanising" the situation. I believed that I could assuage my guilt by saving Robbie;

and to do it I must get him away as far as possible. There was only danger for him where we were, in the Highlands. I wanted to get away, myself, get away. Never come back. I wished desperately I could have got in touch with Don, but I knew he wouldn't be returning to Loch Fourich for a couple of days, and I couldn't reach him by telephone.

I had passed through Birnam on the A9, when I knew that Robbie was dead. I stopped the car, and took him out of the blanket that I had wrapped round him in the basket beside me. He was still warm, but his heart was no longer beating. I pushed him inside my coat, the way he would push himself for warmth and security when he was alive. I turned the car and went back.

Mrs Turk took Robbie from me when I arrived at the Fasganeoin Hotel; but I went with her out to the garden and dug the hole in which we buried him. There was no moon, the sky was swollen with heavy, black cloud; I thought I heard some thunder in the distance. I stayed the night at the hotel.

I don't remember going to sleep, only Mr Klein waking me with morning tea. It was half past eight; I hadn't drawn the curtains before I went to bed, and pale sunshine shafted through the window. Mr Klein said that someone was downstairs wanting to see me. He wouldn't say who it was. I knew it was something to do with Rufus. I knew it wasn't good news. I said I would be down in a few minutes. I drank the tea while I put on some clothes and went down into the hall.

I didn't know the man. He gave his name, but asked me not to mention it to Mr MacCaskill. I promised I wouldn't. (He had called the previous night at Stalker's Cottage, he said, then had been told at the *Fisherman's Rest* that I might be found at the Fasganeoin Hotel – Don and I hadn't been to McNab's since the night of Rufus's disappearance.) He said that on the Thursday following that Tuesday night, he had driven past a friend's house about a mile from Mr MacCaskill's place, and by the roadside saw this fox. He knew his friend kept chickens, you could see them from the road. He stopped his car and went and told his friend there was a fox about – he'd better watch his chickens. His friend took his shotgun, it was double-barrelled, and they came out of the house together. The fox was still there. He looked towards them. As the man raised his shotgun, this fox was "grinning" and chattering, and then rolled on his back, "as if it was a dog, playing". You couldn't miss.

What did he do with the fox? I wanted to know.

He gave a little shrug. His friend got a knife, he said, and cut off the brush for the £1 bounty. "That's what they give you for a fox's brush. A quid." He didn't know what his friend did with the body. I had hardly registered what he had told me. I heard the words clearly; they made sense and yet they didn't make sense. He made it sound so simple, such an ordinary thing to have happened. He went on to explain how when he heard there had been inquiries about a fox that was missing, obviously a tame fox, it had been on his mind a bit. He couldn't forget the picture of this fox by the roadside – obviously, it was Mr MacCaskill's, he thought he should know what had happened. He didn't feel up to telling Mr MacCaskill himself, and, anyhow, he was away. So he had come to me.

I can remember thanking him, promising him again I wouldn't mention his name. I went upstairs to my bedroom. I stood at the window. I wasn't seeing anything. I didn't weep. You couldn't. Not then. The tears wouldn't come. Just this tight sensation in your throat. I remember a knock at the door, and Mrs Turk saying should she keep breakfast for me, or something, but I don't remember what I said to her. I just stood there. The sky was a pale greyish blue, the sunlight was watery. It was dark where the hills met the sky. I heard the sound of a train in the distance.

Mr Klein came in with some coffee. I drank it automatically. As I put the cup down I saw it rattle against the saucer. I started to sob, then.